國寶

TREASURES
OF THE
FORBIDDEN CITY

CHIEF COMPILER: ZHU JIAJIN

CONSULTANT EDITOR: GRAHAM HUTT

VIKING

VIKING

Penguin Books Ltd, Harmondsworth, Middlesex, England.
Viking Penguin Inc., 40 West 23rd Street, New York, New York
10010, U.S.A.
Penguin Books Australia Ltd, Ringwood, Victoria, Australia
Penguin Books Canada Ltd, 2801 John Street, Markham, Ontario,
Canada L3R 1B4
Penguin Books (N.Z.) Ltd, 182–190 Wairau Road, Auckland 10,
New Zealand

First published in Chinese under the title *Guo bao*
by The Commercial Press 1983
This translation first published by Viking 1986

Chief Compiler: Zhu Jiajin
Executive Editor: Chan Man Hung
Arts Editor: Wan Yat Sha
Photographer: Hu Chui
Designer: Yau Pik Shan
English Translation: Chen Tifang, Pei Minxin, Chen Paiken, Gu
Tingfu and Graham Hutt

Type set in Great Britain by
Rowland Phototypesetting Ltd,
Bury St Edmunds, Suffolk

Printed in Hongkong by C & C Joint Printing Co., (H.K.) Ltd

British Library Cataloguing in Publication Data available

Library of Congress Catalog Card Number: 85-51256
(*CIP Data available*)

PUBLISHER'S FOREWORD

This is the second in Viking's series of highly illustrated large format books on the history of the art, architecture and civilization of Beijing's (Peking) Forbidden City.

The first volume, *Palaces of the Forbidden City*, published in 1984, is a stunning and unique pictorial record of the beautifully preserved architecture of the former imperial palace complex in Beijing. For the first time photographers had the full cooperation of the Chinese authorities and access to many buildings which had never previously been photographed. The result is an unforgettable experience both for the visitor to the Forbidden City who wishes to have a permanent reminder of its beauty and to the student of its magnificent architecture.

This second book is also unique in that a number of the works of art illustrated here are reproduced for the first time, and indeed some of the treasures have never been exhibited before. The photography and colour reproduction is of the highest quality with some objects shown from a number of angles or in detail, and others reproduced to their actual size. The 100 treasures chosen for this book represent the work of China's finest painters, calligraphers and craftsmen, and some of the objects illustrated are so rare that few comparable examples exist outside China. The publication of this book is therefore a significant event for the art historian and collector, as well as for the layman.

A third volume in the series on the daily life of the Forbidden City and its emperors is currently in preparation.

We wish to thank the authorities in Beijing, the specialists and photographers of the Palace Museum, and the staff of the Commercial Press in Hongkong for their cooperation, skill and expertise.

May 1985

MAP OF CHINA

Urumqi

XINJIANG UIGHUR AUTONOMOUS REGION

Dunhuang

GANSU

QINGHAI

Xining

Lanzho

XIZANG (TIBET) AUTONOMOUS REGION

SICHUAN

Lhasa

*Chang jiang
(R. Yangtze)*

Chengdu

120   240   360 miles

200   400   600 kilometres

AERIAL VIEW OF THE FORBIDDEN CITY

Kunming

YUNNAN

HEILONGJIANG

● Haerbin

JILIN

● Changchun

INNER MONGOLIA AUTONOMOUS REGION

Shenyang ●

LIAONING

HEBEI   Chengde
           ○
● Hohhot   BEIJING (PEKING)
Huang he ■
(Yellow R.) Yungang ○
           Datong ○   Tianjin ●
           Quyang
           ○
SHANXI   ● Shijiazhuang

SHAANXI   Taiyuan ●

           Ci xian
           ○
           Anyang ○   Ji'nan ●

           SHANDONG

           Luoyang ○ Zhengzhou ○ Kaifeng
           Longmen   JIANGSU

● Xi'an   HENAN   ANHUI

NINGXIA HUI AUTONOMOUS REGION

HUBEI   ● Hefei
                              Nanjing ●
● Dazu   Wuhan ●   Shanghai ●

                              Hangzhou ●

            Changsha   Jingdezhen
            ●   ○
            Nanchang ●   ZHEJIANG
GUIZHOU   HUNAN
                  JIANGXI   Longquan ○
Guiyang ●   FUJIAN

                              Fuzhou ●
GUANGXI ZHUANG   Taibei ●
AUTONOMOUS REGION Dehua ○
                                     TAIWAN
● Nanning   GUANGDONG

            Guangzhou ●

            ○ Hongkong

DONGSHA ISLANDS

ZHONGSHA ISLANDS
XISHA ISLANDS

NANSHA ISLANDS

500 kilometres

TABLE OF CHINESE DYNASTIES

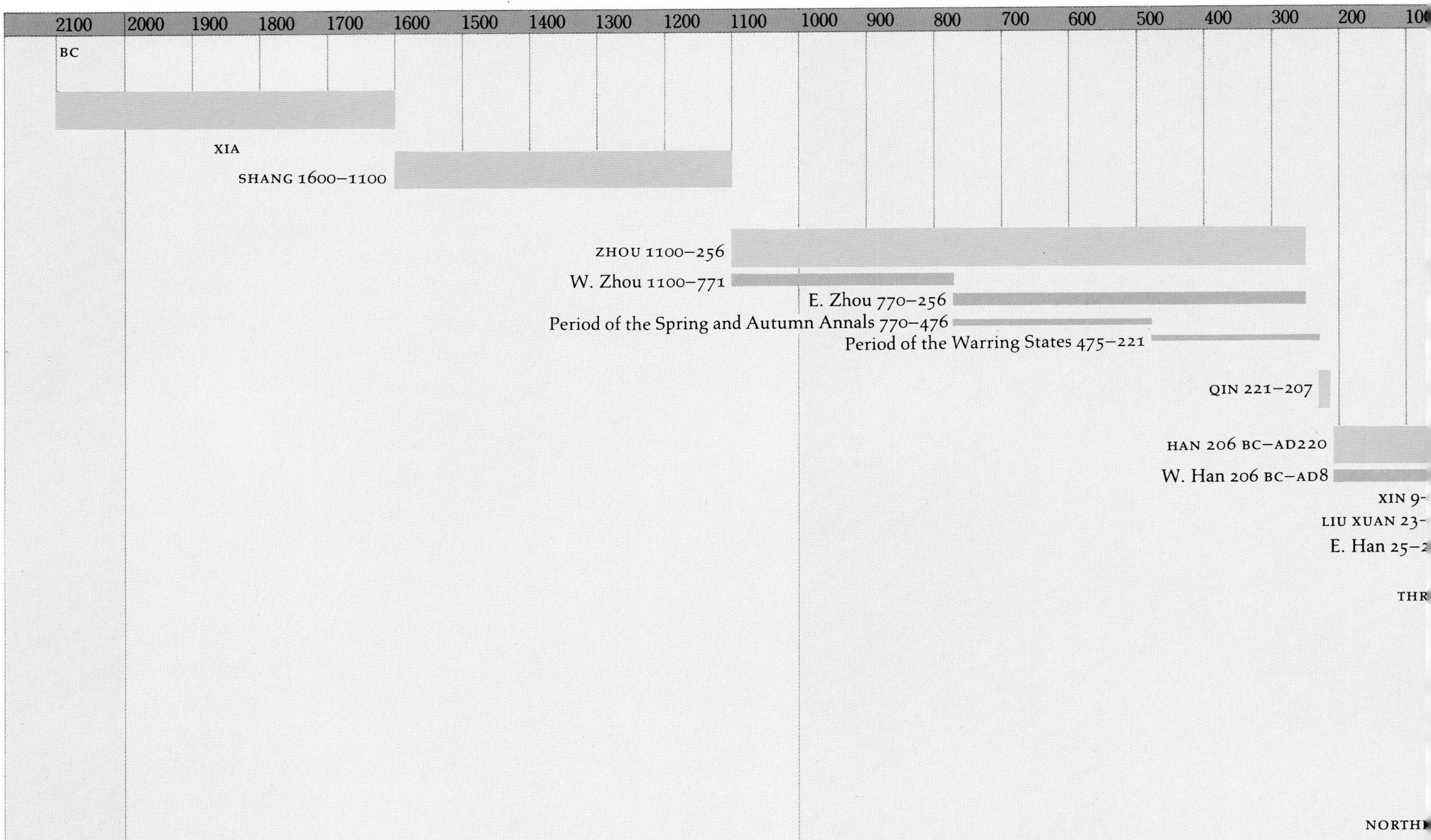

2100	2000	1900	1800	1700	1600	1500	1400	1300	1200	1100	1000	900	800	700	600	500	400	300	200	100

BC

XIA

SHANG 1600–1100

ZHOU 1100–256

W. Zhou 1100–771

E. Zhou 770–256

Period of the Spring and Autumn Annals 770–476

Period of the Warring States 475–221

QIN 221–207

HAN 206 BC–AD220

W. Han 206 BC–AD8

XIN 9–

LIU XUAN 23–

E. Han 25–2

THR

NORTH

REIGN PERIODS OF THE MING AND QING DYNASTIES

Ming dynasty (Chinese)	1368–1644

Name of reign period	*First year of reign period*
Hong wu	1368
Jian wen	1399
Yong le	1403
Hong xi	1425
Xuan de	1426
Zheng tong*	1436
Jing tai (interregnum)	1450
Tian shun	1457
Cheng hua	1465
Hong zhi	1488
Zheng de	1506
Jia jing	1522
Long qing	1567
Wan li	1573
Tai chang	1620
Tian qi	1621
Chong zhen	1628

* resumed government as Tian shun

Qing dynasty (Manchu)	1644–1911
Shun zhi	1644
Kang xi	1662
Yong zheng	1723
Qian long	1736
Jia qing	1796
Dao guang	1821
Xian feng	1851
Tong zhi	1862
Guang xu	1875
Xuan tong	1909

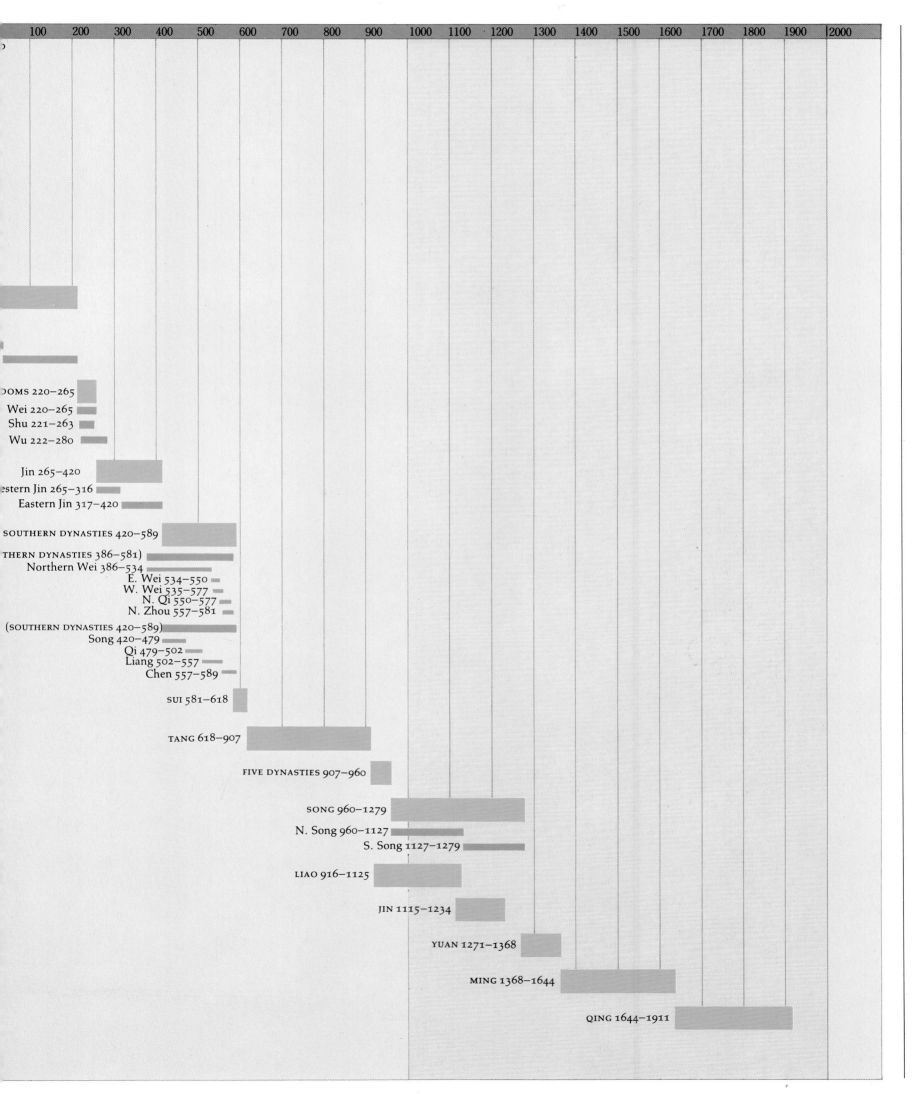

| | 100 | 200 | 300 | 400 | 500 | 600 | 700 | 800 | 900 | 1000 | 1100 | 1200 | 1300 | 1400 | 1500 | 1600 | 1700 | 1800 | 1900 | 2000 |

DOMS 220–265

Wei 220–265

Shu 221–263

Wu 222–280

Jin 265–420

estern Jin 265–316

Eastern Jin 317–420

SOUTHERN DYNASTIES 420–589

THERN DYNASTIES 386–581)

Northern Wei 386–534

E. Wei 534–550

W. Wei 535–577

N. Qi 550–577

N. Zhou 557–581

(SOUTHERN DYNASTIES 420–589)

Song 420–479

Qi 479–502

Liang 502–557

Chen 557–589

SUI 581–618

TANG 618–907

FIVE DYNASTIES 907–960

SONG 960–1279

N. Song 960–1127

S. Song 1127–1279

LIAO 916–1125

JIN 1115–1234

YUAN 1271–1368

MING 1368–1644

QING 1644–1911

CONTENTS

LIST OF TREASURES

INTRODUCTION

The Forbidden City was originally the home of the emperors of the Ming and the subsequent Qing dynasties. The building itself is therefore a cultural and artistic monument to the legacy of China's past.

The 1911 Revolution put an end to the Qing dynasty and, as a result, a Museum of Antiquities was established in the front part of the Imperial Palace in 1914, while the back part continued as the residence of the last emperor, Pu yi. His final departure in 1924 led to the setting up of a committee to wind up the business of the former royal household and the establishment of the Palace Museum in the back part of the palace the following year. After the defeat of Japan in 1945, the Museum of Antiquities was merged with the Palace Museum, which has since remained open to the public. Because ordinary Chinese were physically prevented from entering the vast ceremonial and domestic palace complex of their foreign, Manchu, rulers one of its names was *Zi jin cheng*, the second and third terms meaning 'forbidden city'. Although Westerners continue to use this evocative name, the Chinese refer to it as *Gugong*, 'the old palace', in Chinese and the Palace Museum in English, as all are now permitted to enter.

There are more than 910,000 objects in the Museum's collections consisting mostly of works of art of earlier periods which were handed down by the courts of the Ming and Qing dynasties. A small part of the collections, however, represents the efforts of collecting carried out over thirty years or so. These works of art include examples of famous paintings, calligraphy, rubbings from stone inscriptions, bronzes, ceramics, textiles as well as a host of handicrafts. The 100 masterpieces contained in this volume have been selected from these numerous treasures now stored in the Palace Museum. While some of them have been seen in various exhibition halls, others have not been put out on public display so far.

The fact that the imperial families of past dynasties made a practice of collecting and preserving invaluable objects is witnessed by the existence of the *Xuan he catalogue of calligraphy in the imperial collections, Xuan he shu pu*, the *Xuan he catalogue of paintings in the imperial collections, Xuan he hua pu* and the *Xuan he catalogue of antiquities in the imperial collections, Xuan he bo gu tu*, illustrated catalogues showing collections of such rare objects as calligraphy, paintings and bronze vessels kept in the Song imperial palace. In addition, the *West Qing list of antiquities in the imperial collections, Xi Qing gu jian* and its sequel *Xi Qing xu jian*, the *Ning shou mirror of the antiquities, Ning shou jian gu*, the *Shi qu catalogue of the imperial collections, Shi qu bao ji* (in three volumes), the *Court collection of treasures, Mi dian zhu lin* (in three volumes), the *Tian lu collection of masterpieces, Tian lu lin lang* and the *Complete library in four branches of literature*, or imperial library, *Si ku quan shu*, are the catalogues of ancient bronzes, paintings and calligraphy, and books in the possession of the court compiled by imperial academicians during the Qian long reign period of the Qing dynasty. Many of the ancient relics listed by name are no longer in existence. However, there are still numerous others which have come down to us despite the many vicissitudes that befell them. For example, the stone drums, ten in all, were first discovered in an uninhabited region near Chencang xian. When Han Yu of the Tang period was serving as an academician, he asked for permission to remove them to the imperial college, but without success. These stones were then moved into the Confucian temple in Fengxiang by Zheng Yuqing. They were lost during the turbulent years of the Five Dynasties. It was not until the Song period that nine of the drums were recovered and kept in the prefectural academy by Sima Chi, who then served as a magistrate at Fengxiang. These stone drums, with the tenth finally recovered in 1052, were removed to the then imperial capital of Kaifeng in 1108 and by imperial command the inscribed characters on the stone drums were inlaid with gold. The drums were first placed in the imperial art academy and then moved to the Hall of Preserving Harmony. When the Jin army captured Kaifeng, they transported them to the North and deposited them at the imperial college in Daxing (present day Beijing). During the Yuan period between 1312 and 1313 these drums were installed within the precincts of the Confucian temple. During the subsequent Ming and Qing periods, however, they were placed in the imperial college at one time and in the Confucian temple at another, and there they remained, open to public view until the outbreak of war against Japan, when these drums, together with other antiquities from Beijing, were taken to Sichuan province by way of Nanjing (Nanking) and Wuhan. With the victory of 1945, these treasures were again transported back to the Palace Museum where they remain today. Other examples include 'To Bo yuan' by the calligrapher Wang Xun of the Jin period, which had been included in the *Xuan he catalogue of calligraphy* as well as in the *Shi qu catalogue*; 'Spring excursion', a scroll by Zhan Ziqian of the Sui period; 'Five bulls', a handscroll by Han Huang of the Tang period; and the 'Night entertainment given by Han Xizai' by Gu Hongzhong of the Five Dynasties' period – all these pictures having their names duly recorded both in the *Xuan he catalogue of paintings* and the *Shi qu catalogue*. These famous paintings and pieces of calligraphy, at first in the possession of the Song emperors, were dispersed when the dynasty was toppled by the Mongols. Some were acquired by private collectors and others found their way into the imperial collections of the succeeding Yuan and Ming dynasties. During the Long qing reign of the Ming dynasty, the court decided to sell part of its acquisitions to two brothers, members of the aristocracy, called Zhu Xizhong and Zhu Xixiao. The best of the former's collection ended up in the hands of Zhang Zhujeng whose property was confiscated after his death in 1582. In this way, the best of the original works were returned to their former owners in the rebuilt Forbidden City. Another example recorded in the catalogues is the *Qing ming shang he tu*, 'Going upriver at the Qing ming festival', a handscroll by Zhang Zeduan of the Song period, which has repeatedly changed hands. It belonged for a time to the powerful prime minister Yan Song. Later he was punished and deprived of his property; the painting, along with many other masterpieces, was again recovered by the court. However, it soon fell into the hands of a notorious eunuch Feng Bao.

When the imperial treasures were being put in order during the reign of the Qing emperor Qian long, many of the objects were found to have been handed down from the Ming dynasty. As a passionate collector of antiquities the emperor put all his energies into gathering them together, exploring every avenue in order to obtain for himself almost all the treasures of such famous collectors as An Yizhou, Liang Qingbiao, Gao Shiqi and Bi Yuan. The great abundance of painting and calligraphy listed in the *Shi qu catalogue* and the *Court collection of treasures* was gradually accumulated in this way.

After the reigns of Qian long and Jia qing, although the court no longer laid such emphasis on collecting, the quest for paintings and calligraphy continued as before. Then Beijing was twice invaded by foreign troops, in 1860 and 1900. Many of the treasures stored in the Yuan ming yuan and other places were either looted or destroyed. During the thirteen years between the outbreak of the 1911 Revolution and the flight of the last Qing emperor Pu yi in 1924, further losses were reported.

After its establishment, based on the *Shi qu catalogue*, the Palace Museum compiled a *List of lost paintings and calligraphy formerly in the imperial palace*, the *Gu gong yi shi shu hua mu lu*. However, it was not until 1949 that the Museum, by dint of the list, was able to recover most of the lost treasures through purchase or donation. The recovered objects included masterpieces of the Jin, the Sui and the Tang periods published in this book. Among them, two notable pieces of calligraphy, 'Mid-autumn festival' and 'To Bo yuan', as well as the picture 'Five bulls', were repurchased in Hongkong at great cost.

Despite such problems, the greater part of the treasures has been kept in perfect safety in the palace. The same is true of an even greater number which fall into the category of fine craftsmanship, such as furniture, fittings and furnishings, as well as what may be loosely termed ornaments which have remained in the original places ever since they were presented to the court. For example, a carving of a jade mountain depicting the ancient story of Yu the Great, who controlled the floods and instituted the regulation of watercourses, has remained *in situ* since the day of its installation in 1787. Apart from the jades handed down through the centuries, all the jade articles made in the Qing period, some of them by court artisans, have remained in the palace since they first arrived. So have the *fa lang* porcelain bowl with polychrome enamel decoration of pheasants and peonies, the *cloisonné* vase with underglaze decoration of flowers and birds, the ivory brushholder with a carving showing the life of fishermen, and the *bai bao qian* lacquer hanging screens inlaid with precious stones, all being the works of court artisans which have been selected for inclusion in this book.

So numerous are these works that the porcelain pieces alone, presented annually from the kilns at Jingdezhen in Jiangxi province, now number more than 100,000. It was from these that representative works of the Qing periods of Kang xi, Yong zheng and Qian long were selected. Moreover, there is in store a huge quantity of silks in rolls, woven silk tapestries and embroidered clothes made in the past by the imperial manufacturers at Nanjing, Suzhou and Hangzhou as well as those made after designs specially devised by palace officials. Out of these we have selected a silk tapestry representing the Pure Land of Buddhism, an imperial dragon robe embroidered with gold, silver and peacock feathers and 'Nine suns driving away the cold', a *ke si* woven silk tapestry.

We have also published in this book pieces that once adorned the Ming dynasty palace, such as the porcelains produced during the reigns of Yong le, Cheng hua and Wan li, the *cloisonné* enamel objects made during the reigns of Xuan de and Jing tai, as well as the long black lacquer table inlaid with mother-of-pearl made during the reign of Wan li. These were all made for practical use and kept safely in the palace.

The contents of this album are divided into five categories: namely bronzes; painting and calligraphy; ceramics; the minor arts; and textiles and embroideries, with a general introduction to each section and detailed descriptions to accompany the photographs of each object. Although we have only chosen 100 objects out of the vast number of antiquities, they help to demonstrate the development and achievements of Chinese art and culture from the period of the Shang and Zhou down to the Ming and Qing dynasties.

Zhu Jiajin
Forbidden City, Beijing
1983

BRONZES

青銅器

BRONZES

Chinese bronzes have long been renowned for their fine shapes, elaborate decoration, great variety and exquisite craftsmanship and, because of their unique artistic form, they occupy a highly significant place in the history of art of the world.

Broadly speaking, the term 'bronzes' is applied to numerous categories of artefacts made from an alloy consisting mostly of copper and tin. They include ritual vessels and musical instruments, as well as weapons, tools, chariot fittings, horse trappings and articles for daily use. But in the narrow sense, the term 'bronzes' is generally reserved to refer to ritual vessels and musical instruments.

Of the ten pieces presented in this album the *li* and *gui* are food containers; the *zun, lei, jia, gu* and *he*, wine vessels; and the *bo*, a type of bell.

It has been shown that the ancestors of the Chinese people discovered copper at an extremely early date and had already begun to use bronze at a stage no later than the late neolithic period.

In the same way as other artefacts, bronzes at first appeared as small tools and other objects. Material evidence of this is a bronze knife dating to approximately 3000 BC, the earliest of its kind so far unearthed in China. It was discovered in 1977 at a site of the so-called Majiayao culture at Linjia in Dongxiang xian, Gansu province. Another discovery, made at the site of the so-called Erlitou culture, in Dongxiang xian, Henan province, yielded a large group of tools, weapons and ornaments. Among these were four bronze ritual vessels, called *jue*, which are the earliest known examples of bronze casting to have used clay composite, or piece moulds, in their manufacture which have survived intact.

Ritual vessels and musical instruments were chiefly used on such ceremonial occasions as offering sacrifices and giving banquets. And the nobles at the time were only allowed to use such vessels as befitted their rank; otherwise, they would be condemned as acting contrary to the so-called 'rites'. The most important of these rites were embodied in the many specific functions and ceremonies, and in a system of institutions, decrees and regulations. The performing of sacrifices comprised an essential part of them.

Believing their destinies to be controlled by heaven and holding their ancestors in reverence, the nobility of the time, in offering sacrifices to their ancestors, were usually ostentatious in their display of ritual and musical performances. The sacrifices of numerous slaves and specially designated animals account for the fact that the ritual bronzes consisted in the main of sacrificial vessels. Of the 400 or so bronzes excavated in 1975 from the tomb of Fu Hao, consort of the king Wu ding, at Anyang, Henan province, 210 were used for sacrificial purposes.

The modelling of bronzes demonstrates the consummate artistic attainments of the makers of that time. The style prevalent during the middle Shang to the early Western Zhou periods manifests a dignity and sturdiness which reflect the characteristics of the people who made them. The zoomorphic objects in imitation of birds and animals as well as the decoration in high relief are extremely lively in appearance. After the middle Zhou period the vessels which were made laid more emphasis on the functional aspects and bore simpler and plainer designs. However, graceful shapes and highly decorative motifs appeared once more on some bronzes during the period following the period of the Spring and Autumn Annals.

The bronzes of the Shang and Zhou periods not only retained and developed geometric patterns frequently seen on painted pottery of the neolithic period but also began to utilize animal mask motifs, dragon and phoenix patterns and designs of fantastic animals with their heads as the prominent feature. In this way, many antique myths and legends could be incorporated into the decorative scheme. It was not until the periods of the Spring and Autumn Annals and the Warring States that the Shang and Zhou style of regular and symmetrical composition began to give way to a fine and elaborate method of all-over design. It was during this period also that scenes of everyday life appeared on the bronzes, such as feasting to the accompaniment of music, battle and hunting scenes, and so on. This anticipated the murals of the Han period, executed on stone or bricks, which were greatly to influence the future development of pictorial art.

Another development in the decoration of bronze objects was the art of inlay. Inlaid artefacts were discovered in the ruins of the early bronze age Erlitou culture, but the materials employed at that early stage were restricted to such basic materials as turquoise and copper. With improvements in mining, smelting and casting skills it became increasingly possible for craftsmen to adorn bronzes with other metals, especially gold and silver filigree, thus adding to both the value and appearance of the objects.

Another outstanding feature of Chinese bronzes is their inscriptions, of both few and many characters written in different forms. They first appeared in the late Shang as a sort of insignia or emblem of a clan. Used mainly for making such distinctions as this, written characters at this stage were few in number and were generally graphic representations of objects or pictograms. The inscriptions appearing on excavated bronzes grew in number and content but those which ran to anything up to fifty words were not seen until the closing years of the Shang dynasty. Some of the inscriptions eulogize the owners of the vessels or their ancestors, the important events of the day, transactions of the transfer of land and the outcome of litigation. Others commemorate the conferment of titles and the presentation of gifts to their vassals by the kings, princes and dukes. All these provide reliable material evidence for the study of ancient Chinese societies, cultures and institutions, making up for the deficiency in ancient texts and other historical source materials. After the Spring and Autumn period, accompanying social changes and developments in production, literacy became more widespread. More and more records were made on stone tablets, bamboo slips and silk. Accordingly, bronze inscriptions gradually became redundant as the main vehicle for historical record making.

Apart from their value as cultural relics, Chinese bronzes are in themselves splendid objects of art. The master craftsmen of over 3,000 years ago were skilled in the art of the making of moulds and casting the finished article and were able to produce superb works which were well balanced with a sense of visual rhythm and strength but, above all, exquisite in workmanship, so that decoration and shape were successfully combined in complete harmony. The fine blending of all these qualities suggests a unity of high order and invokes a strong sense of beauty in all those who wish to appreciate them.

The two square *zun* vessels, *Xu ya fang zun* and *Shi jin li*, included in this section may serve as examples. A heavy sacrificial vessel, the former is extremely wide at the mouth, but it curves sharply back to the tall neck, at the base of which the line of the vessel, in profile, turns back out producing a solid, rounded appearance. The tall, square, flaring base offsets the much wider and flatter top, suggestive of formal stability. Eight flanges run up the sides of the body, recalling the system of support bracketing, *dou gong*, of the defiant upward-curving 'flying' eaves found in the sweeping lines of traditional Chinese roof architecture.

The second example, the *Shi jin li*, is a similarly large ritual vessel but is treated in a completely different manner. First of all, in this type of tripod vessel, the principle that 'three points determine the form' is employed so that three large, lobed legs support the fully rounded body. Two side handles, often called 'ears' placed directly opposite each other above two of the legs, are not merely of practical use but serve to enhance the beauty of the vessel. The decoration is in keeping with the shape of the vessel and lends a sense of unity and harmony. The animal mask decoration in high relief on the bulging body evokes a feeling of richness while the elongated scrolling of the snakes and eyes on the low neck gives it its own place in the overall composition while in no way detracting from it. So, as a whole, the vessel exudes a solemn majesty such as befits all large sacrificial vessels.

Apart from their long history and unique national characteristics, Chinese bronzes display features of the periods in which they were made as well as the high cultural and artistic level that Chinese society had already reached, from the Shang dynasty down to the Spring and Autumn and the Warring States' periods.

1. 乳釘三耳簋

The shape of the bronze ritual vessel *gui* originated from a much earlier ceramic form. As this bore no 'ears' at the sides, so, too, did the early bronzes of this type lack handles. Later, owing to its size, and hence the weight of metal, the bronze version was supplied with 'ears', that is handles, for the convenience of handling. When the ancients held banquets seated on mats on the ground, *gui* were placed on the mats within reach of the feasters who helped themselves to the food with their hands, a custom still retained by some of China's national minorities to this day. Because of this, *gui* vessels had to be made in comparatively large sizes. *Gui* with three and four handles, square *gui* and other forms came into being only later. At that time the shoulder 'ears', of course, no longer served merely as handles but as a vehicle for the elaborately moulded decorative motifs.

The *gui* was used to contain such cooked, glutinous grains as broomcorn millet, panicled millet, rice or sorghum. When the nobles came to offer sacrifices and give feasts, many other types of dish were often served, and in such cases more than one *gui* was needed. Ancient texts record that the number of *gui* used ranged from two to twelve, but that they always occurred in pairs.

The bronze *gui* shown has a wide, flared mouth, deep bowl and tall ring foot. The ground is filled with the spiral meander pattern but the dominant design is of rounded nipple protrusions within rhombuses or lozenges and animal mask and eye patterns. All of these retain the basic features of moulding and ornament typical of the handleless *gui* of the Shang period. The only additions are the three handles in the shape of animal heads on the shoulder which separate the panel of designs between the mouth rim and the ring foot into three similar sections.

The spiral meander, *hui wen*, motif appeared at an early stage in geometrical design, formed by lines that turn back in on themselves continuously. Its old name was the cloud pattern, *yun wen*, when rounded in shape, or thunder pattern, *lei wen*, when of squared shape, or cloud and thunder pattern, *yun lei wen*, in general. This motif was used singly on the neck or foot of a vessel, and not until the later Shang did it serve as the ground to set off the principal ornament. The centre of the eye motif looks like the eye of an animal with extensions resembling tails on both sides. It was probably the prototype of the scroll and hook curves which developed later. The distinctive nipple design covering the vessel is made up of bosses regularly placed at the centre of rhombuses which are filled with spiral meanders.

Gui with handles came into being in the later Shang, mostly without any decoration suspended below them. Those which do bear such pendant decoration appeared towards the end of the Shang dynasty and only became prevalent after the beginning of the Zhou dynasty. Based on this fact, this *gui* must have been produced at the close of the Shang period at the earliest; and since the decoration of rhombus-framed bosses was an important Shang device becoming rarer during the Zhou period, it is a fair assumption that this *gui* belongs to the Shang period.

The 'ears' or loop handles on *gui*, since their first appearance, were mostly two in number, and hence two-handled *gui* are now frequently on display. Four-eared *gui* with ears symmetrically placed on four sides are occasionally found, while examples bearing three handles are a rarity.

It is worth noting that, until now, this three-eared *gui* had never before been described or illustrated.

2.醜亞方尊　3.醜亞方罍

FANG ZUN. SQUARE ZUN,
WINE VESSEL. KNOWN AS
XU YA FANG ZUN, 'XU YA
CLAN FANG ZUN'

Shang dynasty. Later period
height 45.5 cm.
overall width 38 cm.
mouth 33.5 × 33.5 cm.
foot 22 × 22 cm.
belly depth 33.6 cm.
weight 21,500 gm

醜亞者（諸）姤（后）呂
大（太）子隕（尊）彝

The *zun* is a wine container, and is also a general name for many types of wine vessel. Bronze *zun* occur in two shapes. One has a flared mouth and a more or less cylindrical body (sometimes with a square body and a round mouth, which is a rare variation). Generally the vessel bulges slightly at the belly above a high foot.

Another shape incorporates a wide, flared mouth, a contracted neck and is broad at the shoulder. Its greatest circumference lies where the belly meets the shoulder, and below this the vessel reduces in size until it reaches a high foot which is either circular or square. *Zun* vessels first appeared in the middle Shang and became more common in the late Shang period. They were still in existence in the early Zhou, although not in any great number. The broad shouldered type is usually quite large and the square *zun* illustrated here belongs to this type.

The *lei* is a container for holding liquids. Before the Han dynasty it was classified as a type of *zun* and named *shan lei* or *shan zun*. In deciding nomenclature for bronze vessels, the antiquarians of the Song period retained the name *lei* because some vessels of this kind were found to have the written character *lei* cast on them. For this reason, *lei* formed a special category on its own.

The shape of *lei* resembles that of an urn, but smaller, or an earthenware jar or pitcher, except that it has a narrow neck and broad shoulder. The distinguishing feature of the *lei* is a handle on the front part of the lower belly, enabling the vessel to be grasped and tipped up to pour out the liquid content. As in the case of the *zun*, the *lei* also occurs as round and, more commonly, square.

The surface of this *fang zun*, or square *zun*, is completely covered in decoration with an elephant head at each of the four corners of the shoulder. Surmounted by two *kui* dragons shaped like horns on the forehead, the elephants' trunks are curled and held high while the tusks are thrust forward from their bases. In between the four elephants are animal heads, also four in number, looking like deer with palmate antlers.

Eight flanges follow the upward sweep of the neck and extend beyond the rim below the mouth, imparting an added grandeur to the vessel.

The vessel was cast in two stages, entailing two distinct methods of execution. One way was to cast a part or parts of the vessel first. When cool, these were embedded in the mould made for casting the main body of the vessel and the molten bronze, when poured in, fused with the ready-cast pieces to form the finished article. Examples of this include the capped posts of bronze *jia* and the body walls of the huge square tripods, *fang ding*.

The second method involved casting the main body of the vessel first incorporating projections or holes in the body wall. When removed from the mould and solidified the holes or projections of the vessel's body were ready to have the clay mould and core attached to them. Molten bronze was then poured in and formed a tight bond with the vessel. Examples of this method can be seen in the handles of the three-handled *gui* and the eight animal heads on this *fang zun*.

The broad shouldered, shrunken-mouthed *fang lei*, or square *lei*, has a lid that looks like a roof topped by a finial knob. With eight flanges, it has a ring hanging from the mouth of an animal head on each side of the shoulder for a cord to run through so that the vessel can be carried about as if it were equipped with a handle, although there is already an animal-head shape lug on the front lower part of the belly.

The vessel bears designs of animals masks and a pattern of *kui* dragons against a background of spiral filler. The *kui* dragon is a legendary creature, a single-horned and single-footed dragon usually depicted with a gaping mouth and a curled tail; hence, such a design is called *kui wen* or *kui long wen* (*kui* dragon pattern). The animal mask motif was given the name *tao tie*, referring to a gluttonous monster and includes the stylized representation of the heads of tigers, cows, rams, pigs and so on. The one on this *fang zun* belongs to this type while those seen on each side of the belly of the *fang lei* belong to another type, formed by a pair of *kui* dragons facing each other across the vertical flange. The protruding eyes of the two dragons in profile make up the two eyes of the monster viewed from the front.

Two *Xu ya fang zun* were originally cast as a pair. The one housed in the Palace Museum, Beijing, is in good condition while the other, now housed in the National Palace Museum in Taibei, Taiwan, has a considerably damaged foot.

Both the *fang zun* and the *fang lei* are inscribed with nine written characters. Xu ya, which gives both vessels their names, was the name of a clan of high standing in the Shang period found to have lived in the region which, broadly speaking, centred on present day Yidu, Shandong province. As many as between fifty and sixty bronzes bearing this clan's name have been discovered to date. There are some ten extant pieces which bear the same inscriptions as those on the *fang zun* and the *fang lei*.

According to verification by the eminent scholar Tang Lan, former deputy-director of the Palace Museum, the two characters *zhe* (者) and *gou* (姤) in the inscriptions are variants of *zhu* (諸) and *hou* (后), together meaning the 'feudal lords'. Hence this series of bronzes, since they were used to offer sacrifices to the dynastic kings and princes, indicates that a close relationship existed between the Xu ya clan and the Yin (Shang) dynasty. These clansmen were most probably the descendants of the Yin royal house.

In 1975 excavations carried out at Tomb No. 5 at Anyang (one of the Shang capitals), Henan province, yielded a large haul of bronzes. Textual investigation revealed that the tomb was that of Fu hao, a royal concubine of a king, Wu ding, of the Shang dynasty. Among the finds were several large *zun* and *lei*, which further testifies that the production of massive sacrificial vessels was the sole preserve of nobility of high rank. The fact that inscriptions gradually became more profuse indicates that the *fang zun* and the *fang lei* illustrated here must have been made later than the Fu hao bronzes and thus doubtless belong to the later Shang period.

FANG LEI. SQUARE *LEI,*
VESSEL FOR LIQUIDS.
KNOWN AS *XU YA FANG
LEI,* 'XU YA CLAN SQUARE
LEI'

Shang dynasty. Later period
height (including lid) 62.2 cm.
overall width 37.6 cm.
mouth 16.9 × 15.5 cm.
foot 19.4 × 16.4 cm.
weight, 20,800 gm

醜亞者（諸）姤（后）吕
大（太）子陳（尊）彝

醜亞
者姤吕
陳彝
大子

4.九象尊(友尊) 5.四象觚(象紋觚)

*ZUN. WINE VESSEL.
KNOWN AS JIU XIANG
ZUN, 'NINE ELEPHANT
ZUN', ALSO YOU ZUN*

Shang period
height 13.2 cm.
mouth diameter 20.7 cm.
greatest circumference of
body 18.7 cm.
foot diameter 15 cm.
internal depth 10 cm.
weight 2,700 gm

These two bronze vessels were unearthed at Yinxu ('the ruins of Yin', the last Shang capital), Anyang, Henan province, in the 'forties. There are three extant wine vessels bearing a design of four elephants. The one shown here has never been published before and is the only vessel of this type, with a design of nine elephants, known. The other two are outside China; one is in the hands of an American antiques' dealer while another is housed in the Museum of Far Eastern Antiquities, Stockholm.

Apart from the designation 'Nine elephant *zun*', from its unusual decoration, it is also known as the '*you zun*' as it is inscribed with the character *you*, the insignia of a clan. The vessel is also very unusual in shape; different from the usual wide-mouthed and broad shouldered *zun*, as well as from the cylinder-shaped *zun*, it is probably a variant of the former type. Shaped as a round bowl topped by a wide, flaring mouth and a slightly contracted neck, it has a bulging belly and a ring foot on which there are three cruciform holes where the moulds were originally held together. It is from this that we can deduce that a composite outer mould was used and from the holes, that the mould was formed from three pieces.

The design of nine elephants, one behind the other, is set against a ground of spiral filler on the main body of the vessel. There is a band of compound spirals around the neck and a broad decorative band of twenty-four blade-shaped plantain leaves just below the edge of the mouth. The decorative bands round the neck and the belly are both sandwiched between two strings of circles, or beads. Of particular interest is the grooved 'tile pattern' around the foot, the pattern so called because of its resemblance to the lines of tiles, scalloped in section, covering a traditional roof. Although it only became more popular during the later Western Zhou and the Spring and Autumn periods its appearance on such vessels created a precedent for its future adoption.

The *gu* is a libation goblet. The bronze *gu* first appears in the middle of the Shang period. Pottery *gu* similar in shape were discovered amongst finds unearthed at sites of the so-called Dawenkou and Longshan neolithic cultures. Broadly speaking, early *gu* can be divided into two types, one with a narrower central section and tall body and the other which is fuller at the centre of a squatter body. The latter was more useful as a goblet while the former, being inconvenient due to its height for drinking purposes, served only as a ritual vessel. By the Western Zhou, the *gu* vessel type had already dwindled in number and finally disappeared altogether, which may be connected with the prohibition of alcohol during the Zhou period.

All the *gu* discovered so far bear no inscriptions of their own

GU. WINE VESSEL.
KNOWN AS *SI XIANG GU*,
'FOUR ELEPHANT *GU*'

Shang period
height 26 cm.
mouth diameter 15.3 cm.
foot diameter 9.5 cm.
internal depth 18.2 cm.
weight 920 gm

nomenclature; they are now named according to the principal decorative themes that appeared thereon, such as the 'four elephant *gu*' shown here. This vessel has a large, flared mouth, tall body and is slender at its centre. Its decoration consists of two animal masks at the centre, front and back; an elephant pattern on the ring foot whose ground is filled with spirals; and a band of circles both above and below the decorations on the belly and the foot.

Despite the shape of the bronze *gu*, which is wider at the top than at the base, there are no problems with its stability as its maker ingeniously gave it a high foot with a wide base, thus causing the centre of gravity to be located below the middle of the vessel.

For decoration, the necks of *gu* are often treated with bands of narrow blade motifs such as plantain leaves while the lower portion often bears animal masks or overlapping scales, so that the structure of the vessel and the surface decoration are ingeniously combined into one integrated whole which embodies perfect equilibrium and harmony.

The principal decorative theme on these two bronzes is the trumpeting elephant with curled trunk held high and prominent tusks and ears. As the nine elephants on the *zun* and the four on the *gu* look like two herds in full flight it is quite clear that neither designer was trying to depict them in an abstract way but to capture a realistic representation of their outward appearance.

Nowadays the elephant lives only in tropical climates but during the Shang and Zhou periods it lived on the central plain of China. Proof is to be found in an ancient text which records that the Shang people were well acquainted with elephants. Further evidence is furnished in the remains of two elephants uncovered in the area of the royal tombs at Xibeigang and Houjiazhuang, near Anyang. Moreover, ornamental devices based on parts of the elephant, such as its ears or feet, are to be found on pre-Zhou bronzes. Complete *zun* in the form of elephants were produced. Most probably the climatic changes combined with the growth and spread of population and agricultural activity caused essential changes in the ecological environment and compelled elephants gradually to move southward.

29

6. 冊方斝

JIA. SQUARE JIA. WINE
VESSEL. KNOWN AS *CE
FANG JIA*, '*CE SQUARE JIA*'

Shang period
height (including uprights)
28.3 cm.
mouth diameter 11 × 13.3
cm.
overall width 16.9 cm.
weight 3,120 gm

The *jia* is a wine container or warmer. It generally does not bear the character *jia*, its own name and, if inscribed at all, bears few characters.

This square *jia* has a lid and slightly curving neck, with a bulging lower body and somewhat convex bottom. A handle is attached to one side of the body. On the mouth rim on both sides of the handle stand two square capped posts, diametrically opposite each other. Its four legs under the belly are splayed. In the middle of the thin, flat lid stands an arched knob formed by two birds back to back with their beaks pointing outward and joined at the crests on their heads. The surface of the lid bears two animal masks, while the handle at the side is adorned with an animal head. The principal decorative motif is a large animal mask against a ground of spiral filler, on each panel. A design of triangles with their vertices pointing upwards can be seen around the neck and the two caps of the posts. The four legs bear *kui* dragons incorporated into a plaintain leaf shape. All contribute to a rare combination of magnificent decoration and graceful shape.

The character inscribed on the vessel is *ce* – an ink rubbing of which is also reproduced here – found at the bottom of the interior. As with all single-character inscriptions it signifies the owner of the vessel or the name of a clan.

Bronze *jia* made their first appearance during the middle Shang period as a derivative of pottery *jia*. In the early stages, most of the *jia* were round in shape, and square ones came into being only after the removal of the Shang site to Yinxu (present day Anyang) when bronze products increased both in quantity and in variety. Such *fang jia* as the one shown here were largely found at Anyang, but most of the finds have been taken out of China and scattered in different parts of the world. The only one that remains within China is a small square lidded *jia* excavated in 1975 from the tomb of Fu hao at Anyang, similar to the one shown. In the light of this fact this vessel should, therefore, belong to the later Shang period too.

Another type of bronze *jia*, with legs forking from the body and hence appearing compartmentalized (see the illustration below left), began to appear in the later Shang and persisted till the early Zhou periods, after which it disappeared.

The reason the vessels for wine proved to be the most popular during the Shang era was that drunkenness was a vice of the time and the lords and nobles indulged themselves in excessive drinking day and night. This reached its nadir during the reign of the last ruler, Zhou wang, who brought the dynasty to ruin because he 'loved wine and woman and licentious music'. Drawing a lesson from Zhou wang, the kings of the early Western Zhou dynasty put a strict ban on drinking and, as a consequence, a great number of types of wine vessels that had been in vogue during the Shang period gradually went out of existence.

Bronze ritual vessels, *jia*, showing variations of the type with 'segmented' body and legs.

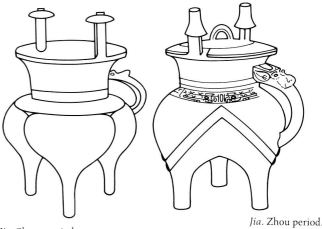

Jia. Shang period.   *Jia.* Zhou period.

7. 堇臨簋

GUI. FOOD CONTAINER
WITH TWO 'EAR' OR LOOP
HANDLES. KNOWN AS *JIN
LIN'S GUI.*

Early Zhou period
height 16.1 cm.
mouth diameter 21.1 cm.
overall width 33.5 cm.
weight 3,660 gm

This bronze vessel bears an inscription of eight characters on the inner surface of the bowl: *Jin lin zuo fu yi bao zun yi*, meaning 'Jin lin cast this ritual vessel for offering sacrifices to his deceased father on the *yi* day'. (*Yi* is the second of the 'Ten heavenly stems' which are used as serial numbers and otherwise called the 'decimal cycle' and combine with the 'Twelve earthly branches' to give times and dates.) It was the custom of the Shang people to make offerings to their forefathers every day in accordance with a fixed sequence. *Fu yi* means that sacrifices offered to Jin Lin's father, *fu*, fell on the second day of the ten day cycle then in operation, which was called *yi* day. However, *bao zun yi*, 'precious *zun* vessel', is a term specifically used by the Zhou.

From the style of the script and from the shape and decoration of the vessel we can be sure that it must have been cast during the early Zhou period. The script characteristic of the time is called the *bo na* style, which admits of a thickening in the middle of each brushstroke with the two ends of the line tapering off into a point; a neat regular style of great elegance and beauty. And Jin lin is probably the name of a noble or adherent of the former, Shang, dynasty.

This Jin Lin *gui* belongs to the type with two 'ears' or handles. It has a flaring mouth with a lipped rim, a slightly bulging body, a round foot and pendant decoration hanging from the handles. It is an example of *shu keng*, that is, a bronze that has been handed down to us with the patina washed off with acid and well polished. The body, front and back, is accentuated with a broad, confident band of animal masks. The ears, eyes, mouths, noses and horns belonging to the masks are in low relief and adorned with lightly engraved patterns. On both the neck part and the ring foot is a border of designs formed by alternate coiled dragon and whorl circles. In the centre of the band on the neck, both on the front and on the back, there is a small animal head, also found on the ring foot but reduced to the shape of a nose. This vessel appears to have been cast using four outer composite moulds; the seams on the two sides are cleverly covered up by the ears and those on the front and back faces are concealed by the two animal masks or the nose-like designs.

The most outstanding feature of this vessel is the ornamental 'ears' or handles. *Gui* 'ears' are generally made to look like some kind of animal, and are represented here by a combination of dragon and bird images. The designer, over 2,000 years ago, has skilfully rendered the upper part of the somewhat oval-shaped handles into dragon heads mounted with two upright, squarish horns. Below the projecting lip of the dragon can be seen two sharp fangs, and a scaly part of the animal's body is joined to that of the vessel. The lower part of the handle is formed from a bird whose head links itself with the cheeks of the dragon above. The bird's beak curves like a hook, with the body and wings sweeping backwards in an arc to form the lower part of the handle and the tail anchored on the body of the vessel. On the rectangular pendant which falls vertically below the handle are hooked decorative lines representing the bird's feet and long plumage.

To find such complexity of design combined with an extraordinarily vigorous realism, almost as if they were sculptures in themselves, on the handles of a *gui*, marks this out as a vessel of extreme rarity.

8. 四虎鎛

BO. BELL. KNOWN AS SI HU BO, 'FOUR TIGER BO'

Western Zhou period
overall height 44.3 cm.
height of handle 10.5 cm.
overall width 39.6 cm.
weight 16,000 gm

Musical instruments form a fair proportion of bronze objects. If it can be said that ritual vessels represent the then rigid social system which was based on rank, then musical instruments may be said to signify the same social stratification. Thus the number of musical instruments allowed to be used at a ceremony can indicate the rank of the noble who used it. According to the Zhou rites, the 'son of heaven' or king could use four sets of bells; princes and dukes, three; senior officials, two; and officials in general, one. At the beginning of the Spring and Autumn period, the 'ruin of the established rules as regards musical and ritual performances' lamented by Confucius set in. This explains why more bells than were permitted to be used under the system of the time have been handed down.

Like ritual vessels, musical instruments also underwent great changes and variations in different periods and regions. The Shang people did not possess bells, but they did have *nao* and *zheng*, which were cymbal-like and were probably the earliest known percussion instruments in China. Such instruments were uncovered at Anyang, Henan province. They are flattened in shape, much greater in width than height, their upper part was larger than the lower and they were held mouth upward on a stem, which was hollow and admitted a wooden rod. A chime of *nao* are generally small and have three to five graduated sizes to a set. Larger *nao*, often unearthed singly, were adorned with animal masks or elephant or tiger motifs. A variation of the *zheng* and *nao* was the *ju ce*, a type prevalent in the states of Xu, Chu, Wu and Yue during the Spring and Autumn and the Warring States' periods.

Nao continued in their development until the establishment of the Western Zhou dynasty, culminating in the fully-fledged *zhong* bell. At first, the bell was called *yong zhong*, with a cylindrical handle on the top, seen earliest in the middle Western Zhou period. The drawing (left) on this page shows the shape of a *zhong*, which looks very much like an inverted *zheng* or *nao* and can be suspended from a rack for striking, usually called *bian zhong*, numbering three to ten bells or more. After the Spring and Autumn period, *niu zhong*, a type of bell with a semi-circular handle on the top, came into being. The Marquis of Zeng chime of bells discovered in Sui xian, Hebei province, consists of sixty-four bells in eight unequal sets. Beautiful in timbre and broad in register, they can be used to play modern music, which shows the high artistic level of Chinese music in ancient times.

The *bo* is related to the *zhong*, the only real difference lying in their slightly different shapes. The rim of the *zhong* is arched in section while that of the *bo* is even. The *bo* emerged much later than the *yong zhong* but earlier than the *niu zhong* bells. In their earliest stages *bo* were used singly, and it was not until the Spring and Autumn period that they appeared in

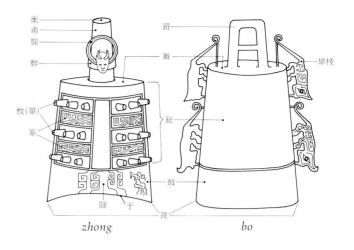

Diagram showing differences between zhong (left) and bo (right) bells

sets (*bian bo*). The *Qin Gong bo*, 'Prince of Qin's *bo*', excavated recently in the city of Baoji, Shaanxi province, and the *Pan hui wen bo*, 'coiled serpent design *bo*', now housed in the Palace Museum, are both sets of three bells of graduated sizes.

The *bo* shown here is spectacularly decorated, compared with *zhong*, as well as with *bo* bells in general. Both the front and the back bear a large animal mask with a notched flange protruding vertically between the eyes and looking like the nose of the animal mask. Although damaged, it appears to be in the form of a bird. On each side of the animal mask is an inverted *kui* dragon. Above and below the masks are decorative bands dominated by whorl motifs. The ingenuity and craftsmanship of the maker are also revealed in the four tigers down the body of the *bo*. Vividly portrayed with gaping jaws and curling tails the creatures are symmetrically attached in two pairs to the bell. Cast flat, in two rather than three dimensions, they form the two stiff side flanges. This design demonstrates an easy integration of the static and the dynamic within what appears as an organic whole. It shows the high level reached by ancient Chinese craftsmen in the art of bronze casting and decoration as well as their ingenuity of conception.

There are three *bo* similar to the one presented in this album: the *Zhou hu zhong* recorded in the *Xuan he catalogue of antiquities*, the present location of which is unknown. Another *hu zhong* is now preserved in Japan. The third one is the *Si hu bo*, housed in the Shanghai Museum. The body decoration of the latter, however, differs considerably from that on the other two and on this *bo*.

9. 師趛鬲

LI. TRIPOD FOOD
CONTAINER. KNOWN AS
SHI JIN LI, 'SHI JIN'S *LI*'

Later Western Zhou period
height inclusive of handles
50.8 cm.
height up to mouth rim
42 cm.
mouth diameter 47 cm.
overall width 57.6 cm.
weight 48,800 gm

孫永寶用□
陳（尊）彝（辱）其萬年子
聖公文母聖姬
寅師趛作（作）文考
佳（惟）九月初吉庚

This vessel, inscribed with a character read as *ru*, is a large sized *li ding* tripod. *Ding* refers to a bronze container with a deep, rounded bowl supported by three legs with two 'ear' handles. There are exceptions, however; for instance, round *ding* whose inner legs are flattened; three-legged *ding* with lobed upper legs; *ding* with a horizontal plate attached between the legs; and single-column *ding*, which are all variants of the more common round *ding*. Another type prevalent from the middle Shang to early Western Zhou periods was the four-footed square *ding*. The huge *Hou wu* or *Si mu wu ding*, a large square tripod weighing 875 kilograms, is a vessel representative of this type.

In the Shang period, the *li* tripod had upright loop or 'ear' handles, a deep, pouch-like body and short legs, but this shape was reduced in height at the close of the Shang and the beginning of the Zhou and was further reduced in the later Zhou and the Spring and Autumn periods, with the bag-like lobes of the leg so lowered and widened that the vessel almost became flat bottomed. Although it had quite a wide lip, it was generally without handles. But at the same time, the *li* tripod with a pouch-like body appeared, which might be a case of reversion to type.

Large sized *ding* always have special nomenclature, for instance, *huo ding*, *ding sheng*, etc. This vessel is called *ru*, which is probably a special term for large *li* tripods. Although there are some differences between *li* and *ding*, they had similar functions as cauldrons for cooking food. Both *li* and *ding* tripods probably shared the same origin in ancient times, with their separation into two types only occurring later. The *li*, however, disappeared from use in the later Warring States' period.

The example shown here has had its patina removed with acid and its surface restored in the past (*shu keng*). It has a wide, flared mouth with a dished rim, and its 'ears' are attached to the neck rather than to the rim. Flanges run down the outside of the deep, rounded bowl, which is supported by three cabriole legs. The decoration is dominated by six large *kui* dragons with averted heads against a ground of spiral filler.

From its shape, the 'ear' handles attached to and bending out and up from the body, and cabriole legs, as well as from the style and content of the inscription, it can be determined as having been cast in the later Western Zhou period.

The inscription on the inner wall of the bowl has twenty-nine characters in five vertical lines. It means 'On this auspicious *geng yin* day during the first part of the ninth lunar month, Shi jin cast this large *li* tripod for his deceased parents. May endless generations of descendants treasure it and use it for ever.' It is for this reason that the sacrificial vessel was named after Shi jin.

The imposing shape of this *li* combines with the solemn decoration to create an air of solemnity. It is the largest and most profusely decorated bronze *li* of its kind so far discovered.

10. 螭梁盉

HE. WINE POURER.
KNOWN AS *CHI LIANG HE*,
'*CHI* DRAGON HANDLED
HE'

Period of the Warring States
height inclusive of loop
handle 23.1 cm.
overall width 19.2 cm.
weight 3,520 gm

The *he* is a wine vessel. From the size of such a bronze vessel and its being mostly three-legged or four-legged, it would seem to have been used as a wine container as much as a wine warmer. But there are other types of *he* with a ring foot and even sometimes without legs at all. As wine could not be heated in the latter case, these must have only been used for containing wine. Because *he* have more often than not been excavated together with a *pan*, a shallow round basin for ritual ablutions, it is not unreasonable for some excavators to regard such vessels as water containers. The *he* underwent many changes in shape between the time of its earlier and later appearance.

The spout of this vessel assumes the form of a realistic bird's head with its mouth slightly open as if it was calling. The hemispherical or, rather, oblate body of the vessel represents the body of the bird, while the base of the spout, which is attached to the body, represents the swept-back wings of the bird with its claws curled in below. A tiger crouching on the bird's head becomes its crest.

The flattened, arch-shaped loop handle is in the form of the body of a *chi*, hornless dragon, its two pairs of legs attached to the shoulder of the vessel on either side. The head stretches forward towards the bird's crest; and the tail hangs, gracefully curved, away from the end of the body. The arched part of the handle is pierced on each side, the main body of the large *chi* formed of nine entwined small *chi* on either side. Above the two legs, on either side of the dragon's body, are a pair of short wings flapping as if ready for flight.

The vertical mouth of the *he* is slightly contracted as it rises from its base and is lidded with a monkey knob. The chain visible around the monkey's neck runs through its right hand to a large ring, cast as part of the animal, to which is attached a real chain, the other end of which is fixed to a loop on the underside of the dragon handle. The monkey assumes a sitting posture, its left arm curled round its drawn-up legs.

Below, the main body of the vessel rests on three legs each in the shape of a strange animal, with a humanoid face, a bird's beak, four clawed feet and a tail. There are two curled horns on its head, while its body is covered with scales and its breasts laid bare. The two hind clawed feet are placed side by side, the legs are a little bent at the knees, and the two front clawed feet each clutch a serpent, the heads of which cling to the strange animal's belly, looking upward. Their bodies are entwined round the animal's trunk and shoulder with their tails hanging at its sides.

The *Shan hai jing Classic of mountains and seas*, an ancient compilation, records a creature called Tuo wei, the god of Mount Jiao, which has a human face but has rams' horns and tigers' claws. This description more or less corresponds to the feature of the animal which forms the vessel's legs.

Except for the plain, undecorated lower portion of the body, the vessel is covered with a granular (or millet) pattern, which acts as the ground decoration. The main design is bounded by three separate bands of decoration. The upper and the lower registers are filled with *gou lian yong wen* (an interlace or chain of clouds otherwise called 'interlocking T's). The middle one contains fairly broad ribbon motifs but the main elements consist of eight separate designs of a single-headed, double-bodied serpent intertwined with a single-bodied, double-headed bird with raised head and drooping tail. The snake, after coiling around the neck of the bird, places its head under the bird's chin.

The edge of the lid bears an ornamental band of twenty interlaced double-headed *chi* hornless dragons. The lid's surface is decorated with a broad circular band of six-foliated and triangular designs in fine thread lines. Scales cover the neck of the bird-shaped spout as well as the snakes which lock around the body of the strange creature which forms the legs of the vessel.

This vessel, peculiar in shape and covered in a profusion of decoration, is a quite outstanding piece amongst bronzes of the Warring States' period. Of special note is the combination of realistic animals such as birds, tigers, monkeys and serpents with fantastic images of spirits and monsters. It fully demonstrates the high level of technical mastery and advances in casting at this time.

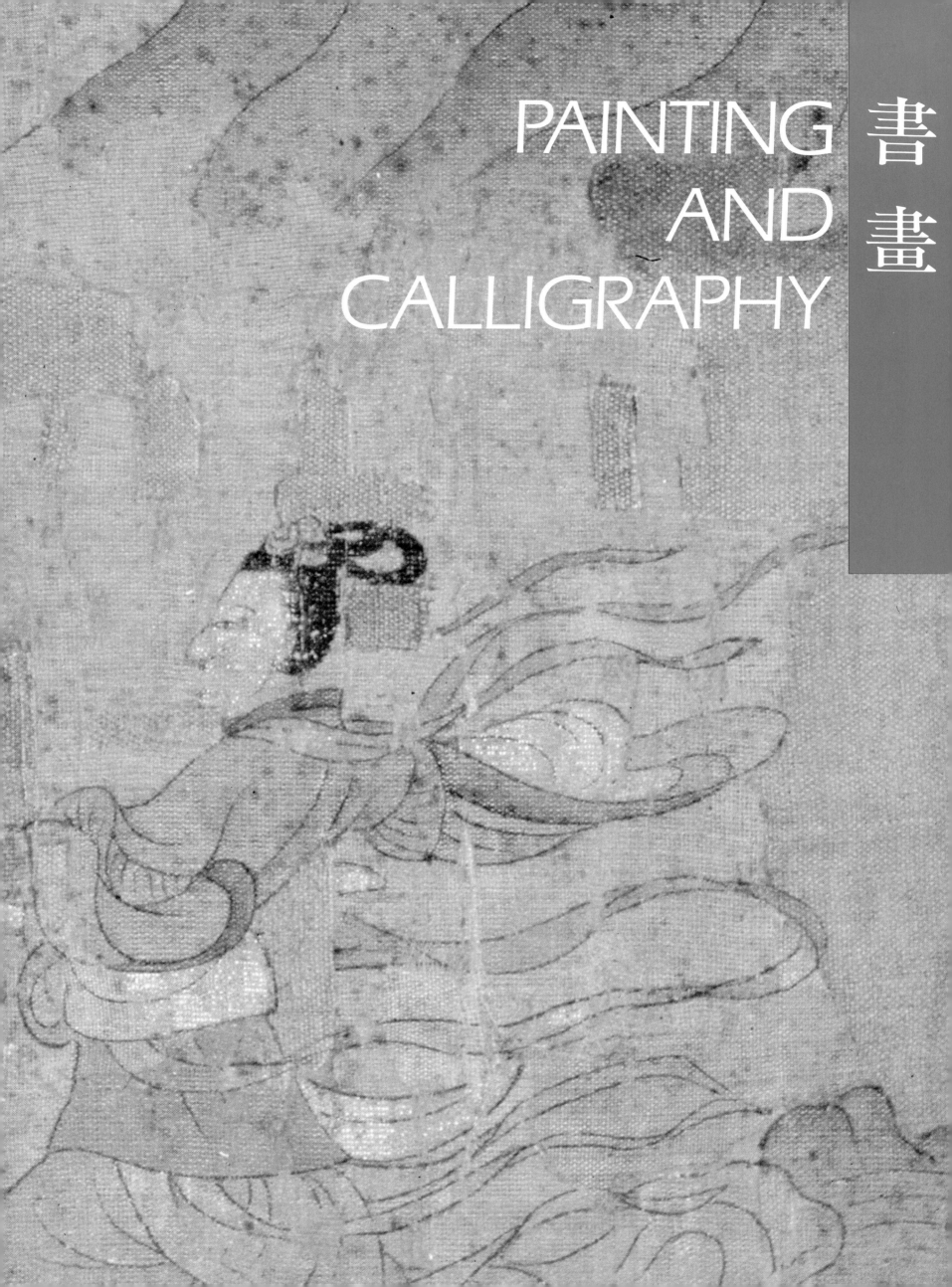

PAINTING
AND
CALLIGRAPHY

書畫

PAINTING AND CALLIGRAPHY

The history of Chinese painting and calligraphy can be traced back over several thousand years. One of the foremost examples of the former are paintings executed on silk during the Warring States' period which were excavated from a tomb of the state of Chu in Changsha, Hunan province. Writing appeared at an even earlier period, with the incising of signs and symbols on pottery of the neolithic period, with written characters beginning to assume the role of an art form, or calligraphy, at least by the Spring and Autumn period.

The figures of paintings on silk of the Warring States' period were first drawn with brush and black ink, and then filled in with colour. This basic technique of using a visible line in pictorial composition has been followed from that time right down to the present day and has become one of the distinctive features of traditional Chinese painting.

Painters of later periods, while seeking to represent images with objective reality, at the same time ceaselessly sought to exploit the aesthetic value of the painted line itself which gave rise to the different groups, or schools, of painters as well as the many different styles of painting. For instance, Gu Kaizhi, who lived during the Eastern Jin period, is the earliest painter whom we know to have been celebrated as such in his day and whose work still survives. His figure paintings, for which he was renowned, all of the highest artistic order, may act as a standard by which we can gain some insight into contemporary painting. He was the first artist to put forward the theory of 'conveying spirit through form'. The efforts of later artists in their search for the expression of 'spirit' or the essence of all animate and inanimate objects extended from figure painting to landscape and bird and flower paintings, stemming directly from this initial concern with figure drawing. This requirement meant that in traditional Chinese painting the need to take nature as the model was always stressed, but never to the extent that it should become nature's slave. Realistic reproduction was not what was called for. As a guiding principle of pictorial composition, 'the beautiful and mysterious' lay somewhere between 'similarity and non-similarity'. Artists concerned themselves as much with inner as with outer reality.

The development of landscape painting began with the withdrawal from its role as a mere background to figures in compositions some time between the Sui and the Tang dynasties. From that time it could be developed gradually as an independent genre to its eventual full maturity. The oldest landscape to have survived is a composition entitled 'Spring excursion', *You chun tu*, by a painter of great renown, Zhan Ziqian. Its artistic accomplishment epitomizes all that was best in landscape painting during the period of the Six Dynasties, as well as initiating a new phase of this genre which blossomed during the Tang era. Zhan's style and technique was carried on by two painters, Li Sixun and his son Li Zhaodao, who brought Tang landscape painting, which was characterized by the use of bright colour, especially blue and green and later gold, to new heights.

Figure painting also flourished during the Tang, a golden period in the history of Chinese painting. The most prominent artists of the time included Yan Liben, Wu Daozi, Zhang Xuan and Zhou Fang. Unfortunately, although he was extolled as 'a sage of painting', no authentic works by Wu Daozi have been handed down to us. We do, however, possess Yan Liben's *Bu nian tu*, 'The imperial sedan', typical of the achievements in portraiture of the early Tang; and Zhou Fang's 'Ladies fanning themselves', *Hui shan shi nü tu*, representative of the middle Tang style.

Other famous Tang painters such as Cao Ba, Han Gan, Han Huang and Wei Yan were well known for specializing in portraying animals, often bulls and horses, illustrating the growing division of painting into different genres as the art continued to develop. The only authentic piece now believed to have been executed by Han Huang himself is 'Five bulls', *Wu niu tu*. All Wei Yan's original works were lost without trace at a very early date, but we are still able to visualize the style in which he worked from 'Herding horses', *Mu fang tu*, a close copy of the original made by Li Gonglin, a celebrated artist of the Song period.

Figure painting continued to flourish during the Southern Tang, one of the dynasties which was in power during the period of the Five Dynasties. Among those serving in the royal Hanlin painting academy as court painters were Gu Hongzhong, Wang Qihan, Zhou Wenju and Wei Xian, all of whom are now regarded as great masters. The merit of Gu Hongzhong's works lies in the meticulous way in which he depicts the innermost being of his figures so that their external appearance is natural and lifelike. His representative piece executed with sovereign elegance is 'Night entertainment given by Han Xizai', *Han Xizai ye yan tu*. The only original extant piece by Wei Xian in China is 'Man of virtue', *Gao shi tu*.

The close of the Tang and beginning of the Five Dynasties marked a period of great change and developments in which great strides forward were taken in the two areas of landscape and bird and flower painting. The newly emerging monochrome ink and wash, *shui mo*, method in landscape painting was gradually substituted for the old 'meticulous gold and green', *jin bi*, style. Guided by concepts such as 'imitating nature outwardly and capturing the spirit inwardly' landscape painters penetrated deep into the mountains to observe nature at first hand and then to explore various new modes of expression and creative ideas. Painters of the North China central plain such as Jing Hao and Guan Tong used a new technique of painting which employed different types of brush stroke which were referred to as 'outlines', *gou*, 'hatchet strokes', *zhuo* 'texture' or 'filler' strokes used for modelling contours of rocks and surfaces, *cun*, and 'use of colour' *ran*, to reproduce the majestic mountain peaks of the North. This method successfully conveyed their bare yet solid cragginess. Painters like Dong Yuan and Ju ran in the area occupied by the Southern Tang dynasty employed 'spread-out hemp fibre' *cun*, *pi ma cun*, and 'dots', *dian zi cun*, to describe and model the luxuriant vegetation and the constantly changing mist and clouds of the South, achieving an effect of grace and lyricism.

Bird and flower painting during the same period was also executed in two different styles owing to the places of their origin. The Xishu (present day Sichuan) school headed by Huang Quan drew materials largely from the rare flowers, exotic fowl and auspicious animals found at the palace. His paintings, executed in fine and meticulous brushwork combined with bright colours, were renowned as 'the richness and splendour that is Huang'. Xu Xi of the Southern Tang, on the other hand, mostly took as his subjects birds, insects, flowers and plants commonly seen in the countryside, and since he gave prominence to ink lines and quiet colours in his works, his style was praised as 'Xu Xi's typical ease and rusticity'. Unfortunately, the works of these two originators of bird and flower painting can only be guessed at. Those of Xu Xi have long since disappeared and the only painting by Huang Quan to have survived is 'Studies of birds, insects and turtles', *Xie sheng zhen qin tu*.

The imperial painting academy flourished especially during the period of the Song dynasty, when a great number of celebrated artists were drawn to the court. Guo Xi, arguably the greatest master of landscape painting of the period, was summoned by imperial edict to the court of the emperor Shen zong of the Northern Song dynasty. 'Rocky lowland with far horizon', *Ke shi ping yuan tu*, is considered to be representative of his work while at court. Apart from his great contribution to art in terms of the colossal number of landscapes that he painted, he fully explored the theoretical side of landscape painting. Another court painter active in the academy of the emperor Hui zong was Zhang Zeduan, whose best known work was 'Going upriver at the Qing ming festival', *Qing ming shang he tu*, an astonishing work. Other court painters include the four great masters of the Southern Song period, namely Li Tang, Liu Songnian, Ma Yuan and Xia Gui, whose works not only display a vast range of artistic skills, but are filled with new concepts of composition marked by a great economy of style. For instance, Ma Yuan, in his twelve 'Studies of water', *Shui tu*, by taking a fairly ordinary subject such as water was able to express new creative ideas by means of the observed linear patterns made by the liquid in its different states.

During the latter half of the Northern Song period, there was a great surge in what was to be termed 'scholar' or 'literati' painting, *wen ren hua*, as a result of the works and theories of such painters as Su Shi, Wen Tong, Mi Fei, Li Gonglin and Wang Shen, whose ideas of creativity placed a still greater emphasis on 'spirit', *shen*, in painting. This contributed to the development of spontaneous expression by means of the wash and ink method of painting. Having undergone its fermentation period during the Southern Song, literati painting emerged as the main trend in the pictorial art of the Yuan period. Of these scholar painters in the early Yuan the most prominent was an eminent official, Zhao Mengfu. While advocating the reinstatement of art of the past masters in opposition to the repetitious and formulaic paintings of the imperial academy since the late Southern Song period, he also advocated the development of 'amateur' literati painting by relying on the past to create the new. The picture 'Horses drinking in an autumn suburb', *Qiu jiao yin ma tu*, was typical of his painting in imitation of the Tang blue and green landscapes but brought within the literati style. Under his influence, the four Yuan dynasty master artists of landscape painting, namely Huang Gongwang, Wu Zhen, Wang Meng and Ni Zan came to the fore. Huang's 'light red', *qian jiang*, landscapes are simple and vigorous with natural, unrestrained brushwork delineating wide, full vistas. Wu and Wang, having modelled themselves after Dong Yuan and Ju ran, used brushes heavily loaded with ink to execute vigorous strokes to produce landscapes of deep refinement. Ni Zan, on the other hand, created a mood of aloofness with his economical strokes and light use of ink. With original styles and features, all four artists independently reached a new peak in literati landscape painting.

During the first half of the Ming period, the art of painting was under the dual influence of the court painters and the Zhe school. Landscape, figure and bird and flower painting continued to be modelled on the works of the Song imperial academy, while the Zhe school found its greatest master in Dai Jin, a painter of great influence and superb achievement. His landscapes, besides inheriting the styles of Ma Yuan and Xia Gui, show the influence of the brushwork of the Yuan artists and are characterized by a vein of robustness and nonrestraint. During the latter part of the late Ming period, painters in the area around Suzhou (Jiangsu province) were particularly active and the four masters of the so-called Wu school, Shen Zhou, Wen Zhengming, Tang Yin and Qiu Ying, became the leading artists of the Jiangnan (the area south of the River Yangtze) region. Shen and Wen were well versed in the art of landscape painting, modelling themselves on Dong Yuan and Ju ran and the four Yuan dynasty masters in order to create their own individual styles. Tang and Qiu took Zhou Chen as their most recent model and studied such artists as Li Tang, Liu Songnian and others from the more distant past. Their virtuosity, however, was not limited to landscapes but in addition extended to figure painting. The fine and spontaneous method of expression, *xie yi*, in the area of bird and flower painting underwent a long formative period before it made a sudden leap in development away from the careful studies with which the genre was associated. Shen Zhou and Tang Yin opened up the confines of this genre and they were followed by Chen Shun and Xu Wei. All of them were able to give full play to the properties inherent in both wash and ink and the freer *xie yi* methods. Xu Wei in particular executed his brushwork with generous use of ink in a style which was completely free from inhibition. Indeed, his impact is felt even down to the present.

The years covering the end of the Ming and the beginning of the Qing dynasties saw the emergence of a multitude of fine painters. In figure painting, Chen Hongshou is prominent. In landscape painting, Shi xi, Shi tao and Wang Hui are counted amongst the great masters, while Hong Ren and Xiang Shengmo developed remarkably individual styles.

Chinese calligraphy, like painting, is an art of linear definition and, similarly, both use the brush and ink stick as their main tools. Throughout the dynastic periods there has been no lack of excellent calligraphers, each bringing in his own innovations. These two have been closely related during the long period of China's rich and colourful culture and art. It is, therefore, no surprise that models of fine calligraphy and famous paintings have always been kept together in collections. From very early times works by celebrated calligraphers and painters have been collected together, their cultural value being seen as much greater than that of precious stones and metals. For example, by the period of the Tang dynasty, a work by Gu Kaizhi (fifth century AD) was already regarded as 'a priceless treasure'. A painting by one of his contemporaries, Wu Daozi, was worth 'twenty thousand pieces of gold'. Down the ages, apart from the royal households who spared no effort in collecting ancient calligraphy and paintings, there were many private collectors, such as Mi Fei during the Song period, Xiang Yuanbian of the Ming, Liang Qingbiao and An Qi of the Qing period, who were widely renowned as owners of rich collections of works of art. Most celebrated of all, perhaps, was the collection gathered together by the emperor Qian long of the Qing dynasty, which was grandiose in the extreme.

11. 石鼓

STONE DRUM AND INK
RUBBING

Period of the Warring States
Stele: 11th year of the reign
of Duke Xian of the state of
Qin equivalent to 374 BC
Ink rubbing of early Ming
period

The significance of stone drum script lies in the fact that it was directly evolved out of the so-called *Zhou wen*, 'Zhou script', named after the official who standardized the shapes of characters in approximately 800 BC. Stone drum script, therefore, can be seen as transitional between Zhou script and small seal script, *xiao zhuan*, a standardization which took place, once again, during the Qin period, in the second century BC.

In the early Tang, Su Xu said: 'Yu Shinan, Chu Suiliang and Ouyang Xun heaped praise on the ancient script', and Zhang Huaiguan when mentioning the great seal script in his *Judgement of calligraphy, Shu duan*, said that 'its heroic twists are like something wrought with iron, yet displaying a dignity coupled with ease and graceful smoothness', which describes the characteristics of the script exactly. The structure of the characters is quite regular, well proportioned, and well knit. The brushwork is at once mellow and tensile, without showing any sharp points. Therefore, the stone drum script has been used as a model by all those who have wished to learn how to write seal characters, throughout history.

Due to their condition, it is difficult to obtain good ink rubbings on paper from the stone drums. At the time that they were discovered, early in the Tang period, they were already badly eroded. Only four rubbings made in the Northern Song period are extant. One used to be kept in the Tian yi ge, First

The oldest extant inscriptions carved into stone are to be found on 'stone drums'. Carved on the ten drum-shaped stone blocks are ten poems whose titles are in the following order: *Wu che, Qian yi, Tian che, Luan che, Ling yu, Zuo yuan, Er shi, Ma jian, Wu shui* and *Wu ren*. The poems consist of more than 500 characters, all in large seal script, *da zhuan*, and record the grand occasion when the king of Zhou dispatched an emissary to the state of Qin to join in the Duke of Qin's hunting expedition along the River Qian. After their discovery early in the seventh century AD in Yong xian, Shaanxi province, the script was greatly admired by the calligraphers of the time such as Yu Shinan, Chu Suiliang and Ouyang Xun. During the period of the Tang and Song dynasties, Du Fu, Wei Yingwu, Han Yu and Su Shi all wrote poems on the stone drum script, and Ouyang Xiu was the first one to record it in his *Record of ancient stone inscriptions, Ji gu lu*. Since then the drums have been popularly regarded as most precious, for from them we can see the stage of development that inscriptions, the Chinese written language, calligraphy and Chinese literature had reached at that time. Thus, the stone drum inscriptions hold an important place in historical and archaeological studies, such as the history of literature, the history of development of the script and the history of calligraphy.

Pavilion in Heaven, a building owned by a family named Fan in Siming. Zhejiang province; and the other three, discovered at the end of the Qing period, used to be in the Shi gu zhai, Studio of the Ten Drums, in Anguo xian, Hebei province, in the Ming dynasty, but are now in Japan.

The reason why no rubbings had been taken during the Southern Song period is that in the final years of the Northern Song dynasty, the Jin army captured the stone drums and took them to the North and the emperor Zhang zong of the Jin dynasty had the drums locked away. The rubbings made during the Yuan, the Ming and the Qing periods reveal further damage to the inscriptions. Previously in the collection of Zhu Wenjun, it is the only rubbing now housed in the Palace Museum to have been made in the middle of the Ming period.

This set of treasures has undergone many vicissitudes. Since their discovery early in the Tang, they had been subjected to inclement weather and the ravages of man and it was not until the Song period that they were removed to the Fengxiang prefectural academy. During the reign of the Northern Song emperor Hui zong, the prime minister Cai Jing first put them in the Biyong preparatory school for the imperial university at the capital, and later took them to the Ji guge, Pavilion for the Storing of Antiques, in the inner imperial palace. As we have mentioned, when the capital of the Song dynasty fell into the hands of the Jin army, the invaders seized the drums and carried them off to the North and put them in the Da xing imperial university (in present day Beijing). At the beginning of the Mongol Yuan dynasty these ancient objects were left in the side halls of the imperial university, and were subsequently removed to buildings inside the Dacheng Gate, where they remained for over 600 years. During the war against Japan, they were transported south over great distances in order to safeguard them and it was not until after the end of hostilities that they were brought back to Beijing where they are now kept in a special room in the Palace Museum.

12. 張遷碑

INK RUBBING. FROM
STELE KNOWN AS *ZHANG
QIAN BEI*, 'ZHANG QIAN
STELE'

The official script or the clerical style, *li shu*, of Chinese calligraphy made its first appearance in the Qin period and became most widespread in the Han period. A pleasing script, it is a modification of the seal character script, with the shape of each character developing from the round appearance of seal script to that of a square. Not only was it more regular and therefore more convenient in writing than seal characters, but it lent itself much more to the soft, flexible tip of the writing brush pen, which had come into use.

The multiplicity of its strokes gives the official script a rich, decorative appeal and it occupies a significant position in the history of calligraphy. The Zhang Qian stele or stone tablet has been regarded as the most representative of the trenchant and robust style of the extant *li shu* of the Han period.

The tablet was set up in the 3rd year of the Zhong ping era (AD 186) in the reign of the Eastern Han dynasty emperor Ling di and was excavated in the opening years of the Ming period. It was originally sited in Dongping xian, Shandong province, but it is now housed in the Tai Temple (for offering sacrifices to the god of Mount Tai, the most sacred of the five sacred mountains of China) in Taian of the same province.

The script contains 16 vertical lines, each with 42 characters, with a line of 12 seal characters at the top which read 'eulogy to the late Mr Zhang, magistrate of Gucheng and Dangyin, of the Han dynasty', followed by a biographical record of Zhang Qian's life, deeds and conduct. On the back of the tablet are engraved the names of those who contributed money towards the raising of this commemorative stone stele.

The style of the inscriptions is characteristically regular and uncluttered. Out of its primitive simplicity and imposing strength there emerges a vigorous and strangely wonderful style. The brushwork typifies a symphony of sturdiness and uprightness, compactness and elegance as well as rich variations. The brush tip is pressed and bent at the start of each stroke to give it a square beginning, but flattens out at the end of it. The structural form looks somewhat rectangular, but the individual characters show immense variations in size, length and shape formed with both thick and thin strokes. The style of the inscriptions on the back of the tablet is much more restrained, free and natural.

This tablet, similar to the Heng Fang stele and the recently excavated Xian Yu Huang stele, contributed to the development of calligraphy in the subsequent Wei and Jin periods. Highly valued and widely imitated by students of calligraphy, the Zhang Qian stele is regarded as representative of the official script in the closing years of the Eastern Han period, and it occupies a very important place in the history of Chinese calligraphy.

Few good rubbings of the tablet are now in existence, and the only early rubbing that clearly shows the four characters *dong, li, run* and *se* in their complete forms is the one shown here. Because the rubbing itself has been produced with such skill, the thick black ink delineating the clear-cut lines of the original characters, incised into the stone, it is a fine and rare object that can be appreciated for its own qualities.

Bao Xi once wrote a title label for this rubbing, and Gui Fu, Guo Shaogao and Lu Shi added postscripts, while Chu Fengchun, Wang Yun, Wang Daxie, Weng Tonghe, Liu Tingchen and Chen Baochen have added their names to it to record their appreciation. Once in the private collection of Zhu Wenjun of Xiaoshan xian, Zhejiang province, it was donated to the Palace Museum in 1954.

13. 伯遠帖

WANG XUN (350–401):
LETTER TO BO YUAN

Calligraphy in running
script
25.1 × 17.2 cm.
Jin period

The period of the Jin dynasty, during which time calligraphy built on in the traditional style of the Han and Wei periods, saw the emergence of many celebrated calligraphers. They not only wrote in all the existing scripts, but had also developed styles of their own. It can be said that it was a great period unprecedented in the history of Chinese calligraphy. Among the famous calligraphers, Wang Xizhi, his son, Wang Xianzhi, and their adherents, were foremost in this art and their influence was to be felt down the centuries in the works of their many imitators.

Unfortunately, original examples of the work of Wang Xizhi and Wang Xianzhi were lost very early on and examples of calligraphy which are said to have been written by them are, without exception, facsimile copies of the Tang period. The only genuine calligraphy in existence from the Wang line of calligraphers is the example illustrated.

Wang Xun was a nephew of Wang Xizhi. He learned calligraphy from his uncle when a child and later earned a considerable reputation as a calligrapher. The composition entitled *Bo yuan tie* is a letter written by Wang Xun to Bo yuan comprising forty-seven words arranged in five vertical lines, and reads as follows:

'To Bo yuan – your fine and successful career deserves deep admiration and emulation by us all. I am feeble in health and therefore take to an easy and leisurely life. Your letter has come to hand, but I don't think I can state clearly how I feel. It seems to be only yesterday that we parted, yet I feel as if it were long long ago. As we are separated by mountain peaks and lofty cliffs, we shall not be able to see each other and look forward to coming together.'

The style is clean-cut, sinewy and forceful, fully displaying angularity with its cutting edges and pointedness. The structure of the characters is well knit, and the strokes are well spaced. There is a slight tendency for the lines to tip towards the left, giving a precipitous and solemn appearance. From this can be seen the harmonious style of Jin calligraphy and it is an invaluable source for the study of the history of calligraphy.

This specimen was kept at the court of the Northern Song dynasty and an entry for it was made in the *Xuan he shu pu, Xuan he catalogue of calligraphy*. Later it found its way into the collections of Dong Qichang and other noted calligraphers of the Ming and Qing periods. It was also described in *Records of paintings and calligraphy, Shu hua ji, Masterpieces seen in a lifetime, Ping sheng zhuang guan*, and *Complete collection of calligraphy, Mo yuan hui guan*. During the reign of the Qian long emperor of the Qing dynasty it was acquired by the court and was greatly treasured by him. He kept this with other calligraphic specimens such as Wang Xizhi's 'Clearing skies after snow', *Kuai xue shi qing*, and Wang Xianzhi's 'Mid autumn', *Zhong qiu tie*, in the west pavilion of the Hall of Mental Cultivation, and eventually reserved a special study called the Room of the Three Rarities, *San xi tang*, referring directly to the Wangs' calligraphy, in which he could appreciate them whenever he wished. After the fall of the Qing dynasty, it was removed by Pu yi, the last Qing emperor, and later passed into the hands of private collectors. After 1949, this piece and Wang Xianzhi's 'Mid autumn' were both discovered in Hongkong but it was not until the end of 1951 that they were bought by the Chinese government and returned to the Museum.

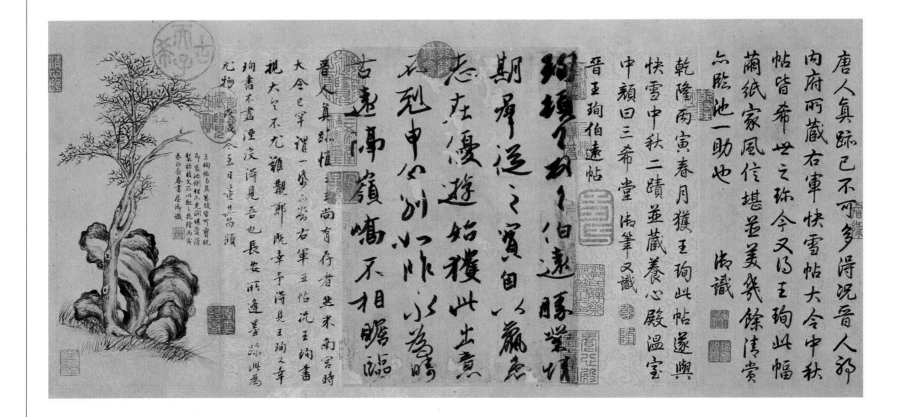

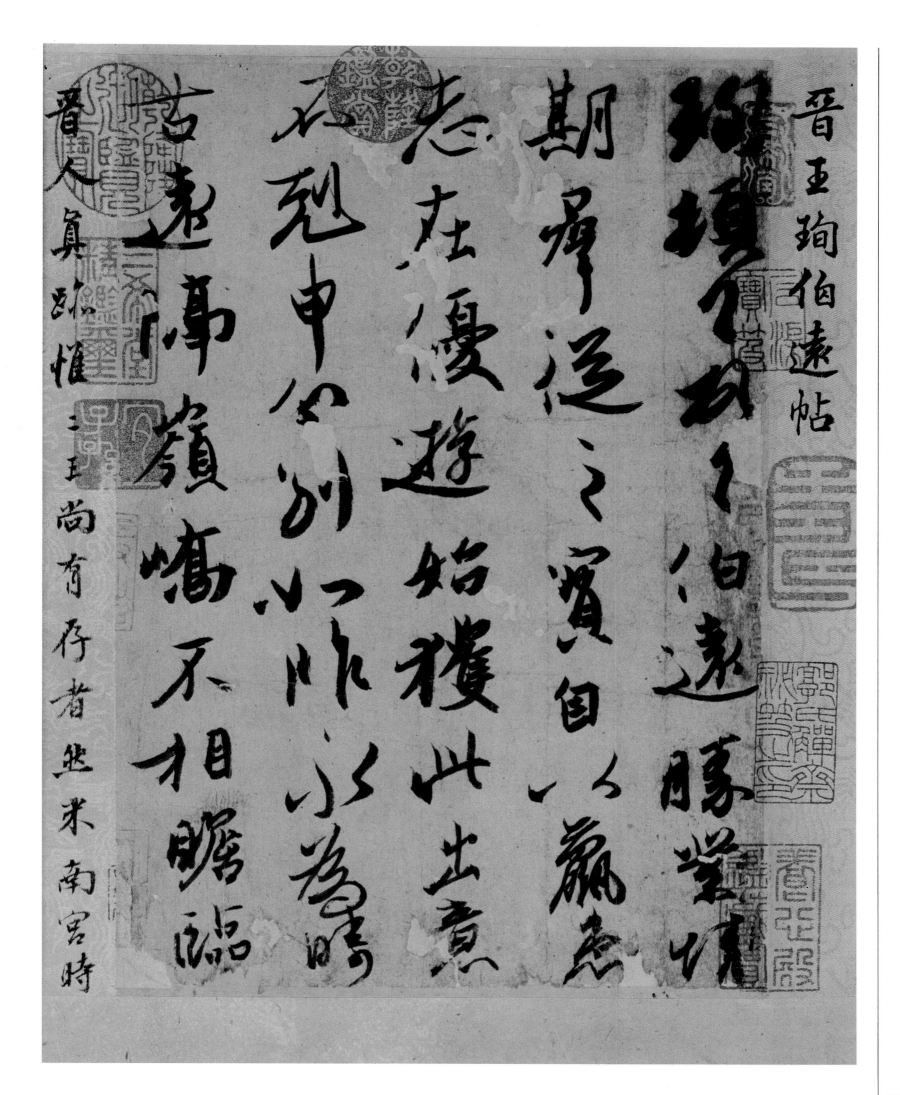

14. 張翰思鱸帖

OUYANG XUN (557–641):
ZHANG HAN REMEMBERS
THE PERCH

Calligraphy in running and
regular scripts
25.5 × 33 cm.
Tang period

Ouyang Xun, whose style or studio name was Xinben, hailed from Linxiang, Tanzhou, present day Changsha, in Hunan province. He first served as an official during the Sui period and continued his official career during the succeeding Tang. He was so successful that he became the counsellor to the crown prince and an academician of the imperial college and was finally created a peer. He was a great calligrapher and an erudite man conversant with the classics and history. Taking Wang Xizhi and Wang Xianzhi as his models, he developed a style of his own, known as the 'Ou-style', which was to exert influence over the styles of later generations of calligraphers. It is well knit in structure and regular in shape, with brush-strokes reminding one of *li shu*, or clerical script. His style in fact marks a transition between the calligraphy of the Six Dynasties' and that of the Tang periods. It paved the way for the establishment of the Tang *kai shu*, regular script, and provides us with a link between the old and new scripts. Alongside Yu Shinan, Chu Suiliang and Xue Ji, he is regarded as one of the four great calligraphers of the early Tang. Extant inscriptions on stone taken from his calligraphy, all in regular style, include 'Inscription in praise of the sweet spring at Jiucheng Palace' and the Huada Temple stele and his calligraphy in running script, *xing shu*, still in existence includes 'Zhang Han remembers the perch', shown here.

This letter is a biographical sketch of Zhang Han in ten lines, with nine to eleven characters to each line. The neatly written characters are tall and slender yet compact, with bold, vigorous brushstrokes forming balanced characters within which can be seen a tendency towards slanting the horizontal lines. The calligraphy itself lacks a signature, but the following has been written on the paper on which it is mounted by Zhao Ji, the emperor Hui zong of the Song dynasty: 'This calligraphy written by Ouyang Xun of the Tang is characterized by its boldness, strength and momentum, so much so that even the monk Zhi yong could not come close to it. Jilin [now Korea] once sent an envoy to solicit his calligraphy. When the emperor Gao zu heard of this, he also expressed his admiration for the widespread fame of Ouyang Xun's calligraphy. In his later years, his strokes became more vigorous than ever as if they would defy everything before them and it is no exaggeration or empty flattery to say that his characters stand sheer and peerless like solitary peaks with precipices on all sides.'

This piece of calligraphy was mentioned in the *Xuan he shu pu, Mo xian hui guan* and the *Da guan lu* as being in the imperial collections of the Northern and Southern Song and Qing dynasties. During the reign of the Qian long emperor of the Qing dynasty it was reproduced in the *Calligraphic masterpieces from the Room of the Three Rarities, San xi tang fa tie.*

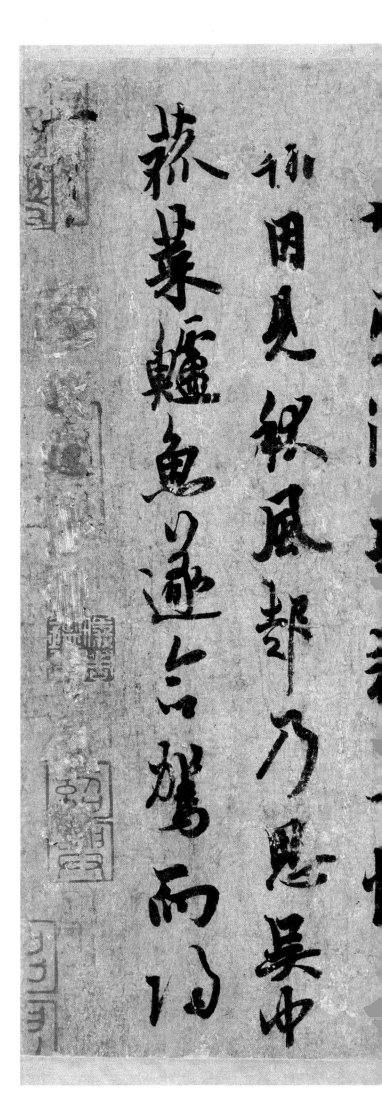

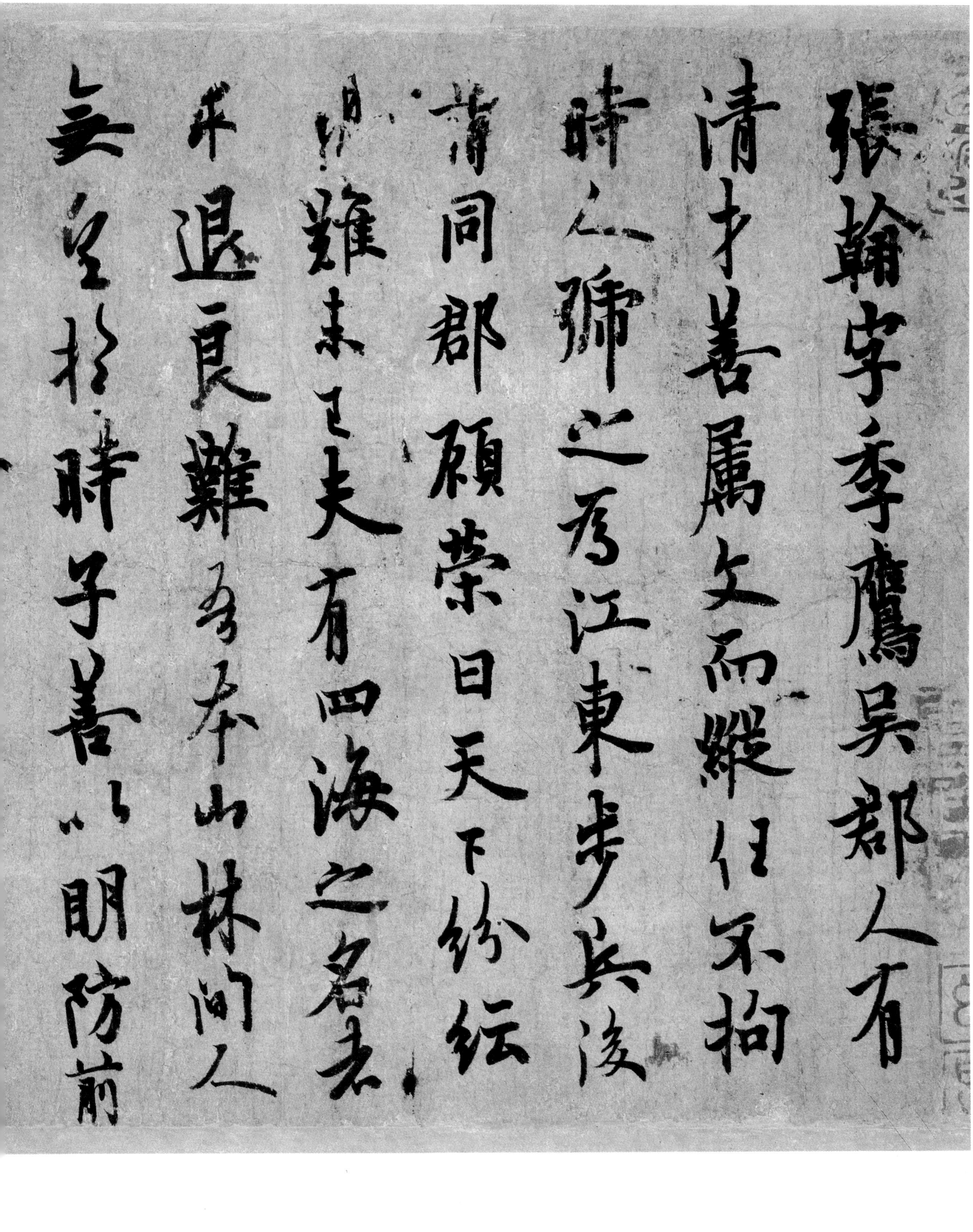

張翰字季鷹吳郡人有
清才善屬文而縱任不拘
時人號之為江東步兵後
謂同郡顧榮曰天下紛紜
禍難未已夫有四海之名者
求退良難吾本山林間人
無望於時子善以明防前

15. 自書詩卷

CAI XIANG (1012–1067).
POEMS BY THE
CALLIGRAPHER

Calligraphy in running
script
28.2 × 221.2 cm.
Song period

In the history of calligraphy, Su Shi, Huang Tingjian, Mi Fei and Cai Xiang are regarded as the four great calligraphers of the Song period. In fact, it was another calligrapher, Cai Jing, rather than Cai Xiang who was originally placed in fourth position after the other three masters. However, as Cai Jing became an object of hatred because of his misgovernment when in power, Cai Xiang was substituted for him.

The oldest among the four masters, Cai Xiang, styled Junmo, was born in Xiangyou, Xinhua, now Fujian province. He was inspired by the Jin and Tang masters and was expert in all types of calligraphy, but he is especially remembered for his running and regular scripts. He had made a close study of works by Zhong You, Wang Xizhi and Yan Zhenqing. Adhering strictly to the disciplines of the old masters, his calligraphy resembles Wang Xizhi's 'both in form and in spirit but never went beyond the scope of Wang'. He was also the most accomplished imitator of the Tang calligraphers. The emperor Hui zong of the Song dynasty once said, 'Cai's well disciplined style is pregnant with force. He is really the Yan Zhenqing of today.' Su Shi also praised Cai as a 'gifted and learned man with such complete mastery of his brush that his mind and hand are in complete harmony. No other calligrapher of this period can match him in the diversity of style.' Even though he never truly developed a completely new style, unlike the other three famous Song calligraphers, during the early Song period when imitation of ancient masters was fashionable, his achievements in calligraphy were by no means insignificant considering the fact that he was able to adopt the best elements of the Tang masters to form a style of his own.

The calligraphy shown here includes eleven poems by Cai Xiang composed during his journey from Fujian, when he was recalled to the then capital, Kaifeng, in 1050 at the age of forty. It is typical of the running script he produced at the time when it was approaching maturity in his middle age. The beautiful flow of the spirited brushstrokes is serious and mellow and the structure is compact and well balanced. The calligraphy begins with characters in running hand, *xing shu*, with a tendency to regular script, *kai shu*, then the flow of running hand begins to predominate, becoming a cross between running, *xing*, and cursive, *cao*, script. This is finally transformed into the complete freedom of the cursive script, *cao shu*. The lightness and beauty of the style without the loss of moderation makes the calligraphy a great masterpiece.

Many famous calligraphers have written their colophons at the end of the calligraphy and it has repeatedly changed hands since the Song with its title mentioned in various catalogues such as the *Shan hu wang, Wu shi shu hua ji, Ping sheng zhuang guan* and *Shi qu catalogue* (volume 3).

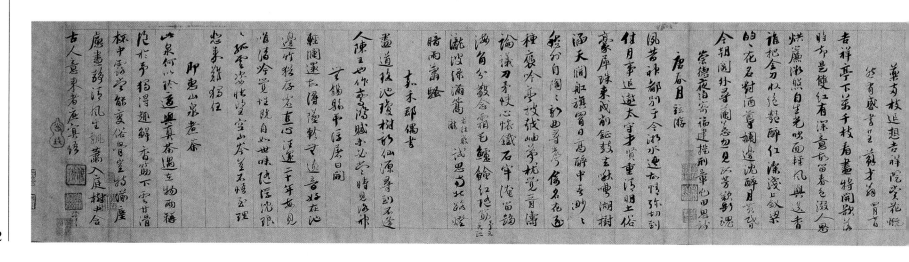

陳王也作喜鴻賦求兄

空野驅車狩远行

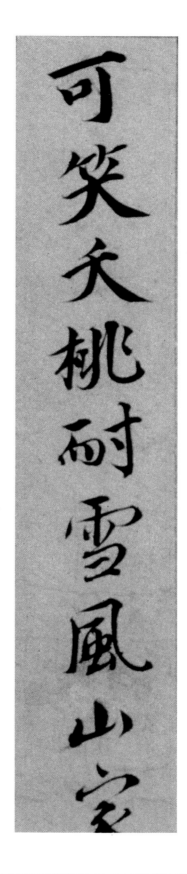

可笑夭桃耐雪風山家

16. 新歲展慶帖

SU SHI (1036–1101):
LETTER, 'SENDING
GREETINGS'

Calligraphy in running
script
30.2 × 48.8 cm.
Song period

Su Shi, also known as Dongpo the Hermit, was from Meishan, Sichuan province. He was a great writer, poet, calligrapher and painter. Moreover, he was included among the 'Eight great essayists of the Tong and Song'. His scripts, both the running and regular styles, were modelled on the works of Li Yong, Xu Hao, Yan Zhenqing and Yang Ningshi. In fact, his brushwork represented an altogether new style which had assimilated the merits of a wide range of leading masters and can be traced back to Wang Xizhi, Wang Xianzhi and the monk Zhi yong. Also referred to as one of the 'Four great Song calligraphers' he was, therefore, ranked alongside Mi Fei, Cai Xiang and Huang Tingjian, who also regarded Su Shi's brushwork as 'second to none of the dynasty under which he lived'.

The example illustrated here is a masterpiece typical of Su Shi's running script. The vigorous and beautiful brushwork in bold strokes is executed in a free and uninhibited manner. The structure characteristic of Su Shi, which appears irregular at first glance, is actually well spaced. The Tang calligraphers, such as Yan Zhenqing and Liu Gongquan, are known for their regular, steady and dignified style, while their counterparts of the Song period sought the novelty of apparent lack of coherence in a structure at once vivid and beautiful, thereby creating a brand new style. The calligraphy shown here is a good example of this tendency. The whole piece, consisting of nineteen lines with a little more than two hundred characters, was written from beginning to end without stopping. Though an ordinary letter, it shows no trace of carelessness or hesitation on the part of the writer who possesses complete control of his brush in achieving a perfectly natural style. As Su Shi himself once said, 'good calligraphy sometimes occurs precisely because there was no original intention that it should be so'.

Su Shi wrote the letter to his good friend Jichang (Chen Zao), asking Chen to meet him at Huangzhou. From its contents, we know that it was written on the second day of the first lunar month of the fifth year of the year Yuan feng, equivalent to 1082, when Su Shi was forty-six. It was also the third year after he was banished to Huangzhou, where he had been granted a tract of land so that he could work the fields and build a house on it. Su Shi wrote in his letter that since the house was not completed at the time, he was unable to enjoy the company of his friend. However, he still wished Chen to meet him at the end of the month. By then the house would most probably have been built. This letter not only exemplifies Su Shi's calligraphy, but also provides important insight into his life and his friends.

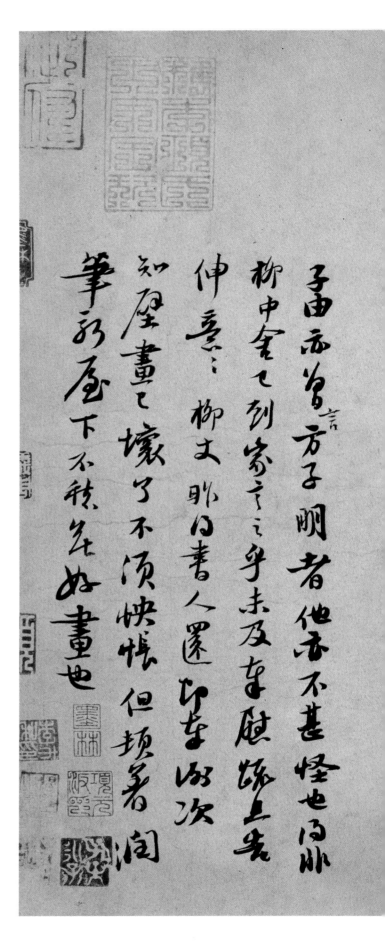

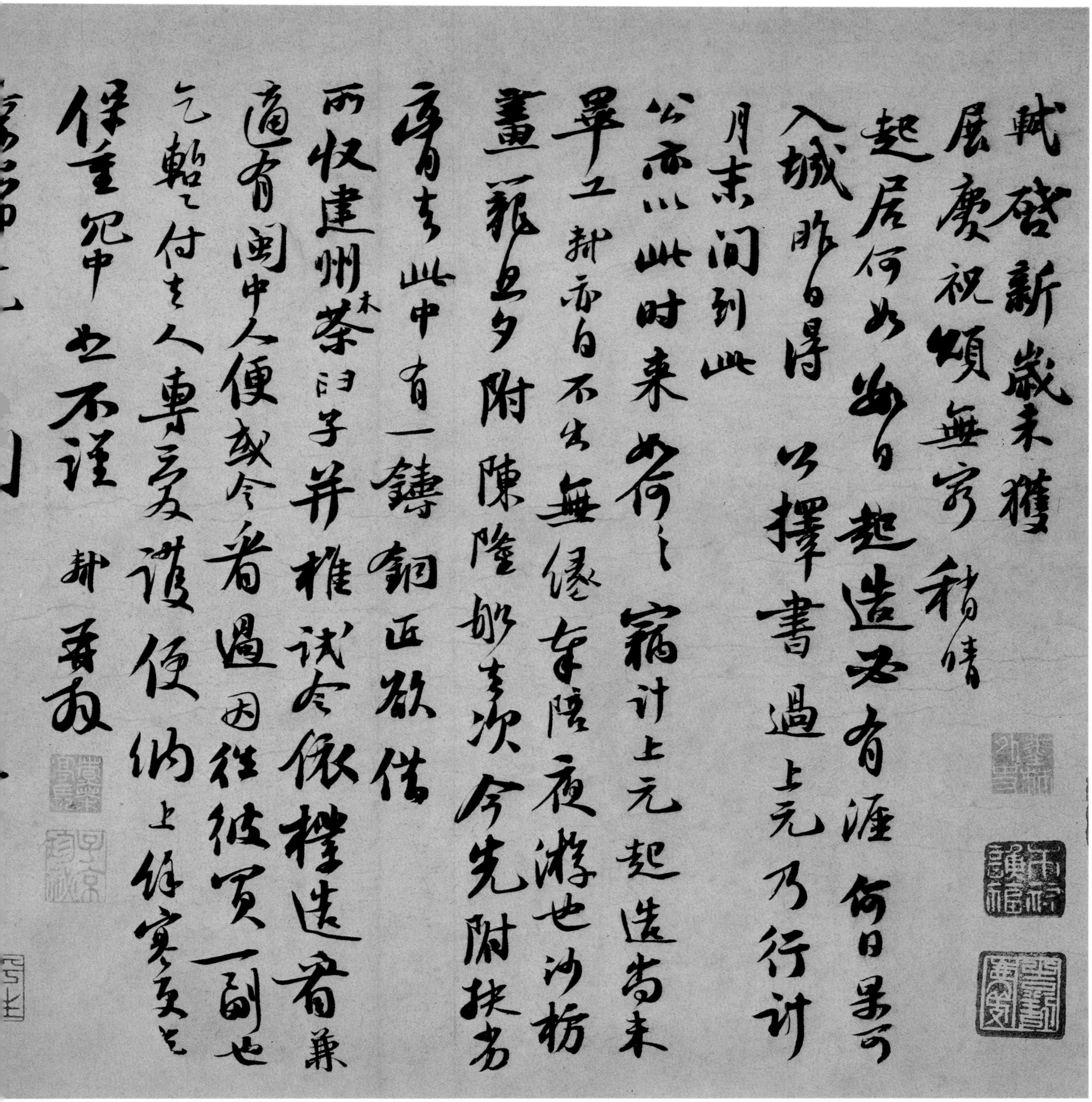
轼启：新岁未获
展庆，祝颂无穷。稍晴，
起居何如？数日起造必有涯，何日果可
入城？昨日得公择书，过上元乃行，计
月末间到此。
公亦以此时来，如何？如何？窃计上元起造，尚未
毕工。轼亦自不出，无缘奉陪夜游也。沙枋
画笼，旦夕附陈隆船去次，今先附扶劣
膏去。此中有一铸铜匠，欲借
所收建州木茶臼子并椎，试令依样造看。兼
适有闽中人便，或令看过，因往彼买一副也。
乞暂付去人，专爱护，便纳上。余寒更乞
保重。冗中，恕不谨。轼再拜。

17. 詩送四十九姪帖

HUANG TINGJIAN
(1045–1105): 'SEEING
MY FORTY-NINTH
NEPHEW OFF'

Calligraphy in running and
regular scripts
35.2 × 130.3 cm.
Song period

Among the running and regular scripts by Huang Tingjian, his two poems written in his own hand, the 'Song feng Pavilion' and 'Seeing my forty-ninth nephew off', are most representative of his style and therefore attract the attention of students of calligraphy.

Huang Tingjian came from Fengning (now Xiushui, in Jiangxi province). He passed the highest imperial examination in 1067 and was later banished for making false entries in the official historical works he was compiling. He was reinstated after the emperor Hui zong acceded to the throne, but was again demoted because of his writings which offended the court. He died in Yizhou (now Yishan, Guangxi province) at the age of sixty-one, and was privately given the honorary title of Wenjie by his friends.

Huang was a renowned poet and calligrapher. He learned poetry from Su Shi, but soon rivalled his master in fame and was a founder-member of the first Jiangxi group of poets. In calligraphy, he learned first from Zhou Yue, then came under the influence of Yan Zhenqing, the monk Huai su and Yang Ningshi. Expert both in running and cursive scripts and considered to be one of the 'Four great calligraphers of the Song', he especially owes his exclusive style to the calligraphy 'Inscription on the tomb of a crane'.

The calligraphy reproduced here records his parting with his nephew after their brief meeting for the first time and their words of mutual encouragement. The poem contains thirteen lines, with a total of forty-six characters. Following the title on the right is the poem itself with five characters to each line.

The characters are constructed with forceful and bold strokes which stand stiff and upright and yet are executed with a smoothness and ease and fill the paper with a sense of power, as if 'a horse were dashing at full tilt into the fray'. This is a new style developed by Huang, based on the best elements he had absorbed from his predecessors. The style is characterized by the pulling in of the strokes towards the middle of each character and the pulling outwards of the slanting downwards strokes in the so-called 'radial' structure, as shown in such characters as *fen*, *fa* and *xiu*, etc. The strokes reach beyond the imaginary outer square shape of the characters of the Jin and Tang regular scripts, while the long strokes have an easy and graceful appearance. This characteristic is especially conspicuous in Huang's later works.

This calligraphy is included in the first volume of the *Shi qu catalogue*, as well as in the thirteenth volume of the *Calligraphic masterpieces from the Room of the Three Rarities*.

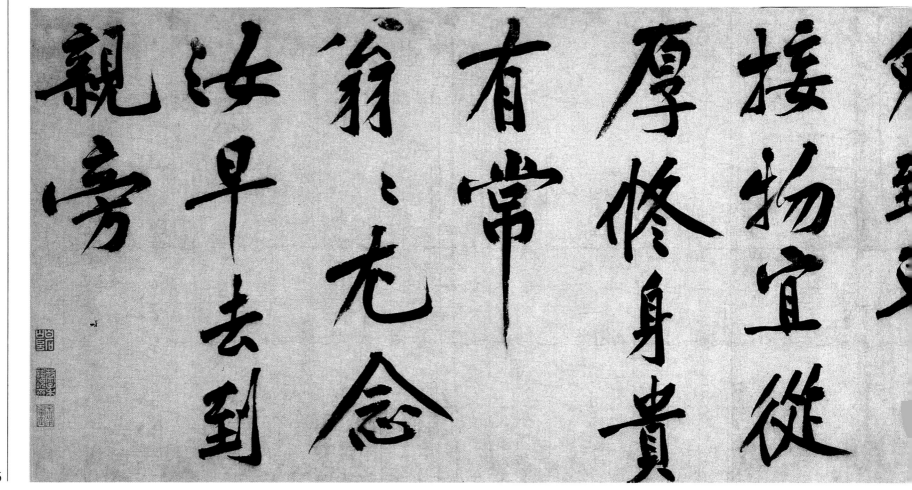

詩送四十
九姪
有娛財相
見何惜舉
別篋共期
同奮發更

18. 苕溪詩

MI FEI (1051–1107):
STANZAS WRITTEN AT
TIAOXI

Calligraphy in running
script
30.3 × 189.5 cm.
Song period

Mi Fei, also known by many other pseudonyms, was born in Xiangyang, but for a long time he lived in Runzhou (now Zhenjiang, Jiangsu province) and lived to the age of fifty-seven. During the reign of emperor Hui zong he held successive official posts connected with painting and calligraphy in the Ministry of Rites, and so on. As one of the greatest calligraphers and painters of the Northern Song period he and three other giants – Su Shi, Huang Tingjian and Cai Xiang – were known as the 'Four great calligraphers of the Song'. As such he occupies a significant position in the history of calligraphy and exerted a tremendous influence over later ages.

He benefited from the calligraphic legacies of the Jin and Tang periods, in particular Wang Xizhi, Wang Xianzhi, Ouyang Xun and Chu Suiliang, making an intensive study of these ancient masters and assimilating the best elements from them to form a style of his own which led to a strong subsequent following. As he said of himself, 'in my prime, people called my handwriting a medley of ancient styles, in as much as it had been derived from the essentials of many masters, without forming a style of my own. Now that I have created an exclusive style in my old age, people cannot locate its ancestry.' Thus he elucidated the method of utilizing the past in order to open up new ground for future developments. That is why, in the words of Sun Di, he was able to 'make innovations and go beyond the limits set by established rules'. Also, according to Huang Tingjian, his script was regarded as 'a sharp sword or arrow that nothing can resist. Never has any calligrapher's brush exhibited such power.'

The calligraphy by Mi Fei represented here, written in 1088 when he was thirty-eight, is representative of his work. From the contents of the poem we learn that, at this time, he was travelling around Lake Tai in Jiangsu province, visiting Suzhou, Wuxi and finally arriving at Wuxing by boat. It was written just before he set out from Wuxi to Wuxing. The eight-line stanzas of five characters to the line are written in running script and total thirty-four lines in all. The calligraphy seems to have been executed in one go, without interruption. A feeling of spaciousness between the lines does not interfere with the compactness of the structure, and the fluid coherence is not at all hampered by the apparent unevenness. A sense of steadiness can be observed in spite of the irregular shape of the characters, and despite the tendency for the vertical lines of characters to veer to the left, each character is written one directly below the other and so the balance is not destroyed. The strokes are sinewy, elegant and extremely skilful. No two strokes are executed in the same way. The multiplicity of the techniques with which the brush is manipulated to produce all sorts of strokes, heavy and light, helps to achieve a work of supreme beauty. It is indeed a great masterpiece and typical of Mi Fei's style.

This calligraphy, mounted in scroll form, was originally part of the Qing imperial collections but was taken by Pu yi, the last Qing emperor, when he fled to Changchun. With the collapse of the government in Manchuria, it disappeared. When it was finally recovered by the Palace Museum in 1963, six of the written characters were found to be missing with two others partially damaged. The inscription by Li Dongyang in large seal script at the beginning and the colophon by Xiang Yuanbian at the end were also missing. However, when the calligraphy was remounted, Zheng Zhuyou of the Museum staff succeeded in restoring Mi Fei's missing characters, based on a photograph taken of the scroll before it was damaged.

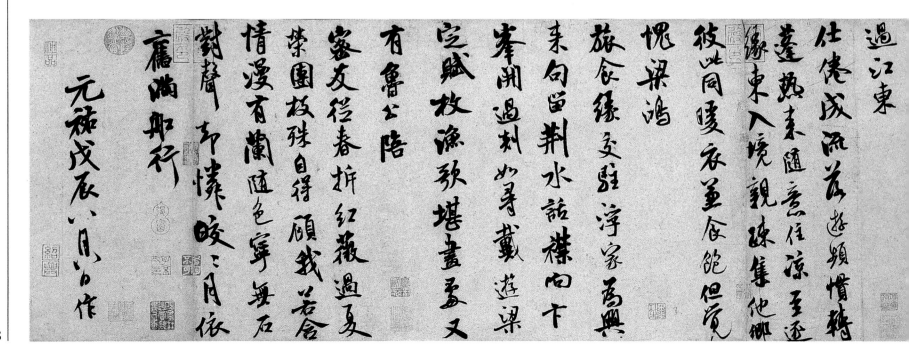

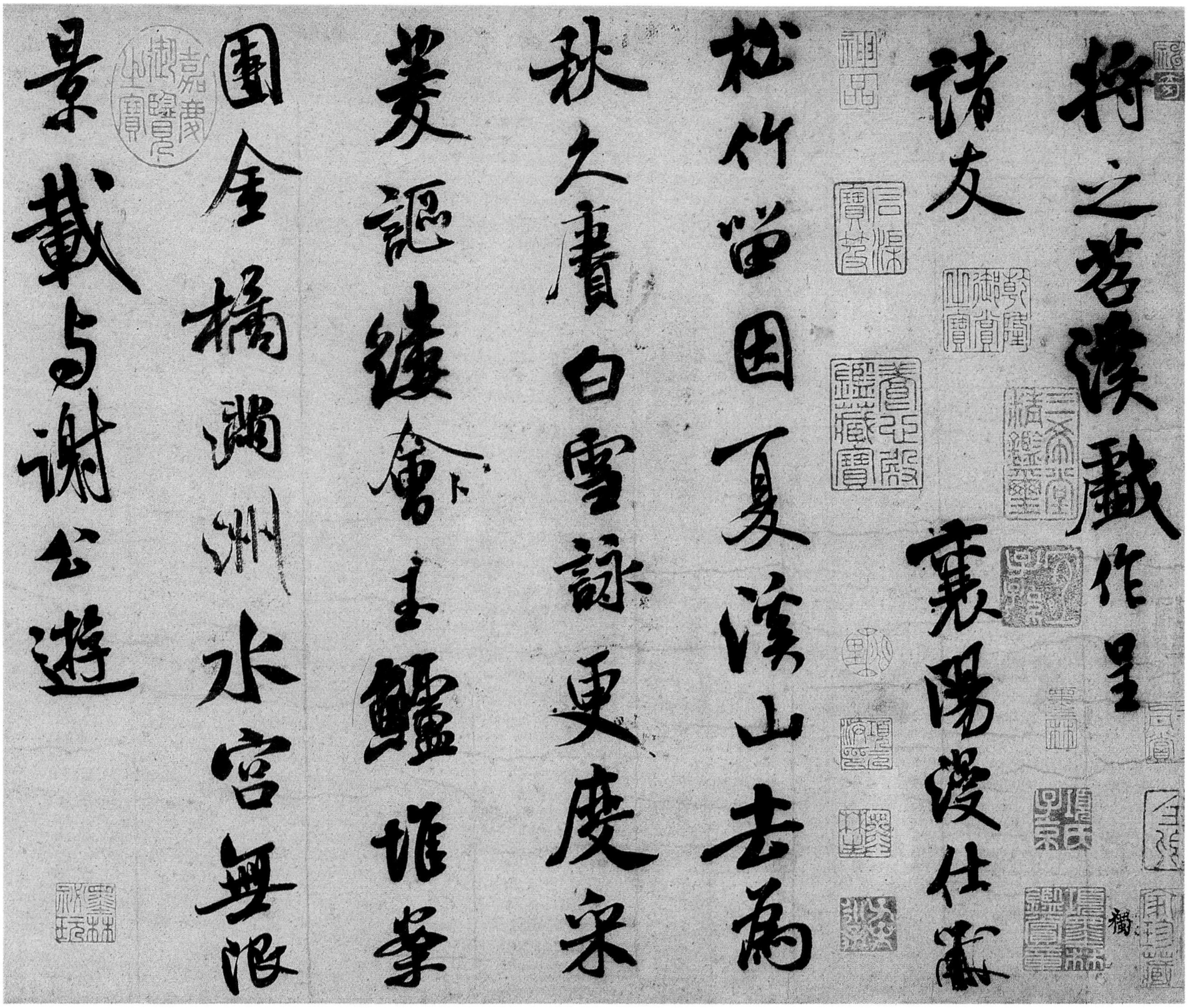

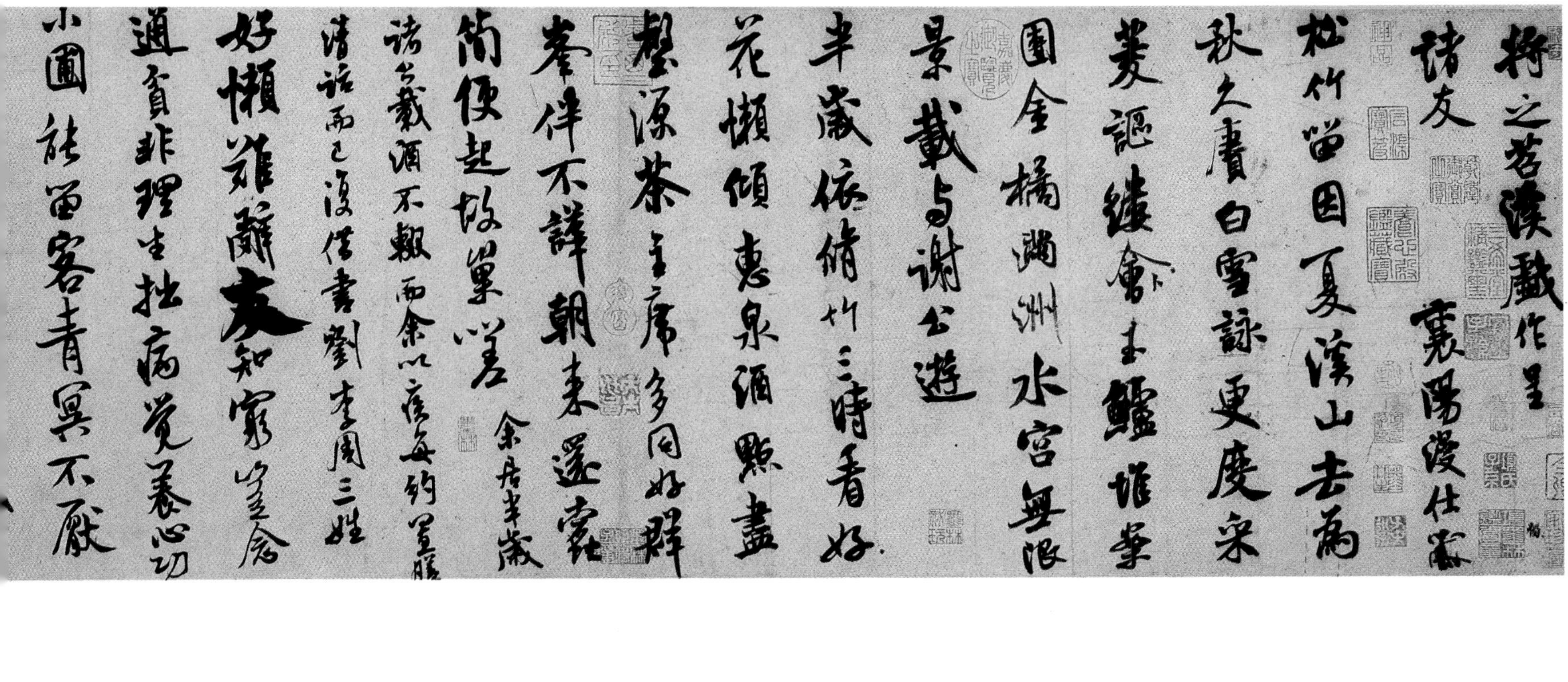

将之苕溪戏作呈
诸友
襄阳漫仕黻

松竹留因夏溪山去为
秋久赓白雪咏更庆衰
菱荗绿会主鳢堆掌
团金橘满洲水宫无波
景载与谢公游

半岁依修竹三时看好
花懒倾惠泉酒点尽
磊源茶主席多同好群
简使起欣巢以莟
奉伴不详朝来遽
诸公载酒不辞而余以
病不疲每约置膳
好懒难辞友知宾至意
通贫非理生拙病觉养心切
小圃能留客青冥不厌

19. 洛神賦圖

GU KAIZHI (345−406):
THE NYMPH OF THE RIVER
LUO (COPY)

Handscroll, colour on silk
27 × 572 cm.
Song period

The first Chinese painter whose work has come down to us and for whom there is any reliable evidence is Gu Kaizhi. An extremely talented man, he was accomplished in the arts of painting, poetry composition, calligraphy and, moreover, because he possessed great wit and humour as well as being by nature magnanimous, he is recorded as being 'extremely silly'.

Especially adept in figure painting, Gu also included landscape and animals amongst his subjects and he was said to have executed a good many religious murals for Buddhist and Taoist temples. His paintings belong to the 'meticulous' style, *mi ti*, characterized by superbly drawn fine, continuous, meandering lines that circulate 'like the threads spun out by spring silkworms'. It resembles 'the floating of clouds in the sky in spring and the flowing of the streams across the land', lithe, smooth, graceful and charged with emotion.

'The nymph of the River Luo', although a close copy made during the Song period, in all likelihood retains all the features of the original and the traditions of painting current during the Six Dynasties' period. Handed down over many centuries it is an invaluable source which allows something of an insight into the artistic achievements of this artist.

The picture is based on the famous prose-poem 'The nymph of the River Luo' by Cao Zhi who lived during the period of the Three Kingdoms. The poet describes his encounter with the mythological spirit of the River Luo by the waters' edge, and confides his grief and longing for a woman whom he could never hope to marry. In this long narrative handscroll, the two chief characters Cao Zhi and the nymph repeatedly appear in a series of pictures known as 'continuous narrative' which relate the whole story stage by stage. It not only faithfully reproduces in pictorial form the contents of the poetical work, but also conforms to them in its artistic treatment of the episodes, thereby successfully expressing the sentiments of the poet through the images it provides.

The scroll begins with a scene depicting Cao Zhi approaching the riverside with his attendants; in the distance he catches sight of the beautiful River Luo nymph for whom he yearns, gliding upwards out of the rippling water. Her hairknot coiled high, the girdle of her robe flowing in the breeze, taking graceful steps away from the river bank, she looks back as if reluctant to tear herself away. The portrayal of her beautiful form and manner fits the written description perfectly 'emerging hesitantly round the corner of the hill', as she reappears. The nymph is surrounded by a riot of blooming lotuses which rise out of the water, with green pines and chrysanthemums growing along the bank. The sun, moon, dragons and wild geese which fill the sky are metaphorical devices used by the poet to symbolize the beauty of the nymph. They reoccur in each scene to remind the viewer of the relevant verse as well as to achieve a decorative effect. They also lend a magical and dreamlike air to the scenes. The nymph appears several times in various sections of the scroll as the narrative unfolds according to the events in the poem, finally riding in a chariot drawn by six dragons and vanishing into the clouds. The poet describes this part of the story with vividness and imagination, and Gu's painting is no less splendid; the conjoining and intermingling of the water and the clouds, all sorts of mythical animals in their strange shapes and rich colours; the nymph sitting in her chariot continues to look back, her yearning and reluctance to leave still apparent. Finally, we see Cao Zhi in his futile search for the nymph in a boat, and then sitting on the river bank, candle in hand, waiting for the dawn in hope of seeing the nymph again. Finally, we share in his departure by carriage in despair.

In artistic composition and technique, 'The nymph of the River Luo' continues in the traditions of painting of the Han period. This is especially true of the mythical images such as the three-legged crows in the sun, the fish swimming in the water, which immediately bring to mind paintings on silk and murals of tombs of the Han period. However, in its meticulous line drawing, precision of structure and composition, and in the emotional coloration, which conveys the interrelationships between the figures and their surroundings, this painting far outstrips any painting from the Han period. It is true that in terms of landscape painting this composition does not compare with the works of later generations in that it abides by the principles that it 'never allows water to overflow' and it 'makes trees spread out like the stretching of the arms and the opening of the hands', but it is typical of artistic concepts of the Six Dynasties' period. Yet it is for this very reason that it is believed to be based on an original by Gu Kaizhi.

20. 列女仁智圖(部分)

GU KAIZHI (345–406):
ADMONITIONS OF THE
INSTRUCTRESS TO THE
COURT LADIES (DETAIL;
COPY)

Handscroll, colours on silk
25.8 × 470.3 cm.
Northern Song period

This scroll, based on the 'Biographies of virtuous women', *Lie nü zhuan,* by Liu Xiang of the Han period, is from an original said to have been painted by Gu Kaizhi. The subject-matter, of long standing, is to be found on Han stone engravings and excavated examples of lacquer paintings of the Northern Wei period. This scroll, part of which is missing, is a copy made during the Song period. Although it is only a copy, it still reflects the flavour of Six Dynasties' art and, to a certain degree, reflects the artistic achievement of Gu Kaizhi.

Not counting those originally depicted in the damaged section, there is a total of twenty-eight figures included in the scroll. Of these, there are eight named women of virtue. These ancient ladies, commended for their honourable conduct and wisdom, served as examples for others to follow. In treating the subject-matter, Gu follows the same compositional arrangement as the Han artists when they depicted the same subject, in that figures are drawn on the same plane, side by side. No background is provided apart from a few necessary objects, so that the 'ancient tradition' is largely preserved.

However, in the area of facial features and the posture of the figures, more emphasis is placed on the capturing of physical movement and the expression of their inner thoughts. Links inherent in the underlying narrative are strengthened by giving expression to the relationship between the characters described. A good example is found in the section describing the Duchess of Wei. While Duke Lin of the state of Wei and his wife were sitting in their palace one night, they suddenly heard the rumbling of a chariot outside. The Duchess at once informed him it must be his minister Ju Boyu approaching. When the Duke inquired of her the reason for her conjecture, she replied: 'A true gentleman behaves correctly even in the dark. Boyu is a virtuous minister. I know it must be him from the sound of the chariot.' The visitor turned out to be none other than the famous minister himself. In the picture (below right) the Duke is shown sitting inside the screens, bending forward with his right hand half raised in an attitude of inquiry. Before and to the left of him his wife attends him, kneeling erect and ready to answer. The courage of her own convictions is apparent from her posture and her facial expression. Again, in the section describing Sun Shuao tearfully recounting to his mother how he had killed the two-headed snake, a heroic act which he knows will surely cost him his life, his manner and expression resemble that of a wronged child. The countenance of his beautiful and richly attired mother, on the other hand, is full of benevolence. The inner as well as the outer qualities of a dignified, virtuous and wise woman are thus brought out to the full. Gu Kaizhi, the first Chinese art theorist to put forward the idea that 'the form should be able to convey the spirit', repeatedly stressed in his writings the importance of conveying the spiritual qualities and the characters of people. This scroll shows how successful he was in the realization of an objective which he pursued all his life.

妻知且亡數諫伯宗屢託畢羊
以免各狹伯宗遇禍州黎奔荆

伯宗凌人妻知且亡數諫伯宗屢託畢羊
屬以州黎以免各狹伯宗遇禍州黎奔荆

靈公夫人
衛靈公

21. 遊春圖

ZHAN ZIQIAN (?): SPRING
EXCURSION

Handscroll, ink and colours
on silk
43 × 80.5 cm.
Sui period

Zhan Ziqian was a native of Bohai, present day Yangxin, Shandong province. No record of the date of his birth or death survives. He successively served in the governments of the Northern Qi, Northern Zhou and Sui dynasties. Skilled in the painting of Buddhist deities, human figures and horses, he was also particularly strong in depicting magnificent buildings and landscapes. He was regarded as a link between the past and future developments in painting as well as a great master for his role in opening up a new era in the art. For this reason he was honoured alongside Gu Kaizhi of the Jin, Lu Tanwei of the Song and Zhang Sengyou of the Liang periods. In landscape painting, he initiated a style which was to be brought to full fruition in the gold and green landscapes favoured by such artists as Li Sixun and Li Zhaodao of the early Tang period, while in figure painting, which occupies an important position in the history of art, he was regarded as the founder of this particular genre as developed by the Tang painters.

This painting was, at one time, kept in the imperial Song palace and it bears the title 'Spring excursion by Zhan Ziqian' written by the emperor Hui zong. Later when it passed into the hands of famous collectors of the Yuan, Ming and Qing periods, they in their turn added their colophons to the picture or mentioned it in their writings. Therefore it is extremely valuable as an historic document as well as a work of art, which can help in piecing together the development of early landscape painting.

This painting, executed in the blue and green style, depicts natural mountain scenery and shows figures on an outing in springtime. The artist has conveyed a most beautiful scenic spot, showing its peaks piled high with lush, green vegetation, by means of methods appropriate to the medium size format. The colours are vibrant while the brushstrokes, although fine, are firmly drawn. A pleasure boat glides across the centre of the lake bearing three young women who sit beneath the high awning contemplating the natural beauty which surrounds them and of which they are a part. Unhurried, the man sculls the boat slowly forward. There are also a number of people on the shore: some walk, some ride or stroll along the mountain pathways, while others stand looking out over the lake. The theme is exploited to the full by the depiction of each minute detail of the elements of the natural landscape and the actions of the people who inhabit it. The scene is exuberant and yet poetic, producing an extremely appealing effect. The artistic techniques employed bear all the hallmarks of early landscape painting. From the point of view of structural composition it is evident that it has broken away from the pattern of Wei and Jin paintings which subscribed to such principles as 'never allowing water to overflow and that figures should be larger than mountains which, in turn, should be set off with rocks and trees that ought to spread out like the stretching of the arms and the opening of the hands'. Instead, landscape now becomes the main element for treatment, while figures assume a subordinate role more in keeping with their environment. The shape of each of the elements and the relationships between them, their relative proportions, distances seen in perspective, their arrangement and spatial relationships, are all arranged as befits true landscape painting. The most important mountains, trees, rocks, buildings and human figures are placed in the upper right quarter of the composition. The mountains extend towards the left until they gradually diminish in size and disappear on the horizon. The expanse of water, forming a diagonal across the painting, follows it natural course between them covered by small waves and ripples caused by a light breeze which strokes its surface. Making a scale-like pattern, they become lighter as they recede into the far distance, eventually merging with a vast sky. A mountain village painted in the lower left-hand corner balances the composition and, positioned where it is, connects the upper right and lower left sections of the painting imparting an illusion of depth so that 'something nearby appears as a great distance'. In brushwork, however, some traditions of previous periods have been retained. For example, rock formations are outlined and subsequently coloured, no texture brushstrokes (*cun*) as yet being used. The needles of pine trees, instead of being shown in detail, are sketched with thin lines and the

space thus enclosed is dotted with green. Trees are depicted singly and are of uniform 'deer antler' shape, they do not intertwine, appear in clumps or set off each other. The theorist Zhang Yanyuan of the Tang period wrote: 'While Yang [Qidan] and Zhan [Ziqian] portrayed architecture with great meticulousness, they gradually modified the surrounding objects. When drawing rocks, they made them appear as if carved, the contours like the sharp edges left on a block of ice shattered by an axe blade. When drawing trees, they brought out the minutest forms of the leaves and supplied them with fine veins.' This shows that early landscape painters, although having transformed the ancient techniques and brought landscape painting to a position of independence, still betrayed a degree of primitive simplicity, due to the restrictions of their visual awareness as well as their powers of expression, inherent in an art during its early stage of development. However, we also see in the picture every indication of landscape painting evolving from its birth towards maturity. There is an awareness of the appearance and qualities of different natural objects and different brushstroke techniques are employed with which to express them.

In the use of colour the same elegant simplicity prevails, yet attention is paid to the proper use of each colour to achieve an effect which is magnificent but not pretentious. Zhan Jingfeng, a collector of the Ming period, said of this picture: 'Being the fountainhead of the blue and green style of landscape painting, although it is meticulously done it appears somewhat rough and sketchy. This is only to be expected because the awkwardness has not yet been overcome and the skill not yet penetrated and although the structure has been established the full achievement is not fully realized.' It was only with later development by Li Sixun and his son, Wu Daozi and Wang Wei, that landscape painting with its multifarious styles gradually came to full maturity. The tradition was continued throughout the Five Dynasties', Song and Yuan periods, attaining great heights, but these much later achievements cannot be separated from the ground which was laid by the early landscape artists.

22. 步輦圖

YAN LIBEN (601–673):
THE IMPERIAL SEDAN *OR*
THE EMPEROR TAI ZONG
RECEIVING THE TIBETAN
ENVOY

Handscroll, ink and colours
on silk
38.5 × 129.6 cm.
Tang period

Yan Liben was a Tang dynasty minister of state famous for his paintings. As a pioneer of the mature Tang style of painting he enjoyed an undisputed position in the early Tang and was praised as 'an all-round artist without peer'. Particularly known for expertise in figure painting he executed many such compositions for the court. Although all these pictures are now lost we can still get some idea of Yan's style and artistic achievements from the painting shown here.

The present painting shows the meeting in AD 641 between the Tang emperor Tai zong and the Tibetan envoy sent by Tibetan King Srongtsan Gampo to escort Princess Wen cheng home to become the bride of his royal master. The marriage of the princess to this distant ruler marks an event of historical significance, symbolizing the friendly relations between different nationalities in a country with a great many ethnic groups. On the right the emperor sits on a litter carried by six palace maids. Three other maids are holding an umbrella and two fans. Three figures on the left attend the emperor. The man with a curly beard wearing a scarlet robe is probably the master of ceremonies while the younger one, in white, appears to be an interpreter, with the Tibetan envoy standing between the two.

The remarkable feature of the painting is the way in which the status of each figure is distinguished in such a lively and precise way as well as their individual characters and temperaments: the seasoned master of ceremonies wearing a serious expression; the interpreter who looks both attentive and uneasy owing to his inferior position; and the emperor and the foreign envoy, the most successfully executed of the figures.

The form and features of the emperor were first carefully outlined in ink and then washed in with colour. His steadfast gaze gives him a grave appearance. The folds of his clothing are painted with only a few strokes with little colour added. His whole appearance is one of an imposing and martial bearing. The painter must have had a deep understanding of the emperor through their long acquaintance. By referring to relevant historical records, it can be seen that the artist has done full justice not only to Tai zong's outer appearance but also to his temperament and manner. The envoy, dressed in the Tibetan style, stands respectfully with folded hands. Deep wrinkles on his broad forehead reflect his long and wearying travels to China, as well as the particular features of his race. His manner, serious and sincere, is expressive of his respect for the emperor and his awareness of the importance of the mission. The strong colours combined with careful brushstrokes contribute to the solemnity of the occasion portrayed, while the fluent strokes, known as the 'iron wire' technique, of subtly modulated lines bring out the quality and feel of the silk clothes. The beautiful pattern on the dress of the Tibetan envoy, faithfully reproduced, also contributes to the significance and position of the figure in the composition.

23. 揮扇仕女圖

ZHOU FANG (?): LADIES
FANNING THEMSELVES

Handscroll, colours on silk
33.7 × 204.8 cm.
Tang period

Zhou Fang, styled Zhonglang, was a native of Jingzhou (now Xi'an, Shaanxi province). He was renowned for his skill in painting temple murals and figure painting, especially of women. The techniques he used for religious murals were known at the time as being executed in the 'Zhou manner', while those of his female figure paintings were firmly based in the traditions of Zhang Xuan.

The picture 'Ladies fanning themselves', a work representative of this style, depicts nine court ladies, two maids and two eunuchs – thirteen people in all – divided into groups of two or three figures. Although sumptuously clad and waited on hand and foot by maids and eunuchs, these court ladies for all their apparent affluence have long faces and worried expressions, as if tired of a life that dragged on endlessly. Their lives were, spiritually, monotonous in the extreme and the artist successfully brings out this contradictory fact and shows his sympathy for these luckless women.

The court women are vividly delineated, with their inner thoughts clearly revealed in the subtle facial expressions and their physical postures. For example, the first of the women sitting listlessly in a chair, at the beginning or right-hand end of the painting, indicates a languor not yet shaken off after a nap. Although she holds a fan, she prefers to be fanned by the servant, demonstrating that, although living in the lap of luxury as her exalted position required, she actually finds life dull and boring. Another woman sits against an embroidery frame. Her right elbow rests on the frame, a fan in her hand,

while her left hand, wrapped over the top of the fan, supports her head. Her body is slightly turned, her head lowered, her brow knitted; the picture is one of depression and sorrow. Court ladies did embroidery solely to kill time, yet this lady shows no interest even in this.

The two women at the end of the scroll are especially lifelike. One of them, her face turned towards the viewer and her head slightly raised, languidly gesticulates with a small fan. To all appearances, these fans serve only as toys with which to while away the time. Her air of perfect self-composure gives the impression that there is nothing that she has not seen or heard within the palace that would ruffle her. Viewed from behind, the woman appears aloof and detached from wordly affairs. However, the lady leaning against the Chinese parasol tree seems, in sharp contrast, so anxious as to be completely unable to endure anything before her. History records that Zhou Fang and Han Gan both painted portraits for Zhao Zong, son-in-law of General Guo Zhiyi, so successfully that it was very difficult to tell which was better. When Guo Zhiyi's daughter returned, the general asked her to judge these two portraits. The daughter, who knew her husband best, of course, replied that Zhou Fang's work not only did full justice to the face, but also captured his expression. This naturally decided the matter. From the painting illustrated here, it is possible to imagine just how fine such portraits as that of Zhao Zong, as well as other examples of Zhou Fang's work, must have been.

ZHOU FANG (?): LADIES
FANNING THEMSELVES

24. 五牛圖卷

HAN HUANG (723–787):
FIVE BULLS

Handscroll, ink and colours
on paper
20.8 × 139.8 cm.
Tang period

The Tang dynasty presided over an unprecedented era, witnessing cultural developments which included the flowering of Chinese painting. The bold innovations based on the traditions of the Jin and Sui periods gave rise to a multiplicity of schools and styles. The art reached new heights in the abundance of the subject-matter treated and in the depth of its expression, giving rise to a completely new generation of artists. Outstanding examples were: Yan Liben, for his portrayals of famous political figures; Li Sixun and his son for their meticulous 'gold and green' landscapes; Wang Wei in monochrome brush and ink landscapes; Wu Daozi in his depiction of human and Buddhist subjects; Zhang Xuan and Zhou Fang for their paintings of court ladies; Cao Ba and Han Gan for horse painting; Dai Song and Han Huang for their paintings of bulls; and Bian Luan in paintings of birds and flowers. Unfortunately only a very small number has survived. Of these, 'Five bulls' by Han Huang, illustrated here, is one of the few authentic paintings still in existence. It is also highly prized as the oldest extant Chinese painting executed on paper.

A native of Chang 'an (now Xi'an, Shaanxi province), Han Huang, styled Taichong, was the son of Han Xi, a former prime minister. Very successful in his official career, he attained the highest civil honours and was finally created a duke. In politics, he advocated the complete reunification of the empire after the long period of disunity as well as the development of agriculture. He also played an important role in the suppression of rebellious provincial governors. Han was also skilled in both calligraphy and painting. His cursive calligraphic style was modelled on that of Zhang Xu and his paintings could be traced far back to Lu Tanwei of the Song dynasty of the Northern and Southern dynasties' period. Taking rural life as his main theme he became known as a genre painter and was skilled in the painting of domestic animals. He touched on a way of life which was far removed from the idle luxury reflected by Zhang Xuan and Zhou Fang in their compositions, both in scope and depth. Indeed, that in his selection of subject-matter he shifted the emphasis away from the palace to the countryside in itself represented a huge stride in the development of Chinese genre painting.

The present painting is executed on a long, narrow sheet of white paper. The five bulls, shown from different viewpoints and in various attitudes, are painted realistically. Using the simplest of close-up compositional arrangements it possesses no more background than a single clump of brambles. Apart from their stubborn side, the painter has brought out the meek, compliant nature of the bulls. Thick and thin modulated lines are used to describe bone and muscle, while delicate lines are applied to depict the thin individual hairs at the base of the horns and at the end of the tail. The ink outlines are filled with colours – ochre, yellow, grey and white – which are used to model the animals in three dimensions from dark to light. Gu Kaizhi had stated: 'The vividness of a portrait relies upon the very touch on the pupil of the eye.' What he was referring to was the painting of the eye, or pupil, as the single most important art in portrait painting. Han Huang has applied this principle to this painting by making the bulls' eyes suitably large but taking great pains in painting them, so that they shine with the spirit of the animals, a great achievement in the portrayal of their physical and spiritual sides. The great Yuan period artist Zhao Mengfu in his colophon at the end of the scroll has added: 'This painting of "Five bulls" is a full expression of their spiritual vitality. It is truly a rare masterpiece.' Kong Kebiao of the Yuan also said: 'The bulls are as lifelike as if they were seen beside the stream here or in the fields there. How wonderful!' Li Rihua, who lived during the Ming period, in his Jottings from the Six Inkstone Studio, *Liu yan zhai bi ji*, also praised the painting as 'So imbued with the vitality of life, that it is without match'. This critical acclaim was not only achieved because of Huang's technical mastery

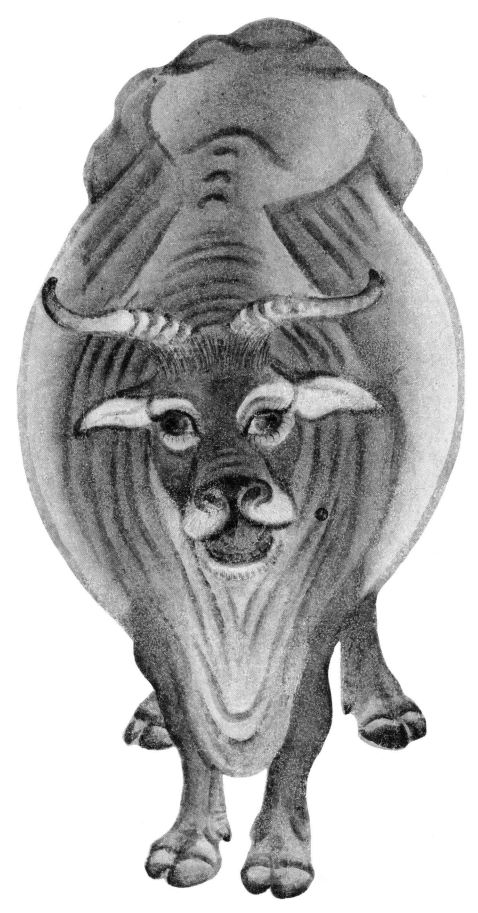

but took into account the fact that he had become well acquainted with the natural attributes of his subjects. Only by close observation had he been able to paint such a picture.

The scroll found its way into the imperial collection of the Southern Song dynasty. It was acquired by Zhao Boang during the early part of the Yuan and then came into the possession of Zhao Mengfu. This accounts for the three colophons by the two Zhaos at the end of the scroll. Later it returned to the imperial collection and was housed in the library of the crown prince between 1314 and 1321 when it acquired the colophon by Kong Kebiao. During the Ming dynasty it was first in the collection of Xiang Yuanbian, then acquired by Wang Keyu who subsequently sold it. Eventually, it became the property of the Qian long emperor of the Qing dynasty and bears colophons by him and other owners. It was also included in various catalogues of the Qing period. When Beijing was occupied by foreign troops in 1900, the painting was stolen and taken out of the country. It was not until 1950, when it was bought back by the Chinese government in Hongkong at great cost, that it was restored to the collections of the Palace Museum.

25. 韓熙載夜宴圖

GU HONGZHONG (?):
NIGHT ENTERTAINMENT
GIVEN BY HAN XIZAI

Handscroll, ink and colours
on paper
28.4 cm × 335.5 cm.
Period of the Five Dynasties

Han Xizai, a high-ranking official of the kingdom of Southern Tang, one of the Five Dynasties, was a talented man, yet he was given to dissolute behaviour and sensual pleasures. He kept a number of women singers and dancers to entertain the guests whom he often invited to his night revelries. Suspicious, the emperor sent his court painter Gu Hongzhong to spy on Han and the picture that Gu painted afterwards from his recollections resulted in this well-known masterpiece which has come down intact to us.

The painter has utilized the same 'continuous narrative' method of expression as Gu Kaizhi employed in his 'Nymph of the River Luo'. The chief character, Han Xizai, appears in five different scenes, the story unfolding in five separate sections. The first composition, 'listening to music', includes the largest single assemblage of characters of the whole painting. The bearded man in a tall hat seated on a couch is Han Xizai (upper right), his head slightly lowered, his hand hanging over his knee. Apparently weighed down with anxiety, he is listening only half heartedly. This is in contrast to the red-robed man, Lang Can, the scholar who had achieved first place in the imperial examinations. The young man has an easy manner. He is apparently enjoying the music and watching the girl playing the *pi pa*, lute, attentively. Two other guests sit in front of Han's couch, one face on, the other shown in profile. They are most probably Chen Zhiyong, a Doctor of Rites and Zhu Rui, a secretary of the royal secretariat. They are both

fascinated by the music and, judging from their fixed gaze and set mouths, the musical composition being performed is neither trivial nor light. The performer is the youngest sister of Li Jiaming, deputy-director of the royal conservatory, who is looking over his shoulder at her. The slim girl sitting next to him is Wang Wushan, a talented dancer. Both she and Li Jiaming's sister were doted on by Han Xizai. Of the two young men behind Wang, one is Han's pupil, Shu Ya. The other women are all singers and dancers. In terms of the composition and structure of this section, the placing of the performer on one side and the audience on the other serves to unify the figures and underline the theme of listening to music. The individual response of each person, all of different rank and status, as well as temperament, is carefully brought out in their depiction. This shows how the artist observed life in minute detail and the way in which he was able to translate this into the superb drawings of human figures.

In the second section, 'watching the dance', Han is shown drumming for Wang Wushan, the dancer. Sitting in front of the drum, Lang Can remains totally absorbed in the proceedings. The others, either beating out the rhythm with a clapper or clapping their hands, are in a joyous mood. Only the monk in the background looks pensive, his hands clasped before him and his head slightly lowered. The incongruity of his presence alone amongst all the merry-making is obvious enough even without his austere manner. The fact that the artist has chosen

to include him has a deep significance designed to provoke thought. According to history, Han found a very good friend in the person of the monk De ming. After Han declined an offer of the premiership, De ming asked him why he had avoided serving his country. Han replied, 'As the North daily enjoys a growing strength and influence over the South, once a true man of destiny appears, the South will surely retreat in disarray. I will not be the prime minister of a decaying state only to be laughed at and scorned by posterity.' The monk in the picture is most probably the said De ming. The literature does not record the effect of any answer that De ming may have given to Han's reasoning but judging from the painting he would have advised Han against his way of life. His meditative mood amidst the revelry is, however, probably more indicative of his brooding over the actual impending doom of the Southern Tang dynasty.

The rest of the scroll includes the following scenes: 'a brief interlude', in which Han is shown washing his hands in a basin held by a maid; 'a performance given by the flute-players' with Han listening; and finally 'seeing the guests off' in which the flirtations between the guests and the women entertainers are described. As a compositional device, the painter has chosen to use the continuous narrative method, and in order to separate each section employs a screen which is a part of the furniture that one would expect to encounter in such a scene. This, combined with the forward and backward movements and gestures of the figures as they interact, provides a cohesion which transcends the sectional aspect of the painting to form a cohesive whole in a way which is both natural and ingenious. Fine yet strong 'iron wire' lines are used very precisely to delineate the form and express the nature of each object and person. The colours are applied as thick and thin washes with intricate balances and changes providing subtle contrasts and harmonies which aptly convey the beauty and the furtive atmosphere. Whether in figure drawing or psychological representation, skill in the use of the brush, compositional design or application and use of colour, this painting symbolizes all that was best in figure painting of the Five Dynasties' period.

77

26. 高士圖

WEI XIAN (?): MAN OF
VIRTUE

Hanging scroll, ink and
colours on silk
135 × 52.5 cm.
Period of the Five Dynasties

Wei Xian was a court painter under the Later Tang dynasty who favoured such subjects as architecture, water-mills, figures and landscapes. Said to have at first modelled his compositions after Yin Jizhao, he later studied works by Wu Daozi. 'Man of virtue' is his only picture still in existence.

The painting describes the story of Liang Hong and his wife Meng Guang of the Eastern Han period, who 'respected each other as they would guests and the wife always served meals with the tray raised to the height of her eyebrows'. Although not as ugly as the description of her in the historical records, the face of Meng Guang represented here is by no means beautiful. Therefore, not completely divorced from the truth, this artistic treatment aims at striking a happy mean between the historical fact and aesthetic demands.

Although this picture is based on the story of the two historical figures, it is the landscape that is the main compositional interest and the mountains, trees, rocks and architecture are a carefully interwoven arrangement. The texture strokes,

cun, used to model rocks and tree trunks are reminiscent of northern artists such as Jing Hao and Guan Tong. Although hailing from Chang'an (now Xi'an) in the South, it was, however, quite possible for Wei Xian to have come under their influence. Commenting on Wei Xian's paintings, the editor of the *Xuan he catalogue of paintings, Xuan he hua pu,* records 'His cliffs and huge rocks, though majestically sketched, lack skilful texturing. His trees are tall and upright indeed, yet their crowns seem out of proportion with their trunks. These are the shortcomings pointed out by the critics.' A comparison of this statement with the landscape illustrated here shows his opinion to be, perhaps, hypercritical. The house and its substructure, the woven bamboo and staked fences, are executed according to traditional techniques used in architectural painting. They are carefully treated and well proportioned and show Wei Xian's talent to the full; a similar evaluation is made by Sun Chengze in his *Geng zi xiao xia ji, A record of a summer holiday in the year gengzi.*

27. 瀟湘圖卷

DONG YUAN (?–962): THE
RIVERS XIAO AND XIANG

Handscroll, colours on silk
50 × 141.4 cm.
Period of the Five Dynasties

Dong Yuan, styled Shuda, was born in Zhongling (present day Jinxian, Jiangxi province), and served as deputy-director of the Northern Royal Gardens under the Later Tang dynasty during the Five Dynasties' period. He was popularly known as 'Dong of the Northern Royal Gardens'. It was he who founded the Jiangnan school of painting with a unique style and blazed a trail for the development of China's landscape painting. His paintings exerted a far-reaching influence upon painters of later dynasties, especially those of the Yuan, Ming and Qing, and occupy a prominent position in the annals of Chinese painting.

During the Five Dynasties' period, Chinese landscape painting had already reached maturity. Many painters, while preserving the traditions of landscape painting of the Tang period had, through close observation and the careful study of nature, produced works with distinctive characteristics. Typical painters of this era were Jing Hao and his disciple Guan Tong in the North, Dong Yuan and his pupil Ju ran in the South. Both Jing Hao and Guan Tong painted realistically from the landscapes along the Taihang Mountains as well as in the central part of Shaanxi province. They excelled at panoramic views of towering mountains and great rivers, precipitous crags and steep valleys, and layer upon layer of peaks giving expression to the power and grandeur of the scenery in the northern part of China. With a view to conveying the northern landscape characterized by the predominance of rocky formations, they developed brush techniques consisting of hooked, *gou*, texturing, *cun*, shading, *hun*, and dotting, *dian*, strokes which, taken as a whole, conveyed an impression of

grandeur and solidity. Typical of this technique are the paintings 'Mount Lu' by Jing Hao and 'Travelling through the mountain passes' by Guan Tong, both having been handed down to posterity. On the other hand, Dong Yuan and Ju ran excelled in depicting the landscapes in the South with their luxuriant vegetation as well as beautiful lakes and distant hills in Jiangnan (meaning south of the lower reaches of the River Yangtze). In order to represent the terrain characterized by vast areas of exposed earth and the abundance of vegetation, they developed a technique of texturing strokes, *cun*, such as the long, fine 'hemp-fibre *cun*', *pi ma cun*, and 'dot *cun*', *dian zi cun*, to convey an impression of unaffectedness and placidity. Dong Yuan's 'Mountain in summer', 'Waiting for the ferry by the Xia jing Mountain Pass' and 'The Rivers Xiao and Xiang', and Ju ran's 'Looking for the Tao in autumnal mountains' are their representative works left to posterity.

In Dong Yuan's 'The Rivers Xiao and Xiang' we see spread out before us a panoramic view: range upon range of mountains and immense forests, the wide expanse of the misty lake, skiffs bobbing on the water and outcrops of sandy, level ground covered with reeds and waterside plants, scenery typical of the watery South. The painting also depicts the everyday lives of figures that inhabit the landscape. A boat slowly approaches the shore, bearing six men of different social status, while a group consisting of a band of five men playing wind instruments and a *se*, zither, awaits their arrival. Further along are three women, two of whom are standing waiting while the third, carrying a small bag, looks over her shoulder. In the distance, small fishing boats can be seen

plying between the sandy bank and the islet overgrown with reeds. Fishermen haul a fishing net up towards the bank. These figures, though small, are full of animation which lends the painting a feeling of the richness of life. As Dong Qichang (the critic and painter of the Ming period) remarks in his accompanying annotation on the scroll, the conception of the painting owed its origin to the following lines in a poem: 'Lake Dongting is the place for music, The Rivers Xiao and Xiang are where deities roam.' The painting is composed according to the principle formulated at this time of the 'three distances', in this case 'level distance', *ping yuan*, in which the mountains in the distance are described over the water in the foreground. Its simplicity and tranquillity give a feeling of deep serenity. The hills and rocks are painted with ink mixed with cyanine and the figures in thick, deep colours. The peaks and vegetation are built up with dots while the slopes and banks and undulations of the mountains are modelled with 'spread out hemp fibre' *cun*, or strokes. The use of striking contrasts between foreground and far distance and light and shade has, through the artist's superb artistry, allowed the scenery of the Jiangnan region to be depicted in a particularly suitable manner. The use of this particular viewpoint draws the viewer into the composition to become part of it.

When the last Qing emperor, Pu yi, left the Forbidden City, he took the painting with him to Changchun in northeast China and after the end of the Second World War it was passed from hand to hand. Finally, in 1952, it was re-acquired and deposited in the Palace Museum.

28. 寫生珍禽圖

HUANG QUAN
(903?–965): STUDIES OF
BIRDS, INSECTS AND
TURTLES

Handscroll, colours on silk
41.5 × 70 cm.
Period of the Five Dynasties

The period of the Tang dynasty saw the painting of flowers and birds in traditional Chinese style develop into an independent branch of the painting categories, attaining full maturity in the Five Dynasties' period. Huang Quan can be said to be an epoch-making figure of his time and his bird and flower paintings represent a landmark in the history of this branch of painting.

Huang Quan, styled Yaoshu, was born in Chengdu, Sichuan province. During the Five Dynasties' period he was an important court painter to the kings of Shu. He learned widely from different painters and was able to adapt their best elements to his own pictures. 'It was recorded that in flower and bamboo painting, he modelled himself after Teng Chang-you; in birds, after Diao Guangyin; in landscapes, after Li Sheng; in the painting of cranes, after Xue Ji; in that of dragons, after Sun Yu. Though he modelled himself after these masters, his brushwork, never hampered by traditional techniques, exhibited an uninhibited freedom and he excelled

his masters in many respects.' Self-disciplined in drawing, he 'never made a stroke without a definite purpose' and was skilled in fixing a mental picture of his subject before commencing. He often sketched directly from the rare birds, exotic flowers and grotesque rocks assembled in the royal gardens. The animals he drew were vivid and lifelike. His paintings, noted for their fine lines and rich colours, offered a striking contrast in subject-matter, technique and style with Xu Xi's works. The latter, a contemporary of Huang Quan, was also a bird and flower painter of the Later Tang period. Critics were of the opinion that 'Huang Quan went in for gorgeous colours, while Xu Xi cultivated an untamed carelessness.' These two styles were destined to affect the course of development of bird and flower paintings for generations to come.

The 'Studies of birds, insects and turtles' is the only credible surviving painting by Huang Quan. The painting includes ten birds of different species and in different attitudes, two turtles and twelve insects. These creatures are evenly distributed over

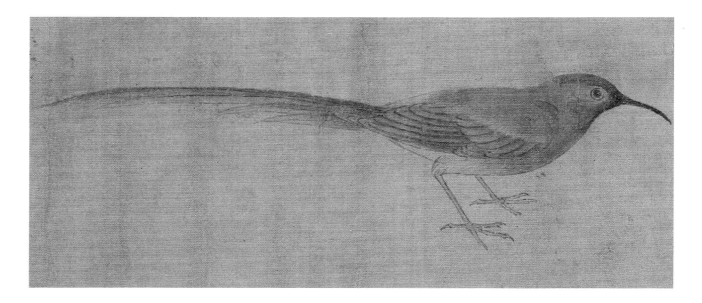

the picture surface with no real structural or compositional relationship between them. It was probably intended as a collection of studies or source material gathered by the artist for future use. Fine contour lines were first drawn in light ink, then several layers of colours, including light ink, were applied on the forms with great delicacy. Generally, the colours cover the original outlines. The characteristics of the paintings are a meticulousness with an emphasis on the application of colours. The wings of the cicadas, bees and other insects appear transparent, while the antennae of the insects are fine and resilient in quality. The outspread wings of the sparrow and the whirring wings of the bee are especially well reproduced. All the turtles, birds and insects are the work of a draughtsman. The picture not only shows the different forms of these creatures, but also observes the changes in their shapes when seen from various angles, which contributes to an overall air of reality.

Literature on painting records many traditional tales con-nected with the real and lifelike qualities of Huang Quan's bird and flower drawings. For example, he once painted six red-crowned cranes on the palace walls which, being so true to life, attracted a live crane which stood next to them. This so aroused the admiration of the king of Shu that the name of the hall that contained the paintings was subsequently changed to Hall of the Six Cranes. On another occasion, after Huang Quan painted flowers and birds of the four seasons on the walls of the Hall of the Eight Trigrams, an eagle chanced to catch sight of the pheasants in the painting and again and again tried to seize one of the birds with its claws. Because of this, the king ordered Ouyang Tong, of the Hanlin academy, to make a record of the episode. All this serves to illustrate how lifelike Huang Quan's birds were and to show the aims of the bird and flower painters of this period. The 'Studies of birds, insects and turtles' clearly reflects this pursuit of realism and the high standards in painting and draughtsmanship attained.

29. 窠石平遠圖

GUO XI (C. 1020–1090):
ROCKY LOWLAND WITH
FAR HORIZON

Handscroll, ink on paper
120.8 × 167.7 cm.
Northern Song period

Guo Xi was considered an unparalleled master of landscape painting of his time after Li Cheng and Fan Kuan. He was also a theorist of the fine arts. The *Lofty message of forests and streams, Lin quan gao zhi*, recorded and collated by his son Guo Si, was the first comprehensive and systematic work on landscape painting ever published in China.

Very few of Guo Xi's works are to be found nowadays. Only six or seven paintings are believed to be genuine, among them, 'Rocky lowland with far horizon', which is actually marked with the date when it was painted, 1078. Produced in his later years, it is a masterpiece which allows of an appreciation of great talent but also helps toward an understanding of his theory of landscape painting.

In the foreground of the painting is a shallow brook, limpid and serene, around which are clustered large outcrops of bare rocks. Close to its banks rocks of various shapes are exposed to view. Amid the rocks grows a clump of trees with twisting boughs. Some of the branches are bare of leaves, while others still bear ageing leaves represented in light ink wash. In the distance, one sees the boundless wilderness and hints of dark green veiled in mist. Mountains lie across the land like a barrier under a clear and cloudless sky in this late autumn scene. According to Guo Xi's theories, a landscapist must first go to the mountains and rivers and observe them at close range before he starts to paint. In contemplating the landscape, Guo Xi developed the method of the observation of contrasts. His writings discuss in detail the different features of the landscapes in various localities. For example, a landscape in the same locality changes its appearance with the change of seasons and climate. Even in the same season, its outward qualities are subject to change, according to whether it is seen in the morning or at dusk, on a cloudy or fine, windy or rainy day. Again, even under similar climatic conditions, a landscape will present a different face when seen from different viewpoints and distances. It was only by means of such probing comparisons as these, using personal observation, that a painter would be able to capture the most subtle changes in natural phenomena and thereby enrich the content of his work, affording variety in composition and endowing his work with the highest artistic qualities. Only thus can he imbue the picture with his own feelings and achieve compositional harmony from the forms he has created.

'Rocky lowland with far horizon' presents a scene characteristic of late autumn in north China. Through personal observation, the artist came to realize that 'mountains in the northwest are mostly grand and imposing', 'towering and extending great distances with their hillocks and mounds, while their massive peaks can be seen rolling and standing out majestically in the wilderness which is crossed by great swathes of land'. All these features are embodied in the rocks and distant hills in the present painting. The artist was the first to make effective use of the 'swirling cloud' *cun* method of texturing brushstrokes, *juan yun cun fa*, to represent the grandiose northern landscape. As for autumn, he felt that 'the clear and bright autumnal mountains appear all dressed up', 'the clear and bright autumnal mountains and falling leaves call forth a feeling of solemnity'. The painting, however, does not give an impression of bleakness and melancholy. On the whole, the force of composition and the brisk, lively brushwork combine to impart a sense of beauty impregnated with solemnity and lucidity. The winding brook, limpid, shallow and tranquil, together with the rocks, each individually painted and yet connected and interrelated, are reminiscent of the saying: 'When the water subsides, the rocks emerge.' Such 'spirit resonance' of this late autumn landscape contained in this picture can hardly have been perceived and expressed so magnificently by a mediocre painter.

Guo Xi, in summing up his rich experience as a landscape artist, formulated the principle of the 'three distances' in the painting of Chinese landscape. The 'three distances' are 'high

distance', 'deep distance' and 'level distance'. The title of 'Rocky lowland with far horizon' suggests that it adheres to the principle of 'level distance' which according to Guo Xi implies 'standing near to the mountain the distant mountains are described'. To draw the scenery, the objects seen along the horizontal line of vision should be concentrated in the lower part of the format, about one-third of its height from the lower edge of the picture frame. The eye is guided from the foreground to the middle ground through which is perceived the far distance, each of the levels clearly demarcated, showing the depth of the vast empty spaces by means of a minimum use of ink, producing a majestic power which instilled the feeling of spiritual inspiration.

Guo Xi, styled Chunfu, was a native of Wen xian, Henan province. In his early years he seems to have been a Taoist priest. He never received a formal training in painting under a master and he had to rely on his own painstaking efforts to gain mastery as an outstanding painter. Later, he taught at the imperial art academy and was subsequently promoted to the highest office in the Hanlin academy. Little is known about the dates of his birth and death. It was during the reign of the emperor Shen zong of the Song dynasty that he was at the height of his creative work, towards which he always adopted a very serious and conscientious approach. To the end of his life his paintings were entirely free from the conventions of method and were always fresh and vigorous.

30. 臨韋偃牧放圖

LI GONGLIN
(1049–1106): HERDING
HORSES (COPY AFTER WEI
YAN)

Handscroll, colours on silk
46.2 × 429.8 cm.
Song period

Horses represent an indispensable part of China's history in warfare, transport and agriculture. They were also major themes for Chinese traditional painting. As both the Han and Tang dynasties laid stress on agriculture and the preparedness for war, much attention was given over to the management of horses. Of the many horse painters since the Tang period the most well-known are Cao Ba, Han Gan and Wei Yan. In the Song period, paintings with horses as subjects began to decline and Li Gonglin was considered to be the best horse painter during this period.

Li Gonglin, styled Boshi, otherwise known as Longmian the Hermit, was born in Shucheng, Anhui province. Noted for his monochrome line paintings using the traditional brush and ink method, he was one of the most influential masters in the final years of the Northern Song period. Skilled in drawing human figures and Buddhist deities, he was equally at home with landscape and bird and flower painting, and took special delight in the painting of horses. History records that he first modelled himself after Han Gan when he started drawing horses but that his works showed slight variation in details. As a painter, he never failed to assimilate the best in his predecessors' works. 'Whenever he obtained a painting, either ancient or contemporary, he always made a copy from it and kept the duplicate.' He also observed horses in the flesh and familiarized himself with them and 'every time he wished to draw them, he always went to have a look at them'. 'There are thousands of horses in Longmian's mind but what he draws is not only their outer appearances [but their souls]', said Su Shi in praise of his skill in incorporating the finer aspects of Cao Ba's and Han Gan's paintings and of the contribution he made in developing the traditional art of horse painting. When he served as an official at the court, 'every time he went to the imperial stable he would look around, and lingered there all day long drawing horses until he had a great feeling of communion between himself and the horses'. This happened to such an extent that the keeper of the imperial stable begged him not to draw pictures from the animals any more for fear that their spirits might be wrested from them.

'Herding horses' was executed by Wei Yan in order to portray the grand occasion in those days of releasing horses for grazing on the open pastures. Li Gonglin made this copy by imperial command in the form of a long horizontal scroll which includes 143 human figures and 1,286 horses. The picture, which unfurls from right to left, presents a grandiose scene. The herdsmen tend the horses on the great plains and sloping fields which are dotted with trees and rocks, brooks and rivulets. The animals are shown in many attitudes: galloping, leaping, cantering, grazing, drinking water, sporting, lying or rolling on the ground. Some of the herdsmen ride on horseback or pursue their course on foot, while others lean against trees to snatch a few moments' rest. Painted with the utmost realism most of them are fully dressed, while a few go barefoot or with their chests exposed.

The painting presents a well-integrated structure with the mass of horses and riders placed at the beginning, thinning out as the scene progresses. The most notable feature of this painting is the clever distribution of the herds along the contours of the undulating terrain, which serves as the setting, to achieve an effect of interconnected order and space amidst the complication and density of the subjects depicted. Due attention is paid to the spatial relationship between distant and near objects and, by making a clear demarcation between the horizontal lines of the undulations, the empty spaces connect fluidly with the painted areas. The human figures and horses are outlined in ink while the slopes, mounds, trees and rocks are additionally treated with texture strokes and contrasting dots after being outlined. The brushwork is forceful and deliberate without being stiff. The use of complex colour schemes and their grouping imparts a richness and reserved freshness to the composition. In short, the conception of such a large-scale composition could not have been so successfully achieved without the consummate skill and careful planning possessed only by a great master. Wei Yan's original work has long been lost, but one can still visualize the scope of the original from this copy. At the same time it affords an insight into the artistic attainments of Li Gonglin. In undertaking the copying of the original he was in fact engaged in the work of artistic re-creation.

This painting has been variously held in the imperial collections of the Song, Ming and Qing dynasties as well as successively in the private ownership of Jia Sidao of the Later Tang, Sun Chengze of the Ming and Liang Qingbiao of the Qing periods.

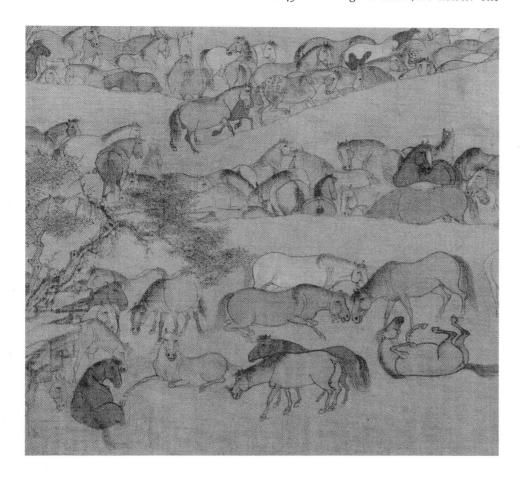

31. 漁村小雪圖

WANG SHEN (1037–?):
FISHING VILLAGE
AFTER LIGHT SNOW

Handscroll, colours on silk
44.5 × 219.5 cm
Song period

By the Northern Song period, landscape painting had already been developed as a new art form and a whole new generation of artists appeared with ingenious techniques, reaching maturity at great speed. Foremost among the founders of various schools were Li Cheng, Fan Kuan and Guo Xi. Having at first modelled himself on Li Cheng and Guo Xi, Wang Shen then went on to develop a style of his own by assimilating all that was best of the masters of the Tang and Song periods.

Wang Shen, styled Jinqing, was from Taiyuan, Shanxi province. He was a son-in-law of the emperor Ying zong. Well versed in poetry, the playing of the zither-like *qin*, chess playing, calligraphy and painting, he was a friend of such well-known figures as Su Shi, Huang Tingjian and Mi Fei. He was later banished from the court for his connections with the conservative party when Wang Anshi, the then prime minister, was pushing through his reforms, and he died in despair shortly afterwards. During his lifetime he collected a great number of famous examples of calligraphy and paintings and stored them in his Hall of Precious Paintings. Thanks to the close contact he had had with works by past masters of various schools, Wang Shen, himself a scholar of rare attainments and wide experience, distinguished himself as an accomplished landscape artist. As stated in the *Xuan he catalogue of paintings*, 'misty rivers and distant valleys, willowy brooks and fishing places, sunny haze and precipitous ravines, chilly forests and secluded gorges, peach blossom-streams and reedy villages, scenes that poets of all ages had often found difficult to describe, were subjects he loved to choose for his paintings. Beautifully executed and conceived, his paintings reflect an artistic superiority found only in the works of the ancients.' Apart from 'Fishing village after light snow' other surviving landscapes by Wang Shen include 'Misty river amid peaks' and 'Mountains and sea', each of which has a style all of its own. 'Fishing village after light snow' is generally considered the masterpiece most characteristic of his artistic achievement and special skill.

'Fishing village after light snow' is a snowscape in the form of a horizontal scroll which takes as its theme the life of fishermen. In the picture can be seen grotesque peaks and graceful ridges, precipitous crags and steep valleys, dangerous cliffs and impassable ravines, hillocks and rapids, clear brooks and winding inlets, sandy islets and river bends, cataracts and springs. Here and there are placed crooked pines and green cypresses, old trees and withered vines, sparse willows and tall

trunks, ancient temples and fishing villages, boats and wooden bridges. A number of fishermen are at work casting nets over the water, or working the mechanical, square-shaped fishing nets on the bank or angling from the bows of a boat. Others are sitting face to face in the cabins. On a hillside path a man walks with a cane and carries a qin, seeking a secluded spot. Flocks of waterfowl circle and wheel between the trees of the mist-shrouded forests. The beautiful setting and lifelike figures suggest a scene from everyday life. The entire landscape is shrouded in haze. The bleak and chilly atmosphere confronts the viewer, imparting a sense of the crisp coldness of early winter.

The artist has made effective use of the 'far distance' method of composition. With consummate skill the elements in the foreground, the middle ground and the background are integrated, with the different parts systematically arranged. Everything depicted is drawn according to its relative natural scale. This scroll is particularly notable for its ingenious and well-formed composition in which the empty spaces and solid areas arise one out of the other, giving an impression of great depth in something – that is to say the scroll – immediately before one. The application of ink and colouring is also extraordinary. With superb brushwork and clear ink colour, most of the subjects have first been drawn out, modelled in ink with *cun* texturing and contouring and ink wash. The upper surfaces of the rocks, trees and reeds were outlined in powdered gold to represent the play of sunlight as it glistens on the light dusting of snow. The horizon, painted with a green-grey wash, lies in contrast to the cold water of the brook and the hazy atmosphere, to represent the boundless sky over the vast expanse of water, with a possible promise of fine weather. The artist has incorporated the techniques of Li Cheng and Guo Xi, both of whom worked in the monochrome ink and wash style of landscape as well as those of Li Sixun of the Tang period who painted in the 'gold and green' style. It was doubtless an innovation never attempted before, and would seem to fit a contemporary statement of his work: 'He is neither ancient nor modern, with a unique style all his own.'

Mention is also made of it in the catalogues *Xuan he hua pu*, *Da guan lu* and *Shi qu bao ji*. The last Qing emperor, Pu yi, took it with him when he fled the Forbidden City and it later turned up in Changchun. In 1950 Hui Xiaotong bought the painting and presented it to the Palace Museum.

32. 清明上河圖

ZHANG ZEDUAN (?):
GOING UPRIVER AT THE
QING MING FESTIVAL

Handscroll, light colours on
silk
24.8 × 528.7 cm.
Northern Song period

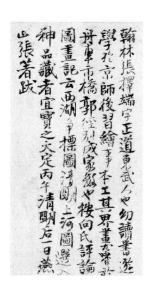

Because Zhang Zeduan's 'Going upriver at the Qing ming festival' depicts so magnificently all aspects of society and everyday life in a realistic and lively way, it has become widely known and holds a significant position in the history of Chinese painting.

Zhang Zeduan held an official post in the flourishing imperial academy of art led by the emperor Hui zong of the Song dynasty, himself a fine painter and calligrapher. He was reputed to have specialized in the painting of market places, bridges, suburban streets and carts and boats. His contemporaries singled out two of his works, 'Competition on West Lake', *Xi hu zheng biao tu*, and the present painting as superb.

The composition portrays the bustling scenes inside and outside the East Corner Gate of Bianjing (present day Kaifeng, Henan province), capital of the Northern Song dynasty, and along the banks of the River Bian. The scroll is divided into three sections: the first section shows the suburbs – a fine mist hanging over the sparse trees, low thatched eaves, crisscross footpaths between fields, willows putting forth buds, a team of donkeys delivering charcoal to the city, travellers going out of the city and sedan chairs coming back from grave-sweeping. The latter group brings out the theme of the painting in a custom observed during the 'clear and bright', *qing ming* (the fifth solar month) time of year, corresponding to spring, when ancestral graves were cleared.

The Shangtu Bridge spanning the River Bian forms the centrepiece of the middle section. The River Bian was the hub of water transport of grain to the capital during the Song period. Huge cargo boats laden with grain pushing upstream one after another and the busy scene of loading and unloading on the wharves provide a pictorial record of the important task assigned to this part of the river. The huge rainbow shaped wooden bridge bore the name of Shangtu Bridge but was commonly referred to as Rainbow Bridge. From both directions horses and carriages stream across the bridge thronged

with hawkers and jostling pedestrians. A boat laden with grain lets down its mast before it passes through the bridge opening and boatmen's strenuous efforts have attracted a large crowd of spectators. It is interesting to note the compositional device employed by the artist in arranging for incidents, like so many dramatic events, to occur at points where land and water routes cross.

The last section depicts a scene in the city centre. A lofty tower over the city gate called the East Corner Gate, is located in the southeastern corner of the inner city of Bianjing. Outside the gate the first bridge to cross the river is the Shangtu Bridge. And on either side of the gate, there are intersecting streets, with row upon row of houses standing on both sides of each of them. There is a wide variety of shops; the fronts of some of the larger ones are decorated with hanging festoons while the smaller shops are simple stalls. There are, besides, official government offices, *ya men*, and temples. The streets are thronged with people and an endless stream of vehicles, horses, camels and sedan chairs passes along the thoroughfares. Among the pedestrians are gentry, officials, servants, pedlars, lackeys, drivers, sedan chair carriers, workers, storytellers, barbers, doctors, fortune tellers, aristocratic ladies, itinerant monks, urchins and even beggars. Their social status can be identified from the hats and clothing they wear. Some of them idle away their time, happy and carefree, while others rush about busy, unhappy and careworn. All inhabit the same streets. The means of transport in the city include sedan chairs, camel teams, oxen, horses, donkey carts, rickshaws and other vehicles of various descriptions. Remarkable for its vivid representation of varied genre scenes, the scroll gives a general picture of the people's life in the capital during the twelfth century at the height of the Northern Song dynasty.

In executing this scroll, the painter shows a masterly skill in making effective use of concrete elaboration and abstract

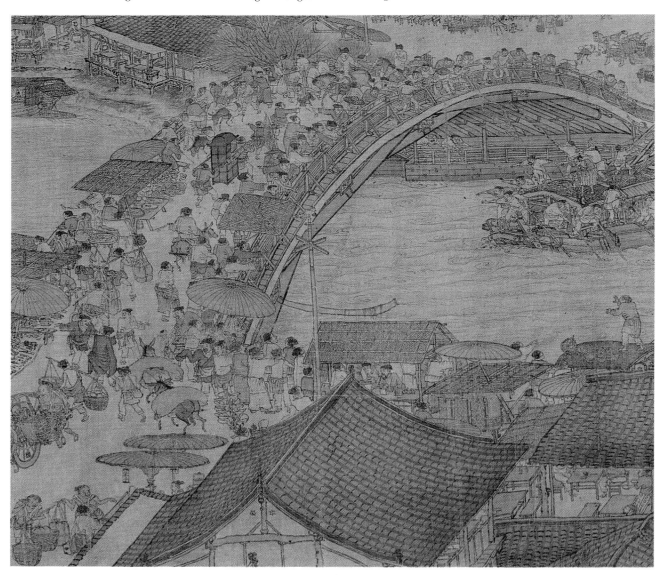

generalization. Its light and elegant colouring, quite unusual in paintings with architecture as their main theme, gives the scroll a unique style. In compositional terms the bird's-eye panoramic view selected allows a clear and concise picture to be built up of what the southeastern corner of Bianjing, a typical district of the capital, looked like in those days. In adopting the traditional handscroll format, the painter makes use of a 'shifting eye perspective' to organize the elements across the picture surface. Despite the great length of the scroll it is far from dull; although complex, it is well organized, compactly laid out and forms a coherent whole. Another characteristic of the painting is the close attention to the details of all the subjects, big or small; from the expansive, quiet, open suburbs, the wide, flowing river and the towering outer city walls to the people in vessels and vehicles, the street pedlars' goods on display and the written characters on the signboards, nothing is missed. Every detail has been treated with faithful accuracy. Even though the composition includes over 500 figures, they are inextricably interwoven in every kind of activity and incident in a systematically organized way that adds further appeal. Not only was the artist a keen observer of human life but also expert in exploring the poetic and dramatic. In translating them into their painted forms, he shows remarkable skill in summarizing and organizing the material he has gathered. At every stage the scene changes completely, so that it is impossible for the eye to take in everything at once. Something different appears at each glance, be it atmosphere or object, so that even after travelling to the end of the scroll, there remains the possibility that this has only been a small part of a much bigger world which continues unbounded beyond the confines of the painting.

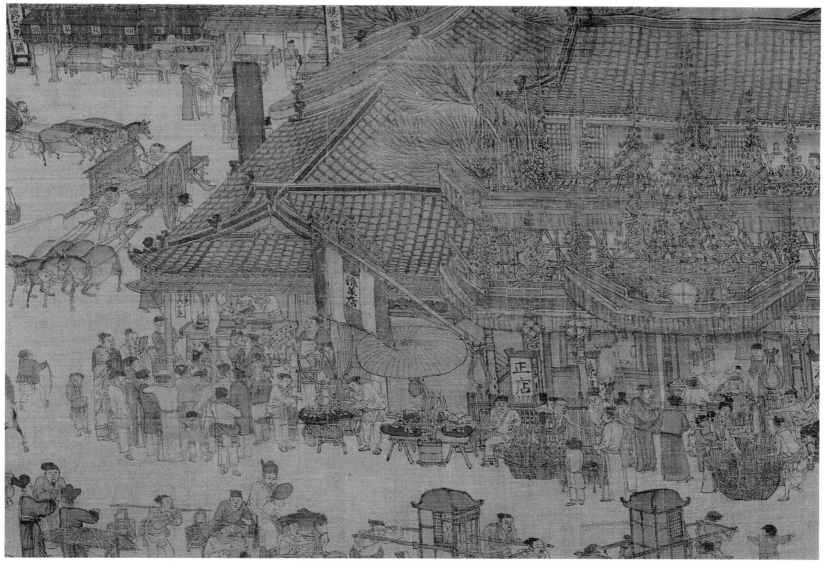

33. 水圖

MA YUAN (1190–1224):
STUDIES OF WATER

Handscroll, light colours on
silk
12 separate sections
each section 26.8 × 41.6 cm.
Southern Song period

Landscape painting underwent a profound change during the Southern Song period. Artists sought to express ideas which were simple and yet complete by means of intense, compact forms to break through the traditional 'panoramic' style of composition in which the whole scene is set down. Thus a new compositional technique was created. Bold and unrestrained brushwork became the order of the day and is a characteristic of paintings during the Southern Song. Foremost among paintings of the time were Li Tang, Liu Songnian, Ma Yuan and Xia Gui, commonly referred to as the 'Four masters of the Southern Song'.

Ma Yuan, styled Yaofu, was from an old family of Yongji, Shanxi province. Under the reign of the emperors Guang zong and Ning zong of the Southern Song, he served as an official in the imperial art academy. The product of such an old and well-known family of painters, he assimilated the techniques of such painters as Li Tang but later developed his own personal style. Specializing in landscape, figures, and bird and flower painting, his favourite technique was the large axe-cut or hatchet stroke brushstroke, *da fu bi cun*. Compositionally he represented the whole scene by reducing it, focusing on a few elements such as rocks and trees, and placing them in one corner. This was indeed an innovation which showed much originality in affording wide views in a small, confined space. Because of this, he was nicknamed 'One corner Ma'. A number of the paintings he executed in the art academy bear inscriptions by the emperor Ning zong and his consort, who was called Yang. This scroll, 'Studies of water', is one of Ma Yuan's works which bears the consort's inscription.

The studies are in twelve separate sections. As the part of the first section which should bear the title is missing, the title is unknown. From left to right, the other eleven sections are respectively: 'Breeze-stroked ripples on Lake Dongting'; 'Surging waves'; 'Cold pool clear and shallow'; 'Boundless expanse of the Yangtze River'; 'Adverse torrents of the Yellow River'; 'Swirling eddies on autumnal waters'; 'Clouds rising over the blue sea'; 'Mighty lake'; 'Unfolding clouds and rolling waves'; 'Dawn sun warming the mountain' and 'Rippling waves'.

Water is the sole subject-matter of all twelve sections except for two which include a corner of the rocky shore and a mountain peak. The scroll, by exploring the many aspects of water, expresses a variety of artistic ideas. By acute observation the painter brings out the shapes created by water at its surface with beauty and admirable brushwork. In 'Breeze-stroked ripples on Lake Dongting' the scale-like waves, gently undulating, are drawn smaller as they recede, finally to merge with the horizon. The effect is one of a gentle breeze brushing the surface of the vast expanse of water and of a pleasant sensation of relaxation and indifference to the cares of the world. In 'Surging waves', the rise and fall of rolling waves are executed with tremulous brushstrokes, as if the water has been stirred by dragons lying dormant below the surface. The tempestuous movement of the waves produces a bracing and grand effect. In the 'Mighty lake' the painter depicts the peaked, pulsating waves with brisk, flowing lines. The irregular arrangement of the crests has been caused by the intermittent blowing of a blustery wind. Even without the painter's light tinges of red, the scene would still appear radiant with sunlight and remind one of the scenic beauty of West Lake in Hangzhou on a sunny day. The 'Unfolding clouds and rolling waves' presents a completely different picture. Drawn in jerky, frozen brushstrokes, a thundering wave soars skyward, crashing with terrifying impetus through the ominous, swirling cloud overhead as if joining in an intensive, noisy battle. Small as the painting is, it presents a scene of magnificent grandeur. The other sections explore individual ideas and forms which allow appreciation from one's own experience.

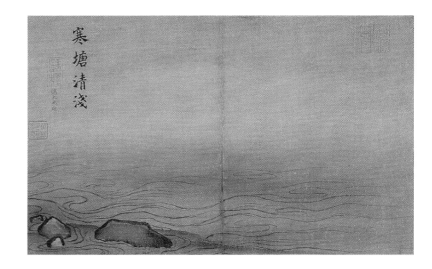

長江萬頃

黃河逆流

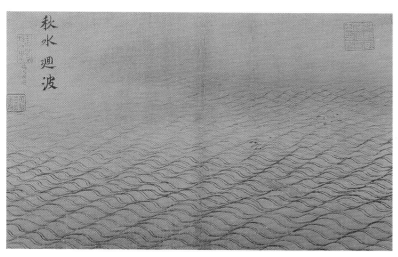

秋水迴波

雲生蒼海

湖光瀲灩

雲舒浪卷

曉日烘山

紅浪漂漂

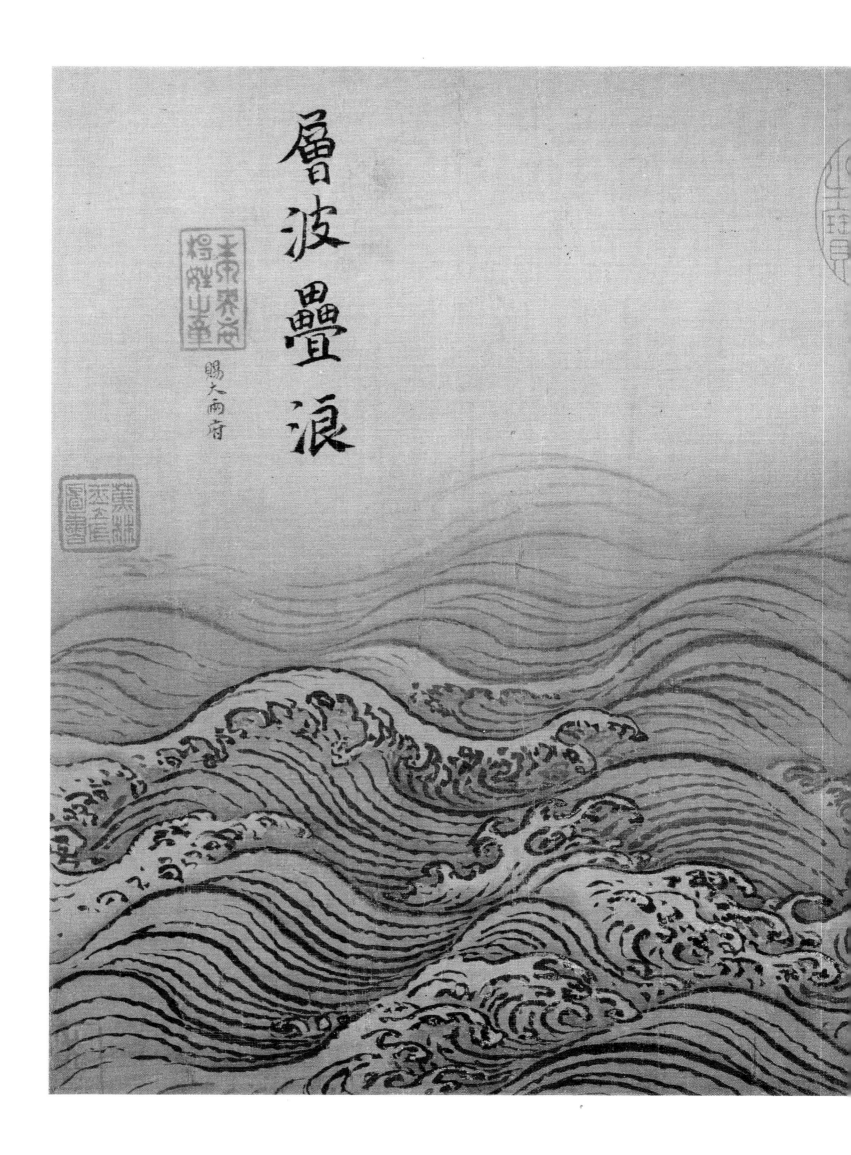

層波疊浪

賜大雨府

34. 大儺圖

ANONYMOUS: DRIVING
AWAY PLAGUES AND
DEVILS

Handscroll, colours on silk
67.4 × 59.2 cm.
Song period

The Song period saw a great development in the area of genre painting of which 'Driving away plagues and devils' is an example. It shows twelve men dressed in strange clothing and wearing all kinds of hats, some of which are bedecked with sprays of blossom. Each of the strange types of headgear is different. Apart from the conical woven bamboo hat, turban-like headscarf and cap, these are an animal mask with horns, a square-shaped box for measuring grain, *dou*, a flat winnowing basket, and a deep open basket all used as hats. The participants hold musical instruments such as bells or hardwood clappers while one has a drum strapped round his body. They also hold fans, baskets, brooms or sprays of flowers, gourds and so on. Each wears make-up of some kind or a mask. The twelve figures form a circle, dancing and gesticulating in a jubilant mood.

The theme of the scroll is derived from the ancient folk custom of driving away pestilence. The *Analects* of Confucius refers to the 'rural custom of exorcism'. According to the *History of the Later Han dynasty*, *Hou Han shu*, 'The day before the beginning of the twelfth moon is the time to perform the ceremony of exorcism. One hundred and twenty children from official families between the ages of 10 and 12 are chosen.' And a passage in the *Yue fu za lu*, *Miscellanies from the Yue fu*, of the Tang period reads: 'they put on hats and square masks with four golden eyes. Clad in bear fur coats, holding dagger-axes and raising shields, they repeatedly cry *Nuo! Nuo!* which means to exorcize evil spirits and pestilence. On the last day of the lunar month, 500 children wearing masks and dressed in green jackets with vermilion pleats perform the exorcizing ceremony in front of the Zi chen Hall which is hung with lanterns and chime stones.' On the whole, these descriptions tally with the activities of the subjects in the painting. By the Song period, of course, ceremonies observed on such occasions might have varied in circumstance and detail. From this scroll, we can see that a number of agricultural implements have been added to the paraphernalia of the ancient custom. We are therefore led to the conclusion that, by the Song period, the proceedings had acquired a wider significance, incorporating prayers and rituals for a good harvest as well as an opportunity for the rural community to enjoy itself. The value of this painting therefore lies not only in its artistic merit, but also in its sociological and historical content.

35. 搜山圖(部分)

ANONYMOUS: HUNTING
IN THE MOUNTAINS
(DETAIL)

Handscroll, colours on silk
53.3 × 533 cm.
Song period

This painting draws on the folk legend of the god Er lang who roamed the mountains in order to expel demons. It is therefore also sometimes referred to as 'The deity Er lang searching in the mountains'. This legend became widespread over many centuries amongst the Chinese people and a great number of literary works have used it as a basis. During the Yuan period there was a *za ju* drama set to music entitled 'Er lang shoots an arrow at the mirror-locked demon', which described Er lang's struggles with the demon king, a nine-headed ox, Nuo Zha and the spirit of one hundred eyes with golden pupils, and their subsequent capture of all the demons and monsters hiding in two caves. Records show that as early as the Northern Song period a painter named Gao Yi had executed a painting entitled 'Supernatural beings hunting in the mountains' which was admired by the emperor. During the Ming and Qing periods, copies of it repeatedly appeared.

The present painting was executed by an unknown painter during the last years of the Southern Song dynasty or during the early part of the Yuan period. The figures are drawn in the careful *gong bi*, linear, style with heavy colours, the lines of the clothes being painted with iron wire lines. The vigorousness of brushwork is a testimony to the skill of the artist who has brought the scene of strange animals and figures to life. In the representation of the mountains, rocks and trees, the artist has employed free, unrestrained brushstrokes similar to the style of Liu Songnian of the Southern Song period. When compared with other scrolls illustrating the same theme, this one is found to be incomplete, the part missing being that which portrayed the leading character, the deity Er lang. At all events, the painting manifests a drawing technique that surpasses that shown in any of the others. The troops from heaven as represented in this scroll make a splendid show of their strength as they hunt down the demons and spirits which inhabit the forests and mountains. These malevolent spirits are embodied in such animals as tigers, bears, pigs, monkeys, foxes, goats, roebuck or river deer, rabbits, lizards and snakes as well as tree-dwelling spirits. As shown in the painting, pursued by the army of divinities some demons have resorted to their original forms while others have taken on the appearance of women in an attempt to flee into caves or wriggle out of being captured, as in the case of the latter. Brandishing such weapons as swords, spears and halberds, the divinities let loose falcons or eagles and dogs in an effort to intercept them and cut off their retreat. Originally Er lang was eulogized as an upright character. Having seen the way in which the army of divinities is depicted one is almost left with the impression that they are vicious and evil, whereas the demons have a kinder and more gentle appearance, while contrary to expectation, the miserable state of these panic-stricken creatures as portrayed by the artist evokes sympathy. Although the intention of the painter in conveying such an impression cannot be resolved it does conjure up a comparable image of the common people who fell prey to the soldiers riding roughshod over them during the period when this painting was executed.

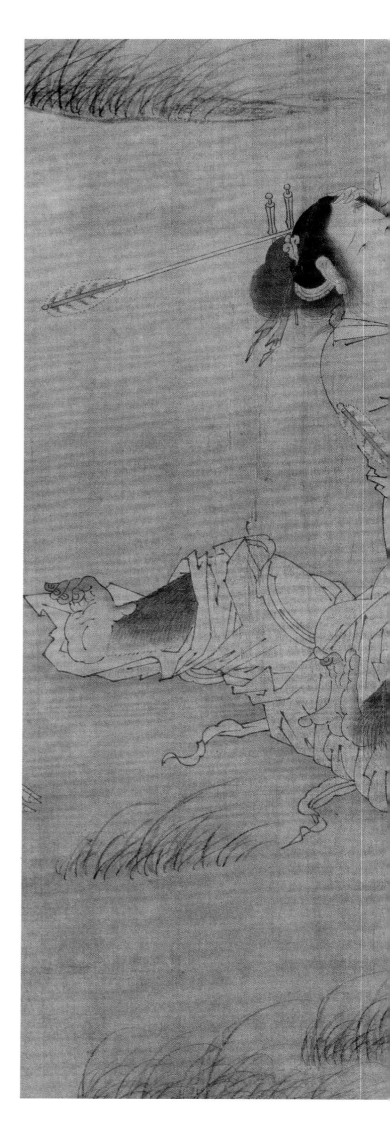

36. 秋郊飲馬圖

ZHAO MENGFU
(1254–1322): HORSES
DRINKING IN AN AUTUMN
SUBURB

Handscroll, blue and green
colours on silk
23.6 × 59 cm.
Yuan period

Zhao Mengfu, styled Ziang, otherwise known as Songxue, came from Wuxing, Zhejiang province. He was the most influential of the calligraphers and painters of the early years of the Yuan period. As an imperial clansman of the Song dynasty, which had been overthrown by the Mongols, he was forced to retire from official life to his home, where he earned a reputation as a scholar amongst the ordinary people. At the age of thirty-four he was summoned by emperor Shi zu (Khubilai Khan) and was subsequently made an official. During his tenure of office he was exceptionally well treated under imperial patronage.

The horse was one of Zhao Mengfu's favourite subjects and he executed a great number of horse paintings during his lifetime. Among his surviving works are 'Men and horses', 'On horseback', 'Bathing horses' and 'Horses drinking in an autumn suburb'.

The latter was painted when he was fifty-nine years old. Horses drink from a clear stream which glides past the long embankment, with the sparse autumnal forest on the grassy slopes dotted cheerfully with red maple leaves forming a pleasing contrast. Reins in hand and holding a whip, a rider dressed in red drives the horses to the bank of the stream. The horses are portrayed in different attitudes: galloping and chasing each other, drinking water, looking back, craning their heads, and so on. Small as the rider and horses are, they are true to life and full of vitality.

Making the fullest possible use of the limited space afforded by the silk format on which they are painted the artist has concentrated his subjects in the middle ground on the right-hand side, cutting off the sky at the top. By representing the view from three different visual angles all in the same composition – straight on, looking up and out into the distance and looking down from above – he integrated his subjects into an organic whole. The different elements are ingeniously dealt with and carefully arranged in relation to whether they are to be fully included or relate to some other, unseen, element. In this respect, the majority of elements, trees, rocks, slopes and the rider and horses, also form the main focus of interest on the right, moving from right to left, in a way that suggests that they have just entered the scene from some hidden place which is cut off by the right-hand edge of the painting. The eye is carried through the composition in this way to a few tree trunks scattered along the top left edge, their branches and tops, as well as the distant hills and water, lying somewhere beyond the picture. A stream in the lower left area is separated by two banks, the lower one of which stops short to disappear beyond the picture frame. The opposite bank, along which two horses gallop and chase, likewise continues beyond the left edge, suggesting the limitless expanse of land, as well as the continuing flow of the river beyond. Thus, the main theme of the picture, on a larger scale than would otherwise be possible if the whole suggested landscape were depicted, is focused within the confines of the space allowed. The overall impression also includes a much greater, unexplained expanse beyond all four edges.

From the brushstrokes and colouring of this painting we can see that the painter, while preserving the fine traditions of the Tang artists, had developed a style all his own. Drawing on his previously acquired skills, he applied calligraphic techniques to drawing. Human figures and horses are delineated with

even and careful brushstrokes which, like the ancient seal script, are characterized by a primitiveness, carefulness, precision, freshness and ease. Strokes used in cursive calligraphy are used for trees and rocks, slopes and mounds and the sandy shore, as well as hooks and *cun* texture strokes, 'broken ink' lines, splitting and shading strokes. Bold and vigorous, his brushwork is nevertheless elegant and smooth. Suitable colours are applied to various objects against a background painted in the traditional blue and green of Tang landscapes. Bright red is used for the maple leaves, green for the embankment and the slopes representing an early autumn scene when the sharp frost has not yet stolen away the grass. The horses are painted in white, red, yellow or an orange-brown colour. Rich, subtle and lucid, the colours do not obliterate the outlines. Clearly the painter has succeeded in incorporating the blue and green and the ink and wash styles of landscape with the horse painting methods of the Tang and Song periods. Furthermore, the artistic talent of the artist is fused with the scholarly attributes of the literatus. If Zhao's 'Men and horses' and 'On horseback', painted at the age of forty-three, still showed the influence of the Tang and Song painters, 'Horses drinking in an autumn suburb' clearly demonstrates the unique personal style he had acquired. This painting embodies all the typical features of the horses he drew in his old age and is, therefore, regarded as a rare possession.

37. 九峯雪霽圖軸

HUANG GONGWANG
(1269–1354): NINE
SNOW-CAPPED PEAKS

Hanging scroll, ink on silk
116.40 × 54.8 cm.
Yuan period

Besides Zhao Mengfu, the most outstanding artists of the Yuan landscape painters were Huang Gongwang, Wang Meng, Wu Zhen and Ni Zan, collectively known as the 'Four great masters of the Yuan'. Inspired by both the theories and paintings of Zhao, they exploited monochrome ink and brush techniques to the full and established the new school of literary men's landscape painting. The main feature of this style was that it raised painting to a new level with its emphasis on the use of brush and ink, and thereby enriched the techniques and methods of expression in traditional Chinese painting. In years to come they were to exert a great influence over painters of the Ming and Qing periods.

Huang Gongwang, the foremost of the masters, was born to a family named Lu in Changshu, Jiangsu province, but he was later adopted by a family called Huang of Yongjia, Zhejiang province, thereby taking the name by which he is known. He

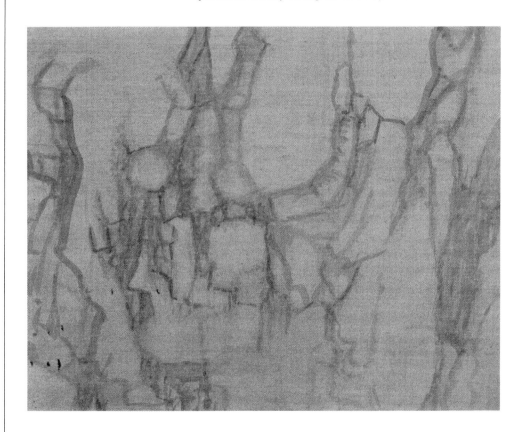

styled himself Zijiu, his other names being Yifeng and Da chi dao ren, 'Idiotic Taoist priest'. After serving for a time as a minor official at the capital, he was implicated in a case of corruption and was convicted. After his release from prison he became a Taoist priest and roamed about Hangzhou, Song-jiang and other places as a fortune teller. Expert in calligraphy, music and painting – especially landscape painting – he made a point of always carrying his ink and brushes wherever he went so as to be able to make studies of picturesque spots. His paintings, spare in their use of colour, were known for their 'bold outlines of mountains and luxuriant growth of vegeta-tion'. He also wrote a famous essay entitled 'Secrets of the art of landscape painting', *Hua shan shui jue*, a distillation of the experiences of his predecessors as well as of his own.

The painting shown would seem to be an example of what Huang called 'the use of a white silk ground to depict snow, in the painting of a winter scene'. Two other extant pictures by the same painter, 'A fine day after the heavy snow' (Palace Museum, Beijing) and 'Visiting Mr Dai at Yan Creek' (in Yunnan Provincial Museum) successfully employ this same technique.

The following text, written in Huang Gongwang's own hand, appears at the top right-hand corner of the painting. 'It was during spring in the first month of the ninth year of the reign period Zhi zheng that I began to paint a snowscape for Yan Gong, and that it straightaway began to snow heavily. Several snowstorms followed and they only stopped when I had put the final touches to the composition. A strange coincidence, indeed! Inscribed by me, the Idiotic Taoist priest, eighty-one years old, to record this event.' The date given corresponds to 1349 and the person for whom it was painted was Ban Weizhi, a well-known scholar of the Yuan period.

'Nine snow-capped peaks' is a masterpiece representing a snowscape of strange towering peaks shooting up in bold jagged outlines, fathomless ravines, withered trees and thatched houses. Enveloped in a snowy white shroud, the scene seems to plunge one into a land of ice and snow.

The composition is compact, with a firm stability built into the precarious rock formations. In this well-structured scheme, the solid forms and cavernous spaces give rise to each other in a natural way. The principle of 'high distance' is combined with that of 'far distance' to construct the painting, so as to permit the inclusion of the towering peaks as well as the fullest possible view of the deep gorges. In placing the main peaks centrally, their sheer sides cut off and falling away to the lower slopes with boulders on either side below, as well as in piling up distant mountain tops in the background, the artist uses a method of primary and secondary construction, at once bringing out the main features and bringing together the many elements to produce a coherent result. The sky above the mountains and the creeks flowing around their bases introduce space to break up the tight mass of the composition and thus avoid overcrowding. The overall effect is an increased sense of solidity in the central, painted areas with open, flowing spaces around them.

The use of brushstrokes is finely and carefully considered. The trees and houses are delineated with *zhuan liao*, or seal script-like strokes, at once firm and vigorous, and the rock formations with *cao shu*, cursive script-like strokes, to pro-duce an effect of grandeur and vigour amidst a scene of spatial neatness and elegance.

The composition is executed on plain silk, the outlines being first sketched lightly in ink, then built up with a combination of *cun* texture strokes, dots and hook strokes in graduated tones. A light wash is used for the mountains and rocks in a way that defines their solid presence. Broken ink, *po mo*, is also used. Small, unpainted areas of silk, where the ink is not intended to take, show through to represent the glittering snow.

38. 秋亭嘉樹圖軸

NI ZAN (1301–1374):
PAVILION AND TREES IN
AUTUMN

Hanging scroll, ink on paper
134 × 34.3 cm.
Yuan period

Among the four great Yuan artists, Ni Zan was noted for his unique style, described as 'solitary, light, concise but strong'. His works, widely emulated by later literati painters, were praised as 'peerless' by critics. He stood alongside the other three giants, Huang Gongwang, Wu Zhen and Wang Meng, and such was his popularity that people of the area south of the River Yangtze judged the taste of a scholar according to whether or not a painting by Ni Zan hung on his walls.

Ni Zan was born in Wuxi, Jiangsu province, and styled himself Yuan Zhen, Yun ling and You xia. Born of a wealthy family, he enjoyed the society of literary luminaries of the day. The social upheaval towards the end of the Yuan period induced him to sell all his estates and, having dispersed the rest of his property, he travelled along the rivers of Jiangsu and around the five lakes of Jiangxi, Jiangsu and Hunan provinces, living in temples and simple rural dwellings. Because of this, he earned the nickname Ni yu, 'Ni the Vague'.

He was skilled in poetry composition as well as calligraphy but he is noted mainly for his landscape and bamboo and rock painting, mostly executed in ink. At first he modelled his works on those of Dong Yuan, but later took up the *zhe dai cun*, 'broken' or 'folded ribbon' texture strokes, originally used by Jing Hao and Guan Tong. He also looked to Li Cheng in the painting of mountains and trees. Most of the scenes were taken from the area around Lake Tai, Jiangsu province, whose sloping shores are sparsely dotted with trees, shallow waters and hills beyond. His works impart a sense of tranquillity and solitude, their richness and strength veiled in apparent simplicity and freshness. Such freshness of expression gave a new impetus to literati landscape painting. Commenting on his own works, he said, 'The sketchy strokes do not aim so much at achieving a likeness as conveying the innermost feelings of the painter.'

Executed during Ni Zan's final years, the painting illustrated depicts tall trees barely covered with leaves in the foreground on a sloping bank. A thatched pavilion and a few bamboos stand beneath them. In the distance are the mountains, separated by an expanse of lake with encroaching sandy outcrops faintly depicted on the left. The picture conveys the desolate atmosphere of late autumn and the accompanying poem reflects the artist's mood and his withdrawal from the mundane to contemplate the beauty of the natural world as he wandered along the waterways. It also contains something of a Buddhist outlook.

The composition is constructed on the principle of a 'level distance' in two sections in which the foreground occupies the bottom part of the picture surface, the far mountains the centre of the upper part, the two separated by a large, unpainted section depicting water. These devices lend clarity and spatial depth to the picture and are the hallmark of his style. In some paintings the distant mountains extend upward as far as the topmost edge of the picture surface.

The brushwork is firmly yet freely executed. Mountains are built up with *po mo* and *zhe dai*, 'broken ink' and 'folded ribbon' texture strokes in a combination of wet and drier washes. Thick, dark ink, also employed to bring out the lower vegetation and leaves, serves to delineate the planes and strata of natural elements. This painting was praised as showing 'a brush of which to be proud' by Wu Kuan, a sentiment later taken up by Zhu Guo, both of the Ming period.

七月六日雨宿雷峯翁幽居文伯賢良以此絹索畫因寫秋亭真樹高爽誌以贈之　風雨蕭條聯作源兩林嘉樹近常窓結廬人境無未歇寫醉御真樂印南渓灵雪而孟情西山青影落秋江眺滾滾翰墨幽意悠有御烟白鷗雙蟄

117

39. 夏日山居圖軸

· WANG MENG
(1308–1385):
HERMITAGE IN SUMMER
MOUNTAINS

Hanging scroll, ink on paper
118.1 × 36.2 cm.
Yuan period

Another of the four great Yuan masters, Wang Meng developed his own unique style. Though he was younger than the other three, his artistic achievements were no less significant and his ink landscapes have been revered and imitated down to the present day.

Wang Meng, who also called himself the 'Recluse of Yellow Crane Mountain' was a native of Wuxing, Zhejiang province, and a grandson of the renowned painter, Zhao Mengfu. He served as an official for a period covering the last years of the Yuan and the first few years of the Ming dynasties. Wrongly accused of high treason, he was thrown into prison where he died.

Although influenced in his youth by the works of his grandfather, he also learned much from the great Tang and Song masters. Inspired by the works of Wang Wei, Dong Yuan, Ju ran and others, his landscape paintings went beyond the scope of those of Zhao Mengfu and took on their own distinct appearance, as witnessed by his application of a variety of brush techniques influenced by other painters, and favoured the use of a dry brush and black ink texture strokes and dots. His landscape paintings are characterized by broad, deep vistas, with views from many angles balanced by a profound elegance. The theme is often one of some kind of retreat or dwelling secluded in mountainous countryside.

'Hermitage in summer mountains' depicts the ideal sanctuary of a recluse tucked away in the folds of high mountains among pines and cypresses, winding brooks and circuitous mountain paths. A building is half revealed in a grove at the foot of the crag; the atmosphere is calm and restful. The picture is so well disciplined and orchestrated that even though composed of a compact mass of elements it is neither overcrowded nor obstructed and in its complexity betrays not the slightest sign of disorder. The lofty peak is counteracted by the tortuous windings of the river and crags which in their turn emphasize the stupendous height and precipitousness of the mountain. The brushwork also shows consummate skill: rock formations are either delicately textured or washed with ink, while trees are finely sketched or casually dotted in, depending on the perspective. The mass of texturing brushstrokes is built up with such carefree precision and combined with such a natural fluidity that each element is defined exactly and light and shade are meticulously controlled, thus holding the whole composition together. The technical virtuosity of Wang Meng is evident in his control of brush and ink. This picture, typical of landscape paintings of Wang Meng's later years, is representative of his style and a masterpiece among his extant works.

In the upper right-hand section of the painting is a vertical three line inscription by Wang Meng: 'While staying in the summer hermitage, in the second month of the year, Wang Shuming [Wang Meng], the Recluse of Yellow Crane Mountain, painted this picture for the respected scholar Tong Xuan in the Pavilion of Tall Trees at Qingcun.' The painting is given a date equivalent to 1368.

40. 三顧草廬圖軸

DAI JIN (1388–1462):
CALLING AT THE
MASTER'S THATCHED
DWELLING FOR THE
THIRD TIME

Hanging scroll, colours on
silk
172.2 × 107 cm.
Ming period

Dai Jin was an important painter who lived during the early Ming period. His achievement stands out against his contemporaries who followed in the footsteps of the Southern Song masters of landscape painting such as Li Tang, Liu Songnian, Ma Yuan and Xia Gui and he is credited as the founder of the new Zhe school. His use of the brush was much freer than that of Ma Yuan. This freedom of brushwork and strong, expressive quality, although a legacy of the traditions found in the paintings of Ma Yuan, was developed into a style wholly unique to the Zhe school painters. These particular techniques were also to be adopted and carried further by Wu Wei who established the Jiangxia school at a later date.

Dai Jin, styled Wenjin, was a native of Qiantang, Hangzhou, Zhejiang province. Working first as a goldsmith, he later took up painting, eventually becoming a court painter to the emperor Xuan zong. However, he was expelled for offending his patron by painting a picture called the 'Solitary fisherman on a river in autumn', in which the fisherman was depicted wearing a scarlet robe, a colour reserved for the nobility. He subsequently earned his living as a professional painter, excelling in all kinds of subjects, particularly natural scenery and figures.

He bequeathed a considerable legacy of works ranging from landscapes to human figures and flower paintings. This particular composition is of the type which employs figures in a landscape to tell a story. It is based on a tale of the period of the Three Kingdoms which recounts how Liu Bei, the founder of the kingdom of Shu, went in the company of Guan Yu and Zhang Fei to ask Zhuge Liang to come out of retirement and join him. The scene is composed of stupendous mountains, steep precipices, rushing, cascading waterfalls, twisted pines, tall cypresses, dense groves of bamboos and thick grass. The

wicker gate stands wide open, with part of the thatched house showing between the bamboo thickets at the foot of the crag. At the gate, Liu Bei bows slightly to salute a boy who, with a gesture of his hand, invites the visitors to enter while Guan Yu and Zhang Fei stand behind Liu Bei, deep in conversation.

Zhuge Liang sits solemnly inside the hut clad in the robe trimmed with crane's down for which he is famous. Fan in hand, he is waiting to receive his guests. The lifelike figures blend naturally with their setting. Their characters – the amiability and modesty of Liu Bei, the military bearing of Guan Yu, the fiery and straightforward nature of Zhang Fei, the superior wisdom of Zhuge Liang and the youthful caution of the boy – are each suitably expressed according to the historical event here described.

In composition the artist has generally followed the styles of Ma Yuan and Xia Gui in that the main element occupies one corner of the painting. In brushwork and use of colour it also owes much to the same painters. In composition, the artist has generally followed the structural techniques of Ma Yuan and Xia Gui, in that the one of two main elements, the foreground, unfolds from one corner, in this instance the left, and proceeds to carry the eye up through the high distance of the mountain, which balances it. The shattered mountains and rocks are described in the 'axe cut' or 'hatchet' brush-stroke, *fu pi cun*, while the folds of clothing are depicted in angular, calligraphic lines which end in *jue tou*, 'pick' or 'hoe-heads'. These expressionist brushstrokes using moist ink washes are characteristics of Dai Jin's style that can also be traced back to Ma Yuan and Xia Gui.

41. 仿黃公望富春山居圖卷

SHEN ZHOU
(1427–1509): DWELLINGS
IN THE FUCHUN MOUNTAINS
(after Huang Gongwang,
1269–1354).

Horizontal scroll, colours on
paper
36.8 x 85.5 cm
Ming period

During the mid Ming period, a new group of painters appeared around Suzhou, Jiangsu province. Taking its name from the ancient kingdom which included this area, it became known as the Wu school. Founded by Shen Zhou, it took its final form under Wen Zhengming and eventually replaced the Zhe and court styles of painting. The most significant feature of Wu school painting was the restoration of the tradition that stressed the importance of the use of the brush and ink, in line and wash, catering for the artistic tastes of the scholar-gentleman and eventually resulting in the further development of literati painting.

Shen Zhou, often referred to as Shi tian, another of his names, was born into an old Suzhou family and soon showed himself to be talented in the arts of poetry, painting, calligraphy and literature, and although he maintained links with the local gentry and bureaucrats in connection with these interests, he lived the life of a commoner. His calligraphy, dynamic and robust, emulated that of Huang Tingjian of the Song period while in painting his eclectic style owed a great deal to such past masters as Dong Yuan, Ju ran and the leading painters of the Yuan period. He also drew inspiration from the natural scenery through which he travelled around Lake Tai and by applying the disciplines of painting that he had learned from these artists, he created a completely individual style. In his later years especially, he became adept in using the tip of a thick, coarse-haired brush which contributed to his unique style. Combining this with simple colour schemes and strong brushstrokes he thus laid a firm foundation for the style associated with the Wu school. Apart from landscapes he also painted flowers in a spontaneous manner which anticipated the type of paintings for which Chen Chun became renowned.

'Dwellings in the Fuchun Mountains' is but one of many fine, extant works by Shen Zhou. The original on which it is modelled (now in Taiwan) was painted by Huang Gongwang who took several years to complete it. At one time owned by Shen Zhou himself, it was passed on by him to a friend for the latter to write a colophon on it. Unfortunately, when the friend died, the son kept it for himself and when it was offered for sale Shen Zhou lacked the means to buy it back. Regretting its loss, he made the present copy from memory. Thus the painting cannot be expected to reproduce the original in every detail. As Shen Zhou himself wrote at the end of the colophon, he appended 'Its image never left me and so I tried to visualize it but the original eluded me and I faltered as I approached the

paper'. However, apart from the section showing a ridge covered with stones and trees in the final position and a few other minor details, it is remarkably close to Huang Gongwang's composition. The brush and ink technique on the other hand differs completely and the use of colour is distinctively that of Shen Zhou. Therefore, in attempting to reproduce Huang's original, the artist has created a completely new composition within the framework of the artistic rules employed by the former painter. The large size horizontal format incorporates connected lines of mountains beneath a boundless sky that merges in places with the large expanses of water which are defined by the islets, mud flats, stony shores and inlets. Pavilions and buildings, flat bridges and winding paths, fishermen's huts and boats are dispersed throughout the landscape. Few human figures are to be found, apart from the solitary men who walk, staff in hand, across bridges and through the hills. A couple of fishermen dangle their lines into the water from boats, and one man watches the geese from a thatched pavilion on stilts which stands at the water's edge. Taken as a whole, the composition brings out the beauty of the mountainous landscape of the area depicted.

This painting was executed when Shen Zhou was sixty and as he lived to a very old age it is representative of works done in his late middle age, the most productive period of his life. Also, as Shen Zhou had developed his own distinctive style and methods by this time, it incorporates the brushwork and use of colour so characteristic of his mature style. The individual elements are often painted with the tip of a well used brush. Mountains and rocks are modelled throughout using both short and long 'spread-out hemp fibre' texture strokes. Texturing, using the tip of the brush, is sometimes used for banks and slopes. Horizontal dots are used for foliage and vegetation with dry and moist or light and rich ink appropriately applied and blocks of a grey-blue wash brushed over forms which have been outlined first in black ink. Blue and ochre washes are carefully placed according to the spatial relationships of different natural elements. The sky and water are mostly left unpainted. The subdued colouring and the innate strength of the brushwork is everything that would be expected of the founder of a new school of painting, a sentiment originally conveyed by the Ming period theorist and painter, Dong Qichang, in the colophon he inscribed in praise of the composition: 'This matches the old masters and surely surpasses them.'

大癡翁此段山水殆天造地設平生不見多
作作輟凡三年始成筆踈墨當與
巨然亂其真身認乃甚惜此卷嘗為余所
藏日靖請題于人遂為其子乾沒其子後不
能有出以售人余貧又不能為真以後之
徒系矣於思耳即其思之不忘延以意餘之
物遠之其臨紙惘然
成化丁未中秋日長洲沈周識

42. 綠陰清話圖

WEN ZHENGMING
(1470–1559): CHATTING
IN THE SHADE

Hanging scroll, ink on paper
131.8 × 32 cm.
Ming period

Except for Shen Zhou, Wen Zhengming was the most outstanding and influential literati painter of the mid-Ming period. If Shen is seen as the founder of the Wu school, we may with good reason regard Wen as the leader who helped shape the group.

Wen Zhengming's original personal name was Bi. He changed his sobriquet, Zhengming, to Zhengzhong and adopted Hengshan as his poetic name. Born in Changzhou (now Suzhou, Jiangsu province), to a family of officials, he learned literature from Wu Kuan, calligraphy from Li Yingzhen, and painting from Shen Zhou during his early years and became well known for his talent in all three. Skilled in painting landscape, figures and plants and rocks, he was placed with Shen Zhou, Tang Yin and Qiu Ying, and regarded as one of the four masters of the Wu school. Though a follower of Shen Zhou in landscape painting, he made a thorough study of the paintings of the Song and Yuan, gradually shaping his own style on the basis of the tradition he had inherited. Moreover, he painted in a variety of styles, including monochrome ink, blue and green coloured ink paintings, rough sketches or fine drawings. His strokes are fine and vigorous, his ink colour fresh and elegant, and the result is a particularly delicate, graceful style. He lived for a long time in Suzhou, then a centre of business and literary activity, enjoyed the society of the luminaries of the day and shone out as a central figure amongst men of letters. Thus, the intellectual pastimes of these scholars became the subjects of his pictures. Dozens of his clansmen and followers were known for calligraphy and painting, contributing vastly to the growth of the Wu school.

As a prolific painter who lived to a ripe old age, Wen left behind a great many paintings, of which many are still extant. The painting shown here is representative of his later years. In the long, vertical format, the artist imaginatively depicts the scenery at the height of summer, using a structure which has been painstakingly thought out and built up with delicate brushstrokes. The picture shows majestic mountains, steep precipices, tall pines, green cypresses and tumbling, gushing springs. Placed between these elements are bridges spanning creeks, thatched houses scattered along the snaking mountain pathways, as well as a Taoist temple, whose ornate roof can just be made out, in the top left of the picture, nestling between trees and rocks. The atmosphere is serene and tranquil. A youth walks over a bridge carrying a *qin*. On the ground, beside the pool of water, two scholars sit facing each other in the shade, one holding a rolled up scroll, the other holding an opened scroll in apparent appreciation of the poem or painting mounted on it. Though the figures are very small, the observer can tell their status at a glance. In the top left-hand corner is a poem inscribed by the painter, 'The green foliage, the chirping birds and the sweet grass; endless is the conversation on the cool shaded ground. In the capital with its noisy traffic and street dust, which of them knows the coolness of the mountain in the fifth moon?' It conveys the poet's dislike of political life and his desire to shun the busy world by indulging himself in the contemplation of natural beauty, an ideal way of life for some of the intellectuals of the time who chose not to take office.

Because of its long, narrow format, the painting employs the high distance method and shifting eye, or moving viewpoint, so that as much subject-matter as possible may be included on the two-dimensional picture surface. Therefore, maximum use is made both of depth along the imaginary horizontal plane and height in the drawing of the mountains by piling rocks in steps behind and above each other. The details of the sky, pool, flat banks, paths and prominent features of the mountain are barely described and this sparseness of texture lends a simple, ethereal vacancy to the studied complexity of the composition. The artist leads the viewer from one secluded spot to another by means of the concealed lines which cleverly link rocks, trees, slopes and circuitous pathways. As the eye is guided along, its gaze is arrested at different points of interest. At one moment one has been left in a deep canyon, at another ascending a peak high above the clouds, at another strolling beside a spring. Thus there is no single focal point. The brushwork shows great delicacy and vigour; a semi-dry brush has been dragged over the surface to depict mountains and tree trunks, the pine-needles are shown with fine strokes and those of the cypresses with tiny dots. The fine lines bring out the neat, overall arrangement in which delicacy is not sacrificed to weakness and an ordered complexity. Each individual brushstroke in the mass of dots and lines is clearly and purposefully yet easily applied; not one stroke is wasted such is the consummate skill of this great master.

43. 事茗圖

TANG YIN (1470–1523):
ENJOYING TEA

Handscroll, ink and colours
on paper
31.1 × 105.8 cm.
Ming period

Tang Yin was born in Suzhou, Jiangsu province. He also called himself Liuru jushi, 'Liuru the Hermit' and Tao hua an zhu, the Master of Peach Blossom Monastery. His talents were well known locally even when young; he and several other noted figures, including Wen Zhengming, Zhu Yunming, Zhang Ling and Xu Zhengqing, were called the 'cultivated elite of Wu' (Jiangsu province), and they were proud of their literary talents and unconventionality. Then misfortunes beset Tang. He was accused of dishonesty in the civil service examinations, had his degree withdrawn, was for ever struck off the list of candidates and debarred from ever taking office. Thereafter he lived unconventionally, devoting himself to literature and art for the rest of his life.

In his early years, Tang Yin learned painting from an old painter, Zhou Chen and, soon surpassing his teacher, his fame quickly spread. His paintings embody traditional styles with his own creative instincts, are full of freshness, elegance and freedom and have an air of cultivated refinement.

Although he emulated Li Tang in the painting of landscapes he did not simply imitate, but incorporated particular elements and techniques employed by past masters. His all-round artistic ability justifiably places him as one of the four great Wu painters.

The picture 'Enjoying tea' is a rare example of Tang's mastery. Huge, steeply overhanging rocks occupy the foreground on each side of the composition enclosing the swirling waters of a rapidly flowing stream which winds its way out of the composition. Thatched dwellings with exposed timber frames stand on the bank partly screened by a pair of majestic pine trees. Behind, the green of the encircling bamboos contrasts with the houses they protect, while the distant peaks rise indistinctly out of the clouds and mist below. Waterfalls cascade from these heights to reappear through the mist as the swirling stream below. By uniting all these elements the composition becomes ordered and well knit and exudes an air of calmness and composure. Shelves packed with books and scrolls run along the walls of the main facing hall while someone sits reading at a desk on which are placed a teapot and cup. In the side room of the rear building a servant boy is preparing tea. Outside a visitor, staff in hand, crosses a bridge which spans the stream followed by a lad carrying a *qin*, zither. In the unpainted area to the left is written a poem in running hand, *xing shu*, which echoes the mood of the painter, and reflects the ideal way of life coveted by the intellectuals of the time, who sought to 'withdraw from officialdom' and lead the 'leisured life of the countryside'. It is, therefore, a painting with an unmistakable theme, drawn with fine strokes, which manages to be both serene and lively. The figures take their vividness from the economical use of the lines used to depict them. The structure and modelling of the pines and rock formations are reminiscent of the works of Li Cheng and Guo Xi of the Northern Song period, testifying to the influence of masters other than Li Tang on such works. However, this is a technique rarely seen in Tang Yin's compositions.

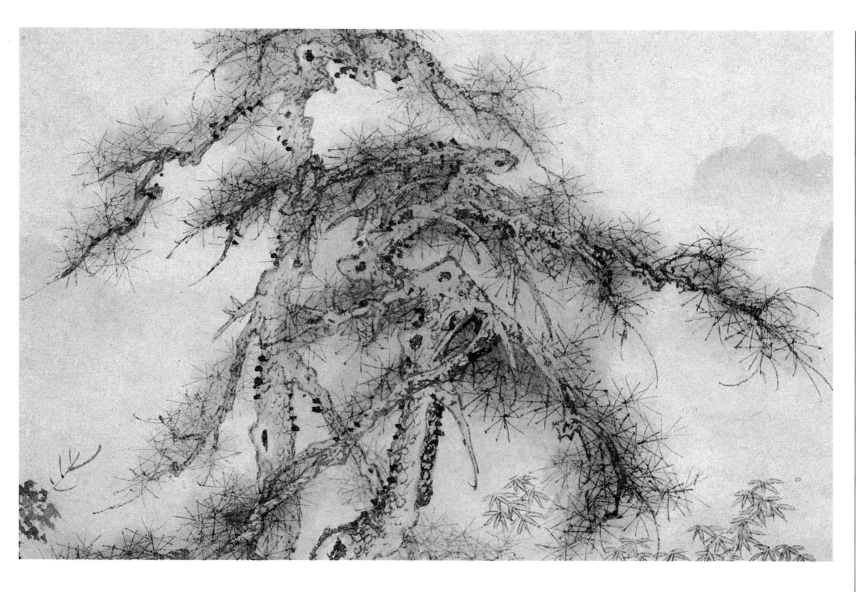

記得惠山精舍裏竹鑪瀹
茗孫杯持解元久筆閒相
仿消渴何芳
玉戌孫
甲戌閨月雨
餘熊眼偶展
即用案中石楠
興來回暮甘意
題之并書於此
御筆

44. 明妃出塞圖

QIU YING (?–?1552): THE
IMPERIAL CONCUBINE
GOING BEYOND THE
GREAT WALL

Hanging scroll, colours on
silk
41 × 34 cm.
Ming period

Qiu Ying was born in Taicang, Jiangsu province, but he made his home in Suzhou. He was said to have worked as a lacquerer in his youth, but was discovered and taught by the famous painter Zhou Chen after he came to Suzhou, and devoted the rest of his life to painting. At one time he worked for the great art collector Xiang Yuanbian, making copies and restoring old paintings in Xiang's possession. So skilfully executed were these copies that it was difficult to tell them from the genuine articles. As a result of a combination of his natural talent and hard work and his close contact and free access to works by the old masters, he became adept in many different styles. Apart from his ability to paint the whole range of traditional subjects he also acquired a facility in the meticulous *gong bi* style of figure drawing, as shown in the present painting, as well as the free and spontaneous *xie yi* method. His female figure drawings especially were taken as models and admired for many years to come.

The subject of the present painting is the story of Wang Zhaojun, an imperial concubine of great beauty, who was later married off to a chieftain of the northern nomadic tribes, as part of the appeasement policy adopted by the Han dynasty government. It is in fact one of ten leaves taken from a pictorial album entitled *Ren wu gu shi, Stories of prominent people*, executed in colour and in the meticulous style of painting typical of Qiu Ying.

45. 墨花九段卷

XU WEI (1521–1593):
INK FLOWERS IN NINE
GROUPS

Handscroll, ink on paper
46.6 × 622.2 cm.
Ming period

Qi Baishi (1861–1953) once composed a poem to the effect: 'The peerless Qingteng and Shi tao, the gifted Wu! I would fain become a running dog in the next world and serve these three great masters in turn.' Among the three great exponents of the spontaneous style of painting most revered by Qi he placed Xu Wei first.

Born in Shanyin (the present day Shaoxing), Zhejiang province, Xu Wei styled himself Wenzheng. A tragic figure who suffered a life of hardship, he achieved much in literature, drama, poetry, calligraphy and painting. Only gaining recognition after his death, his work was admired and treated more seriously with each passing generation.

Xu Wei's chief contribution was to push the impressionistic styles of Shen Zhou and Chen Shun to their limits. With a simple, bold style he tried, with the unrestrained sweep of his brush, to express an idea of the forms rather than the exact reproduction of, for example, plants leaf by leaf. Thus, the quality of the ink tones and washes and the use of the brush became the important factor in expressing the ideas of the artist.

The composition shown here, characteristic of Xu's style, is in the form of a handscroll in nine sections, each containing a particular species of plant in a setting of bamboos, rocks and grasses. The nine kinds of plant are, in order, the peony, lotus, chrysanthemum, narcissus, prunus, grape, banana, orchid and bamboo. These are drawn confidently in moist ink washes with vigorous, uninhibited strokes. A poem recording the artist's feelings accompanies each of the subjects. For example, the brushstrokes used to depict the grape recall those employed in the calligraphic cursive script, intertwining and curving, resembling the dancing and writhing of a dragon. The accompanying poem reads: 'Last year when the mid-autumn moon appeared wonderfully round, the mother-of-pearl had a sleepless night. With no one taking care of the lustrous pearl, to whose possession will it fall?' It clearly shows the poet's frustration over his own hard lot. In another section is painted a bunch of chrysanthemums in full bloom, growing around a strangely shaped rock, and intertwined with thin, tensile young bamboos. As one of his last works this scroll and its inscriptions executed in 1592, only a few months before his death, bears witness to his stubborn and uncompromising attitude to the last, and the exuberant vitality of his art.

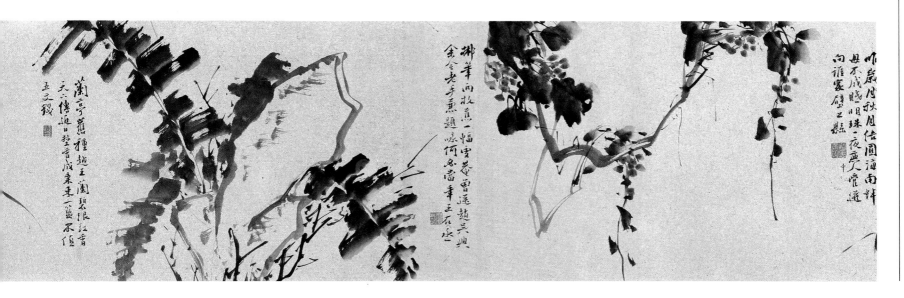

46. 昇庵簪花圖

CHEN HONGSHOU
(1598–1652): SHENG AN
WEARING FLOWERS IN HIS
HAIR

Handscroll, colour on silk
143.5 × 61.5 cm.
Ming period

Chen Hongshou was born in Zhuji, Zhejiang province. In the last years of the Ming dynasty he was made a royal attendant, because of his artistic ability, to copy the portraits of the emperors of past dynasties. Following the collapse of the Ming dynasty he became a Buddhist monk, adopting the name Hui chi. Fond of calligraphy and painting from youth, he studied under Lan Ying and became known for his expertise in all subjects, especially figure painting, in which the imposing forms are mostly drawn in a strangely exaggerated manner. His lines are thin, yet strong and clear, with a decorative quality. His style in figure painting, unmatched during his lifetime, was evolved from the Tang painters Li Gonglin and Zhou Fang. Chen also drew for the popular woodcut illustrated novels such as the *Water margin, Shui hu zhuan,* and *Romance of the Western Chamber, Xi xiang ji,* making a lasting contribution to the art of the woodblock print in China.

The picture shown here concerns the story of Yang Shen (1488–1559), who adopted the name Sheng an. Having come out top in the imperial examinations, he served as an annalist in the Hanlin academy, then became a teacher of the classics at court. He so offended the emperor with his insistence on a point of ceremonial procedure that he was banished to the area of present day Yunnan province, where he lived in exile from the age of thirty-seven to his death. Under such depressing circumstances his melancholia is demonstrated in the following anecdote. It is recorded that 'when he was in Luzhou, once, in his intoxication, painting his face with powder and tying his hair into two knots stuck with flowers, he shamelessly asked his pupils to carry him through the streets, with female attendants holding pots of wine following behind him'. The picture is a faithful portrayal of this strange behaviour, although it omits the students who were said to have carried him through the city. In the painting Yang's portly form is enveloped in a voluminous, large-sleeved robe. Wearing a colourful bunch of flowers in his hair, and with hands dangling down from his drooping shoulders, he holds up his head, sticks out his stomach and totters along with popping, lowered eyes, as if singing in a half-drunken stupor. The picture fully conveys the fantastic and irregular behaviour of a scholar in the face of adversity. The attenuated figures of the two girls who follow him holding a basin and fan contrast strikingly with the portly figure as well as the spirit of the scholar. The winding shape of the maple tree behind frames and emphasizes the chief character. Old and stunted, its flaming leaves symbolize the tenacity with which it clings to life despite the chill of approaching winter. The tree, therefore, also symbolizes the spirit of Yang, and the picture reflects the artist's sympathy with the ill-used Yang Shen and his dissatisfaction with the punishment inflicted on such an able official. Needless to say, the painter approves of Yang's defiance of convention as a protest against his unjust treatment. The placing of the gnarled tree in the background and clump of rocks and vegetation in the foreground, represented so simply, sets the main characters firmly in the centre of the composition.

47. 放鶴洲圖

XIANG SHENGMO
(1597–1685): AUTUMN
VIEW OF FANGHEZHOU
WATERFRONT

Hanging scroll, colours on
paper
65.5 × 53.7 cm.
Ming period

Xiang Shengmo came from a family of calligraphers and painters. Disinclined to follow an official career, he devoted himself to calligraphy and painting from an early age. The fall of the Ming dynasty and the conquest of the Manchus, who established the Qing dynasty, filled him with despair. The numerous poems and paintings that he produced afterwards show his yearning for the old order and his defiance of the conquerors.

His unique style bore no similarity to the works of the early Ming masters, the influential Songjiang painters such as Dong Qichang, the Nanjing painters or even those of his own area in Zhejiang. Neither was it directly derived from one great master but rather the result of an appreciation of a wide range of painters from the past which can be put down to his exposure to the rich collection of paintings in his family's possession. It was said by later critics that he took his 'brush-work' from the Song and 'spirit resonance' from the Yuan masters. Thus Dong Qichang, the Ming theorist-painter, recognized and admired him as 'a painter of scholarly spirit and ordered structure'. One of the rare qualities which marks him out is his insistence on painting real scenes and from life, a completely different approach to contemporary painters who regarded calligraphy and painting as a matter of theory and aesthetic appreciation.

The landscape illustrated is of an actual place, Fanghezhou, which was situated on the shores of Lake Yuanyang in Jiaxing and was the abandoned site of an ancient garden of the Tang period. It was restored by Zhu Kuishi at the end of the Ming dynasty and became a famous park. Xiang visited the place at the invitation of the owner and later painted the picture to record his impressions.

The scene is of Fanghezhou in its autumn colours. It is painted realistically with fine brushstrokes and light, harmonious colours, using a single, flat compositional plane which spreads out upwards across the picture surface. In the foreground is the lake, its shores pierced by bays and inlets and covered with fertile fields and clumps of trees. Only vaguely visible in the distance through the haze are the roofs of a village and the outline of the city wall. On the narrow paths formed from the banks of earth running criss-cross through the fields, the peasants return happily to their homes after their day's labour, and along the river some women are busily picking water chestnuts. The picture is filled with fascinating details of rural life, imparting an air of intimacy achieved without the slightest trace of artificiality.

書于朗雲堂
項聖謨
登高後五日
遠是矣
林泉之樂不
圖以紀其勝
列録而補是
子丹沈有詩
癸巳九月招今
深山監閣今
四十年宛若
口後八樹將
朱蓁石陵萊
畔兹庚火三
吾禾駕夫湖
於鶴洲也在
東公美列景
此洲即鹿時
鶴洲赋帋

137

48. 陶庵圖軸

HONG REN (1610–1664):
TAO'S RETREAT

Hanging scroll, ink on paper
109 × 58.4 cm.
Qing period

Besides the orthodox literati painters symbolized by the so-called 'Four Wangs', the 'Four Buddhist monks' – Hong ren, Kun can, Ba da shan ren and Shi tao – represent the most creative landscape painters during the transitional period between the last days of the Ming and its replacement by the Manchu Qing dynasty. Ming loyalists and survivors of the imperial household, they survived the social and political upheavals of the time and, refusing to give their allegiance to the new dynasty, retreated to Buddhist monasteries deep in the mountains, there to contemplate nature. The protracted chaos which tore the empire apart seems to have left a lasting impression on them which is manifestly reflected in their paintings. They occupy an important position in the development of Chinese painting, and their influence reaches down the generations of painters to the present day.

Hong ren was the oldest of the four. A native of Shen xian, Anhui province, his lay name was originally Jiang Tao. He took the religious name Hong ren and was also called Monk Jian jiang and, posthumously, Mei hua gu na. He learned from the works of Sun Wuyan in his early years, and later turned to the Song and Yuan masters and was particularly influenced by Ni Zan. This can be seen from his thin, vigorous, clear lines, the sombre and graceful style as well as the simplicity of the composition, all characteristic of Ni Zan. Yet owing to his long residence on Mount Huang and his frequent visits to other mountains, the compositions are completely different from those of Ni Zan. The breathtaking beauty of the high, piled-up rocky masses, the fathomless ravines, the contorted age-old trees and the countless charming spots which form the subjects of most of his pictures contrast sharply with the flat vistas of Lake Tai and its sparse trees, distant hills and modest elegance as represented in Ni Zan's paintings. His unique style made him the leading painter of the Xin'an or Huang shan school of landscape painting.

'Tao's retreat' was painted for Zi weng, a Buddhist devotee who had also retired from officialdom in 1660 during the painter's later years, the secluded home of the recluse giving the painting its title. The picture shows five willow trees and scattered clumps of young bamboo. Beneath the willows, beside a deep pool of water, stand a thatched house and a pavilion. Resting upon the banks a single stone slab serves as a bridge, by which the main hall can be reached from the willow-clad banks. Behind the house the rocks rise and fall in great piles as they progress towards the peaks, the ridges clothed in green vegetation. A brook splashes its way down past the rocks into the large pool below. The mountains are dotted with rocks and trees, while the edges of the pond are studded with stones and tufts of rushes sticking out of the water. All these elements impart the tranquillity of a serene and secluded place, an ideal home for a recluse.

The composition again employs the high distance method: the eye is carried into the painting from the bottom left, along the bank by means of the trees, to the buildings in the middle ground and thence along the piles of rock to the distant peaks which balance the composition on the right. The thrust is therefore through the left-hand elements up to the top right which, apart from the few peaks jutting upwards, is left empty, as is the portion of the format below them, in order to suggest a vast, undefined space.

The brushwork is clear, forceful, graceful and calm, mostly done with dry ink dragged over the surface. Textural strokes consist mainly of the *pi ma*, 'split hemp fibre', type and occasionally *zhe dai*, 'broken' or 'folded ribbon', type while horizontal ink dots using the side of the brush are employed to depict lichens. Though monochrome ink is the sole medium used, the painter puts his knowledge of the tonal qualities of ink to such good use that each element is described fully using dark black, dry or moist ink. This shows Hong ren's technical facility as well as his ingenious departure from strict classical convention; he derives his artistic creativity from nature itself and builds on the traditional techniques he had mastered in order to portray real scenery. His works, therefore, conform both to the disciplines of traditional landscape painting while remaining true to the scenes he actually observed.

49. 仙源圖

KUN CAN (1612–?1674):
EARTHLY PARADISE

Hanging scroll, colours on
paper
84 × 42.8 cm.
Qing period

Shi xi was born into the Liu family of Wuling, now Changde, Hunan province. After he became a monk he adopted the religious name of Kun can, also calling himself Shi xi. His patriotic fervour led him to take part in the popular resistance movement against the invading Manchus, but when that resistance collapsed he was forced to take shelter in the mountains of Taoyuan, living in great hardship. Later he wandered around the country, finally settling in Nanjing (Nanking), where he moved from temple to temple until he established himself in the mountains at the Youqi monastery. A strong character, he had only a few friends, all of whom were adherents of the Ming dynasty. He enjoyed high prestige among these loyalists because of his unfailing patriotic ardour.

At first Kun can's painting rivalled that of the Taoist priest Qing xi (Cheng Zhengkui) and they were jointly referred to as the 'Two Xis' (from his other name, Shi xi). The painter Gong Xianzeng compared Kun can's painting with Wang Duo's calligraphy because he considered that their work resembled a 'carelessly dressed woman'. He also compared Qing xi's art with Dong Qichang's handwriting in its purity and delicacy. Since both Wang and Dong were the leading calligraphers of the day, the critic was in no doubt as to the pre-eminence of the two artists he was comparing. When the painter Shi tao became known in art circles, he was also rated highly by Shi xi and, since their names sounded similar, they were frequently referred to as the 'Two Shis'.

That Kun can's work should be compared to a 'carelessly dressed woman' is due to the spontaneity of his style which is quite free from artificiality. He developed his innovative style from the techniques and compositional structures of Wang Meng and Huang Gongwang of the Yuan period. His paintings are notable for their great complexity and coherence of composition which is unpretentious and well knit.

Shi xi's brushstrokes are vigorous, dignified, reserved, succinct, graceful and tensile, and the force of his paintings recalls Su Shi's poem about 'The eastward flow of the great River Yangtze', with its symbolic power and depth. His paintings usually represent lofty mountain peaks piled upon each other, wreathed in clouds and clad in luxuriant vegetation set in a sweeping, majestic panorama. Zhang Geng, an art critic, considered that Kun can's paintings introduced to the viewer entirely new concepts of depth and mystery, and he remarked with regret that 'such mastery of the brush has not been seen for years'.

'Earthly paradise' was painted in 1661, when Kun can was fifty and at his most prolific. The title is taken from the first two characters of the artist's inscription at the top of the composition. The scene he outlines describes the famous Huang shan 'Yellow mountain', rather than paradise, with a forest in the foreground and towering, cloud-wrapped peaks in the background. Temples and houses peep out from behind the folds of the mountains. The brushstrokes are forceful and bold, with the light colours blending in with the black ink. In the lower part of the painting a man rows a boat and this seems to represent Shi xi's own dilemma, as suggested by a line from the poem, 'On a river amidst the cloud-veiled mountains, whither shall I go?' Such poetry indicates his great love of natural beauty and the grandeur of the picture embodies the affection he feels for the beauties of his country and for its people.

50. 貓石圖

ZHU DA (1626–1705):
CAT ON A ROCK

Handscroll, ink on paper
34 × 218 cm.
Qing period

A descendant of the first Ming emperor, Zhu Da became a Buddhist monk after the overthrow of the Ming dynasty. He began signing himself Ba da shan ren, the name by which he is best known, at the age of fifty nine and lived to the ripe old age of eighty.

His anguish over the fall of the Ming and his fear of persecution by the new Manchu rulers compelled him to feign madness in public. Yet the style of his calligraphy and painting is, strangely, very sober. His landscape painting, usually depicting bleak and desolate scenes, reflects the style of Dong Qichang. Once he wrote a colophon on one of his pictures with the words: 'This is describing the land of Song.' The word 'Song' actually implies 'Ming'. His signature Ba da shan ren, written closely together with the four characters joined, at first glance looks like the two Chinese characters *ku*, 'cry', or *xiao*, 'laugh'. It denotes a situation in which one can 'neither cry, nor laugh'. And it is in this way that Zhu Da expresses his grief.

Proficient in painting bird and flower in rich, easy, strong ink tones, Zhu Da was able to make good use of raw *Xuan* paper and to manage the density of wet ink to such a degree as to bring out the full advantages of this kind of painting; the result was a new style founded on the discipline of Chen Shun and Xu Wei. His brushstrokes are round, mellow, substantial, refined and full of variations, which made it difficult for later painters to imitate.

Zhu Da excelled in ink paintings of birds, flowers and animals executed in the spontaneous *xie yi* manner, but with a freedom and confidence in the use of the brush hitherto unrealized. His particular skill lay in becoming familiar with the inherent qualities of the absorbent *Xuan* paper (made in Xuan cheng, Anhui province, it was of the highest quality) which he used so that he could control the spread of wet ink as it was soaked up by the material. By exploiting this interplay between paper and ink, in which diffusion was almost uncontrollable, he took the legacy handed down by the painters Chen Shun and Xu Wei a great deal further, and thus created a completely new style. His full and generous use of moist ink is so rich in its range of tones that his imitators have had great difficulty in copying him. Fish and birds – subjects so often selected by him – are somewhat exaggerated or distorted and the colophons which accompany them, an integral part of the composition, are often difficult to untangle in terms of their legibility as well as meaning.

The present painting was executed when Zhu Da was seventy-one, in 1696. A fragrant plantain lily appears at the beginning, closely followed by a lotus plant, showing its buds and leaves, and then a pile of rocks from which sprout orchid flowers and leaves. A striped cat crouches, eyes tightly shut, atop a rock which is a continuation of those in the foreground. The animal is perfectly described in just a few deft strokes. On the left of the composition a spray of freely drawn camellias brings the composition to a close. Although sparse in its elements and economical in its use of brush and ink the painting, in characteristic Zhu Da style, is full of interest, especially in the sleeping cat, whose outline makes it hard to distinguish from the stone on which it crouches.

丙子夏日寫

51.巨壑丹巖圖

SHI TAO (1642–1707):
PRECIPITOUS ROCKS AND
DEEP VALLEY

Handscroll, ink and colours
on paper
104.5 × 165.2 cm.
Qing period

144

非凝非夢豈非
顧別有關心別
有傳一夜西
風解脫書
萬峰青插
碧雲之天郎

145

Shi tao traced his ancestry back to an elder brother of the founder of the Ming dynasty. Therefore, as a member of the imperial Zhu clan, the young man was taken into hiding from the encroaching Manchu armies as they crossed the River Yangtze and, having wiped out the Ming troops, subjugated the South. In common with other loyalist contemporaries, he shaved his head and entered the Buddhist monastic life as the monk Yuan ji. His style was Shi tao, otherwise known as 'Bitter Gourd Monk', Ku gua ceng ren, but preferring painting to religious discipline he subsequently settled in the cultural centre of Yangzhou, in Anhui province.

Shi tao was a master of the art of landscape, possessing a fertile, creative talent; he also developed his own artistic theories in his *Hua yu lu, Remarks on painting*. He insisted that artists should travel deep into the remotest mountain regions and 'hunt out the most wondrous peaks and get down a spontaneous, rough sketch'. Opposed to the prevailing conservatism he had no use for the sterile copying of the established techniques of past masters but emphasized individual creativity. Thus his brushstrokes vary greatly but are consistently light, flowing, spontaneous and uninhibited. Similarly, in composition, his landscapes are innovative, bold, ingenious and rich in variety. He was often compared with his contemporary Kun can. It was said by Qin Zuyong, in comparing the different styles of the two, that Shi tao's 'brush is deliberately uninhibited in use and has completely shaken off the set patterns of the artist. Yet Kun can, for all his uninhibited style, excels in the meticulousness of his detailing, while Shi tao is superior in the irresistible momentum of his animated brushstrokes'.

The above-mentioned characteristics are all present in the painting 'Precipitous rocks and deep valley' which has a characteristically slanting promontory jutting out menacingly over the lake. Its surface is covered with a mass of luxuriant vegetation including grass, pines and other trees. Water cascades from two sources in the craggy rocks on the right-hand side. Dense forests stretch back towards the distant, sombre mountains which push up through the mist to be lost from view in the sky. A man sits fishing from a boat moored in a cove while a boy makes tea at the back. The whole painting is bathed in the clinging moisture and dripping wetness borne by the swirling mountainous mists and clouds.

52. 巖棲高士圖軸

WANG HUI (1632–1717):
LOFTY SCHOLAR IN THE
MOUNTAINS

Hanging scroll, ink on paper
122.7 × 31.5 cm.
Qing period

Of the six great artists representative of early Qing landscape painting – Wang Shimin, Wang Jian, Wang Hui, Wang Yuanqi, Wu Li and Yun Shouping – Wang Hui is the most prominent in terms of artistic achievement.

A native of Changshu, Jiangsu province, Wang Hui took amongst others the names the 'Hermit of Mount Wumu' and the 'Woodcutter of Jianmen'. He excelled in the art of landscape painting although he occasionally turned his attention to bird and flower painting. He successively learned from Wang Jian and Wang Shimin, who would frequently bring out paintings from their fine collections for him to copy and study. He also accompanied Wang Shimin in his tour round the country to view and imitate treasured Song and Yuan masterpieces in the possession of famous collectors. Thus he was able to assimilate the best elements of the various schools so as to create a style of his own. Ever since Dong Qichang had classified Chinese painting into two schools, the Northern and Southern, a tendency to frown upon the former and to glorify the latter seems to have dominated the opinions of early Qing artists. In spite of the endorsement of this stand by his two teachers, Wang Hui was able to ignore this sectarianism to adopt what he considered best in both. This is best demonstrated in what he said of himself, 'employing the brushwork of the Yuan, the construction of mountains of the Song and the spirit resonance of the Tang'. This is really a distillation of his own experience in the selective study of traditional landscape painting, which explains his unrivalled achievements.

Wang Hui was called to Beijing at the age of sixty by the Qing dynasty emperor, Kang xi, to head a group of painters working on a painted scroll, 'The Kang xi emperor's tour of the South'; this was to be a visual record of the event which, measuring some 250 metres, would take six years to complete. As a result of his work on this his reputation spread far and wide. People came from all over the country to seek his pictures and so numerous were his followers that they formed a new 'Yu shan school' with Wang Hui as its founder. He was honoured posthumously as the 'Sage of painting'. However, few if any meaningful works were produced after he was seventy. They mostly belong to a class of paintings done merely in polite response to the request of a friend or as a form of goodwill.

'Lofty scholar in the mountains' was painted in 1672 when Wang was forty-one years old. At the top of the painting is a poem jointly composed by Wang and the painters Da Chongguang and Yun Shouping. From the two sections we learn that the picture was painted on a boat at Piling (now Wujin, Jiangsu province), where they had met to discuss the art of painting for more than a month. As a result of this meeting they became great friends and presented each other with poems, their own calligraphy and paintings. This was considered an important event amongst literary and art circles of the time. In fact, this picture was a gift to Da Chongguang from the painter.

The painting is composed of lofty, elegant peaks, a deep mountain gorge, with two tall pines in the foreground and other large trees scattered over the mountainside. The mountain stream rushes between boulders and plummets over layer upon layer of rocks, finally emerging from the deep clefts to flow into a large, placid lake. Pavilions and houses, some built on timber stilts, are partially visible between the precipitous drops overhanging the raging torrents. There is also a flight of stone steps leading to some secluded spot. On the level ground at this side of the lake a man sits beneath the pines, his face upturned, contemplating the wonders of his surroundings. The whole combines to convey an atmosphere of peace and solitude, a feeling which is emphasized by the poems.

The high distance employed in the construction of the composition brings out the grandeur of the mountain. It is tightly knit, yet not overcrowded. The water, in the middle, and the sky are left unpainted, imparting a strong sense of space. The tall pines, rooted in the foreground, provide a two-dimensional link with the distant mountains as they stretch up towards them, thereby lending coherence to the whole composition. The artist uses many different texture strokes and qualities of ink to put the objects in perspective and make them appear three-dimensional, testifying to his great skill in the techniques of traditional painting.

This masterpiece, typical of Wang Hui's style in middle age, was once in the imperial collections of the Qing court. Stamped with the seals of the Qian long and Jia qing emperors, it is also recorded in the *Shi qu catalogue*.

53. 哨鹿圖

LANG SHINING (GIUSEPPE CASTIGLIONE, 1688–1766): DEER HUNTING

Handscroll, colours on silk
267.5 × 319 cm.
Qing period

Giuseppe Castiglione was an Italian, born in Milan, who travelled to China as a Jesuit missionary in 1715 at the age of twenty-seven and took the name Lang Shining. Upon his arrival in Beijing, he was summoned to court where he served as an official painter. He died in China at the age of seventy-eight and was invested with the posthumous title of Vice-minister of Public Works and buried in a church in the western suburbs of Beijing; a stone was raised to his memory on which was inscribed a eulogy composed by the emperor. As a painter to the imperial household for more than fifty years, Lang modified European painting techniques by discarding projection and diminishing the contrast between light and shade while retaining three-dimensional effects and perspective. Working alongside Chinese painters he succeeded in blending Chinese and Western techniques into a new style. His extant works include figure, animal and flower paintings, in the form of hanging scrolls, handscrolls, albums. Many portray the activities of emperors in different spheres and some, in particular, describe political activities conducive to the national unity of a country with many ethnic groups; 'Deer hunting' is one such example.

The painting records a deer hunt attended by the Qian long emperor which took place in 1741. The third rider at the head of the cavalcade, astride a white horse and with a red case carrying his bow by his side, is the emperor, who was then thirty years old. He wrote a prose-poem to accompany the painting in 1774, relating how it had been executed by Lang Shining on his orders after he had hunted in Mulan for the first time. Quite a number of ministers had accompanied him. Most of them, like Laibao, were older than him, while a dozen others, including Fuheng, were somewhat younger. He was grieved to note that all these men were now dead. As we know, Laibao was then Minister in Charge of the Royal Household and Fuheng a bodyguard, both attaining the highest civil honours before they died. As shown in the picture, the beardless man at the head of the procession is most probably Fuheng, but Laibao remains unidentified.

Situated in the north of Rehe (Jehol), the original home of the Manchus, Mulan was a mountainous region once covered in vast forests. It measured 100 kilometres from north to south and 150 kilometres from east to west, its circumference, being irregular in shape, totalling some 650 kilometres. This area was filled with wild life, especially deer. After an imperial resort was established in 1709, every year until 1820 the reigning emperor would go hunting there for some forty days to escape the arid heat of Beijing; with him went his retinue of princes, ministers, imperial guards and the members of the minority ethnic groups in the North. Before the hunt, horns were blown in imitation of the sound of the deer to lure them out of the forest. This formed one of the important parts of the hunting procedure. The picture depicts the scene just after the hunters have entered the hills. The figures of the emperor and other important personages all accord with rules of Western portraiture. Men and horses are obviously painted from life, for there is close attention to detail in the drawing of riders and horses as well as a strong sense of solidity. On the other hand the contrast between light and shade is much less obvious but, together with the Chinese method of using hills and trees as a backdrop, it conforms with the principles of traditional Chinese painting. The cavalcade on the move is vividly and realistically painted and the fact that the sizes of the various figures and objects are in correct proportion to their relative distances lends a sense of depth to the composition. Indeed, there can be no question that the figures of the emperor and those in the foreground must have been the work of Lang Shining himself. But one would hardly expect a single man to be able to complete so large a painting. As it was the practice at this time for a team of artists to work together on the same picture, it goes without saying that some others must have contributed. Therefore, this painting actually represents the combined efforts of Chinese and Western artists.

54. 蓼汀魚藻圖軸

YUN SHOUPING
(1633-1690): FISHES
AND WATERWEEDS

Hanging scroll, colours on
silk
135 × 62.6 cm.
Qing period

A native of Wujin, Changzhou, Jiangsu province, Yun Shouping's given name was Ge, which he replaced with the styles Shouping and Zhengshu. He had a number of sobriquets, the most commonly used of which was Nantian, the 'Scholar of the South Garden'. He was expert in landscape and flower painting. His landscapes, especially the smaller and simpler works, have an uninhibited style and a matchless delicacy, but it is in flower painting that he stands out. In developing the 'boneless' technique of painting flowers, first used by Xu Chongsi of the Northern Song period, and by adopting all that was best in the paintings of Ming artists and combining them with his own detailed observations of plants of all kinds, he was able to create a new style which used extremely light colours. This broke new ground and rid the early Qing flower paintings of the use of hooks and dots to represent flowers and leaves, a common technique since the last days of the Ming. His new technique was called 'the orthodox school of painting from life'. So wide was its influence that it lasted through the reigns of Kang xi, Yong zheng and Qian long when it continued to be known as the 'Changzhou school'.

The chief characteristic of the so-called 'Yun style' of boneless flowers is the absence of outlines; all the drawing and brushwork is entirely executed in colour. Thus the graduated tones achieved by colour give the flowers a more natural appearance than that which the usual black outlines or wash would allow, and the method was considered to be the ultimate in painting from life.

'Fishes and waterweeds' is typical of Yun's later works. It shows a clear pool with three fish in it. The weeds at the bottom, barely visible, seem to ripple in the current. Next to the pool is a delicately shaped rock, behind which grow a bamboo and a kind of reed bearing yellow flowers. Two

knotweed flowers in full bloom droop their heads towards the water's edge. This group provides a balance with the fish and the submerged weeds. The painter's inscription in the top left-hand corner reads: 'I caught sight of this scene of knotweed flowers beside a pool in Qingshan Garden.' This picture is a good example of the artist observing subjects in their natural state, and this is why he was able to grasp the nature of things and reproduce them so successfully in his compositions. The rocks are in the main painted in a blue wash mixed with a little black ink. The bamboo, the rush, the knotweed leaves and the aquatic plants are also painted in blue washes, each executed in one stroke, except for the veins of the knotweed leaves which are traced with a deeper colour. The reed and knotweed flowers are dotted with pale ochre and pink respectively. The fish are ingeniously painted with a few strokes in alternate dark and light washes. The unerring strokes and use of colour lend a sense of liveliness to a picture of particular elegance, ingenuity and freshness; such are the characteristics of Yun Shouping's boneless technique.

55. 桃潭浴鴨圖

HUA YAN (1682–1756):
DUCK SWIMMING IN A
PEACH BLOSSOM POND

Hanging scroll, colours on
silk
271.5 × 137 cm.
Qing period

During the mid-Qing period, the great city of Yangzhou, Jiangsu province, attracted a great many artists. It was economically prosperous, advantageously placed on the Grand Canal and was an important centre of the country's cultural life.

Hua Yan came from Tingzhou, Fujian province. He left home to live in Hangzhou as a young man and later moved to Yangzhou, there earning his living as a professional painter. Poor but highly gifted and diligent, he became proficient in poetry as well as painting, as witnessed in his collected poetical work *Li gou ji, Distancing oneself from disgrace*. Indifferent to wealth and fame, he stuck to his own talents to the end. He was born to an ordinary family and is reported as having painted murals for a local temple when he was quite young. Despite the drawbacks of birth, he read widely and studied as much as he could, eventually gaining a reputation as a scholar. Although his compositions tend towards subjects with instant, popular appeal, such as are found in folk art, his paintings also take in the refined, poetical and deeper sentiments associated with literati painting. It is for precisely this reason that he was to be appreciated at all levels of society.

Hua Yan was a versatile artist which was unusual at a time when the art of painting was breaking up into more and more specialized branches. Not only are his figure paintings precise, lively and well constructed, but his landscapes too have a fresh, elegant and uninhibited quality. He also excelled in his paintings of birds and flowers which could be drawn in the meticulous or freer styles. In such examples, birds are often appealingly lifelike with almost human qualities.

This picture was painted in 1742, when Hua was sixty-one, at a time when his art, already mature, was approaching its peak. The upper part of the picture is filled by cascading branches of peach blossom and weeping willow. The flowers, freely expressed in the boneless style, catch the eye with their light and dark shades of orange which glow like burning coals. Below the branches, a few rocks and fine grasses jut above the rippling surface of the pond on which a duck playfully paddles, seemingly turning on the willow leaves whose tips penetrate the water. This charming effect is achieved partly by the use of a semi-dry brush to describe the texture of the duck's feathers. In terms of composition, it provides a focal point whereby the three main elements of the composition are drawn together. In this painting Hua Yan is also seen to be an artist of consummate skill, able to translate things he observed in nature into a visually attractive and pictorially disciplined art.

偃素循墨林異麻漱洞覽
幽叩紗無垠趣理神可感剖靜
汲動機揆輝暨掬間洪桃其屈
苔鹽炫燁平彎蹊布護靡間疏麗
茶欲搽歛羽沈悅清洞貌象媚
漱灘純碧黎游情美嬉亦愛晴
洞邊添溫靈照薄兩崦眞會崇優
明脩榮德霜奄
　壬戌小春寫于洞雅堂
　新羅華嵒弁題

CERAMICS 瓷器

CERAMICS

China is famous throughout the world for its ceramics and has long been referred to as the 'home of porcelain' – or 'China'.

As far back as the Eastern period, some 1,800 years ago, porcellanous stoneware was already being successfully fired at Shangyu, Zhejiang province. This type of ware used ferrous oxide as the colouring agent which, having undergone firing at a high temperature, produced a glossy, light green colour. Produced continuously from the Eastern Jin to the Song periods, when their output declined, these wares have the longest unbroken history of all the many different types of ceramic made in China. And it was also in the Zhejiang region that such green-glazed ware underwent its developmental phases, during the Six Dynasties' period, where kilns were most widely distributed and the quality of the ware itself was improved. A fine example of this is the green glazed jar excavated in the ancient kingdom of Wu which encompassed this area, with a date equivalent to 260. Rich in decorative features, it is typical of early examples of this type. During the period of the Northern and Southern dynasties, due to the spread and influence of Buddhism, the lotus petal, honeysuckle and other patterns began to appear as part of the decorative repertoire. Being foreign in origin, all such elements went through a period of assimilation and blending with indigenous elements, finally to be transformed into the decorative styles that we now identify as being uniquely Chinese.

The ensuing period saw the breakdown of the empire into many kingdoms ruled by many indigenous and foreign dynasties, with eventual reunification under the Sui dynasty. Under the Sui, Tang and Five Dynasties, there was an economic and cultural upsurge from the foundations laid much earlier by the Han, and the splendid achievements in ceramic technology were one manifestation of this.

White wares gradually developed during the Sui towards maturity under the Tang in the North while green wares continued to be produced and to predominate in the South. Here, many famous kilns were mentioned by Lu Yu in his *Cha jing, Tea classic*, said to have been written in the eighth century and concerned with the best porcelains for the making of tea bowls. They include Yuezhou and Wuzhou (Zhejiang province), Yuezhou (Hunan province), Shouzhou (Anhui province) and Hongzhou (Jiangxi province). Xingzhou (Hebei province) was said to produce the best known white ware at that time, while the kiln at Quyang (Hebei province) and those at Mixian and Gongxian (Henan province), all in the North, were also centres of production.

New types of ceramic also appeared under the Tang dynasty, such as *san cai*, three-coloured ware, *jiao you*, marbled ware, *hua you*, mottled ware and *you xia cai*, underglaze colour, all of which broke new ground in the art of ceramic decoration. Underglaze decoration, a technique invented at the Changsha kilns, of Hunan province, was a process whereby colour in the form of a metal oxide was first applied to the ceramic body and over which a glaze was added before firing took place. Combining the art of painting with pottery-making, it laid the basis for porcelains with underglaze painted decoration produced at the Cizhou kilns, Hebei province during the Song period as well as for blue and white and underglaze red ware of much later periods. Amongst the multifarious shapes and glazes of the Tang period, the mottled glazed wares made in the general region of Henan province form a distinct group on their own.

The waisted drum, illustrated, with a black glaze covered in large splashes of blue, made at the Lushan kiln, Henan province, makes use of the chance decorative effects produced by transmutation in the kiln of areas of the glaze during the firing process. Such developments under the Tang and Five Dynasties were to provide the favourable conditions which gave rise to a flourishing ceramics industry during the Song period.

Officially and privately operated kilns developed side by side and by the middle of the Song period the industry was at the height of its prosperity with the famous kilns producing such famous wares as Ding at Dingzhou, Hebei province, Ru, at Ruzhou, Henan province, Guan, Hangzhou, Zhejiang province, Ge, at Longquan, Zhejiang, and Jun, in Junzhou, Henan. The Ding kiln had already been established as early as the Tang dynasty and was, therefore, the oldest of the five. It was also the only one of these wares to employ incised, carved and impressed decoration, the others relying on shape and colour of glaze to enhance their beauty. The Ding piece illustrated, a headrest, is vividly made in the shape of a child. Of the kilns run by ordinary people, Cizhou, in Henan, is the most representative of the privately run kilns producing pieces with a strong popular or folk flavour during the middle Song. Variously decorated – using such techniques as incised designs under a clear or creamy glaze, *sgraffiato*, in which designs were scratched through the white slip to the body beneath and covered with glaze, and bold designs painted in black on the white slip beneath the glaze – this ware was far-reaching in influence and unique in its system of ownership.

An endless stream of these different types of wares flowed from the famous kilns during the Song period. There was Jun ware with its lavender glaze flushed with crimson or purple produced by transformations in the copper which occurred during the firing process; Ru, noted for the 'massed animal fat' appearance of its unctuous glaze; *qing bai*, 'bluish-white', ware from Jingdezhen, Jiangxi, in which the quality of white glaze resembled jade; the greyish green or blue of the Longquan type glazes; the 'cracked ice' pattern of the crackle produced in the glaze during cooling; the Guan and Ge wares as well as the minutely detailed incised designs of the Yaozhou wares of Shaanxi province. All served as models to the later potters who earnestly sought to imitate them.

Porcelains made during the Mongol Yuan period also occupy an important position in the history of Chinese ceramics. The most outstanding achievements were obtained in the successful firing of blue and white, underglaze red as well as high-fired enamels such as copper red and cobalt blue at the Jingdezhen kilns. Boasting a fresh, simple elegance, blue and white porcelains have remained the principal type produced at Jingdezhen to this day. The lidded jar illustrated in this volume excavated in 1964 at Baoding, Hebei province, is an example which fully demonstrates the high standard of underglaze blue and red manufacture at this time.

Based upon this legacy of important skills acquired and handed down over many years, the ceramic arts, dominated by multi-coloured porcelains, entered a golden era, presided over by the Ming dynasty. At the centre of production was Jingdezhen whose name became synonymous with the production of exquisite porcelains. Here too the imperial workshops and kilns were established to cater for the needs of the court, as well as to produce articles used as presentation pieces, both inside and outside China, and for exchange. Apart from the official kilns, privately owned establishments were to be found scattered within the vicinity. While the majority of the huge numbers of pieces they produced were for everyday use, they also were known for fine, showy porcelains.

The introduction, during the Ming period, of high-fired coloured glazes such as the deep, rich ruby-red *sang de bœuf*, the rich, dark blue *ji lan* (or *ji qing*) of the Xuan de reign period, the *jiao huang*, 'bright yellow', reserved for imperial use, of the Hong zhi era, and the *kong que lü*, 'peacock green', contributed greatly to the traditional store of monochrome glazes. But what should really be seen as most representative in terms of standards and achievement during this period are the polychrome enamels. Such examples include blue and white of the Yong le and Xuan de reigns, *dou cai*, 'contending' or 'dovetailed colours', in which an underglaze blue outline is filled in with overglaze translucent enamels, of the Cheng hua era, as well as *wu cai*, 'five colour', polychromes of the Wan li period. All have been greatly admired down to the present. Specifically, mention should be made in this context of examples illustrated in this volume including the 'press hand cup', *ya shou bei*, a bowl with a flared mouth in blue and white, and the *dou cai* stem cup with a design of grapes, both historically recorded as rarities from the official kilns. Also shown is the Wan li *wu cai* reticulated vase with a cloud and phoenix design, an example of the amalgamation of two skills – the piercing of the ceramic body and painting in polychrome enamels – in one splendid piece.

Privately run kilns were to be found everywhere, including the provinces of Hebei, Henan, Shanxi, Gansu, Jiangsu, Jiangxi, Guangdong, Guangxi, Fujian and Zhejiang, during the Ming period. Among their products the following should be mentioned particularly as perhaps the most perfect: the reddish-brown buff, unglazed, stoneware of Yixing, in Jiangsu; polychrome enamelled *fa hua* vessels, utilizing clay slip threads (similar in use to the copper wires of *cloisonné* decoration) or incised lines to contain the flow of the decorative lead silicate enamels, produced in Shanxi; the fine white porcelains with a clear glaze, called Dehua, from the site of the kiln known by the same name in Fujian. The standing figure of Bodhidharma illustrated is representative of the superlatively beautiful results that could be achieved in Dehua porcelains, in this case by He Chaozong who modelled it.

Still greater strides forward were made under the Qing dynasty, especially during the early years which covered the Kang xi, Yong zheng and Qian long eras. The magnificence of the decoration, the consummate skill of the workmanship and rich variety of shapes and sizes surpassed anything ever before seen in China or elsewhere. Jingdezhen, at the same time, enjoyed unprecedented prosperity and success. In addition to the multiplicity of coloured glazes handed on from the Ming period, a number of quite new types appeared. Of the red wares made during the Kang xi era there were: *Lang yao hong*, rich red or *sang de bœuf*; *ji hong* 'sacrificial' (referring to the colour associated with the Altar of the Sun) or bright red; *jiang dou hong*, 'coral red', an iron red enamel used as a monochrome glaze. Blue glazes included: *tian lan*, 'sky blue' with no tinge of green; *sa lan*, 'sprinkled blue'; and *ji lan*, 'sky-clearing blue'. In addition there were: *cha ye mo*, 'tea dust', in which green enamel was blown through a fine gauze on to a brownish glaze; *song shi lü*, 'turquoise green'; *xie jia qing*, 'crab shell green' with a large, irregular crackle pattern; *gua pi lü*, 'cucumber green'; *kong que lü*,

'peacock green'; *qie pi zi*, 'aubergine purple' and *wu jin*, 'mirror black'.

Blue and white, underglaze red and *dou cai* enamels apart, the following polychromes were employed during the Qing: the pale, powder colours of *fen cai*; *fa lang cai* polychrome enamelling; *su san cai*, which included the colours yellow, green and purple but not red; as well as a monochrome black glaze. All served to increase the scope within which the potter and decorator could work. Not only were they more than proficient in imitating the fine ceramics of earlier periods but also artefacts made in bronze, lacquer, bamboo, timber, jade and jadeite. They were also extremely skilled in producing *tuo dai* pure white, extremely thin, high quality porcelain sometimes called 'eggshell', fine openwork decoration in which intricate patterns completely pierce the body, vases with these latter reticulated exteriors and independently revolving interiors, or rotating necks, as well as other novel and ingenious techniques. All this demonstrates the extent to which the art of the potter had reached full maturity in every aspect. Several examples of some of the techniques described have been selected for inclusion in the present volume.

The history of Chinese ceramics can be traced from its distant origins by means of pottery excavated from Peiligang, Xinzheng, in Henan, and the remains of the Cishan culture at Wuan, in Hebei, some 8,000 years ago, down to the present. Yet, to the best of our current knowledge, some 2,000 years elapsed between the first appearance of a type of high-fixed or porcellanous stoneware during the middle phase of the Shang period and the re-emergence of 'proto-porcelains' at some time during the Eastern Han period.

Porcelain is one of China's great inventions, achieved through an amalgamation of the two disciplines of science and art. Furthermore, it is not only of value in economic terms but also possesses a cultural and aesthetic value which can be appreciated by everyone alike.

Each period of China's history produced fresh, new types of ceramic which are unique to that period alone. From the simplicity of the early neolithic pottery, through the huge expansion in types and techniques in the Han to Tang periods, to the full flowering of the ceramic arts from the Tang period onwards, combined with the subsequent discovery of true, white, translucent and impermeable porcelain, the achievements of Chinese potters will always be marked out as being of the highest order.

56.青釉罍

GREEN-GLAZED JAR

height 46.6 cm.
base diameter 16 cm.
belly diameter 29.1 cm.
Period of the Three
Kingdoms
Inscribed Yong an era, 3rd
year, equivalent to 260

This green-glazed jar, otherwise known as a granary, is a funerary object which was excavated in Shaoxing, Zhejiang province, during the late 'thirties.

The area on the eastern seaboard of China which takes in Shangyu, Yuyao and Ningbo and which is centred on Hangzhou, was occupied by the ancient state of Yue during the Spring and Autumn Annals' and Warring States' periods. It already boasted a long tradition of pottery-making, as well as nurturing 'proto-porcelains'. By the late Eastern Han dynasty, Shangyu was already producing green-glazed wares, or celadons, more usually referred to as Yue ware. The region is therefore considered important in the development of Chinese porcelains. It was the first ware to be given the appellation *ci* which generally refers to types of porcelain in Chinese and in this case is a high-fired stoneware.

The period of the Three Kingdoms saw rapid developments in the ceramics industry in Zhejiang, with kilns mushrooming everywhere. Besides vessels for everyday use such as pots, jars, bowls and so on, funerary objects in the form of granaries, pigsties, sheep folds, dog kennels and chicken coops were also produced. The green-glazed jar illustrated bears an inscription 'Yong an third year', a date equivalent to 260.

The body of the jar shows a greyish colour through the thick but transparent greyish-green glaze. Attached to the top of the jar are two gate-towers and a four-storeyed building surrounded by eight attendants playing different kinds of musical instruments. Small birds, their heads uppermost, flapping their wings, appear at the top. Watchdogs lie, heads erect, before each door. Small, bounding dogs, lazing pigs, standing deer, crawling tortoises and swimming fish are placed around the shoulder of the jar. Fishes, dogs and dragons roughly scratched into the clay surface appear to have acted as position markers around which the potter could arrange other moulded forms. There are also carved on the surface the written characters for 'fly', 'deer', 'five kinds' and so on. Characters are also inscribed on a stele, or commemorative tablet, which stands on the back of a tortoise's shell and read 'The third year [of the reign] of Yong an. Prosperity and good fortune. Let

things be of benefit to the high official. May his descendants multiply. A long life infinitely free from calamity'. All twenty-four characters are incised into the body under the glaze. The figures of men and animals are moulded in an extremely vivid way, reflecting a happy scene after the bringing in of a good harvest as well as the opulence and power of the aristocracy. The piece is a fine example of the technical expertise of the potter in realizing a complicated set of forms and is typical of stonewares of this type and date.

The granary is evolved from the 'five-in-one' jar, a type seen in the Han period with five small pots moulded around the outside of the belly of an oval-shaped jar, the central one being taller and larger than the other four. Gradually the size of the middle pot grew bigger until the others grew so small as to become insignificant and these were replaced by modelled accessories stuck onto the body.

The shape and the decoration of this jar are rich and complex but in no way succumb to disorder. The granary characteristic of the times not only reflects the high, technical, artistic achievements, but affords an insight into the architecture, customs and methods of preserving grain of the time.

57. 黑釉藍斑腰鼓

WAISTED DRUM WITH
BLACK GLAZE MOTTLED
BLUE

length 59 cm.
diameter of open ends
22.2 cm.
Lushan yao, Henan province
Tang period

The outstanding features of this fine piece lie in its well-proportioned, perfectly symmetrical lines and the lustrous black glaze accompanied by the large splashes of light blue which cover it. A harmonious blending of shape and decoration accord with its function, in imitation of a waisted drum.

In a consideration of China's historical cultural intercourse with the outside world, music should not be overlooked as an active component. History shows that a good number of musical compositions and instruments that had come into China from the western regions, including Central Asia as well as from the national minorities in the North, greatly enriched Chinese music both in form and content. A story relates that the first emperor of China, Qin Shi huang di, 'beat *fou*' which, though in fact an earthenware vessel for holding wine was also employed as a musical instrument to 'keep time when singing' in ancient times. Beating time on earthenware vessels led to the practice of using tea bowls to produce music in the Tang period.

However, this elongated waisted drum with 'wide open ends, and a slender belly' is certainly not a tea bowl and neither is it 'pottery arranged on a frame' used in ancient times, but a replica of one of the musical instruments imported from the west of China and beyond. In order to make the drum usable, animal skin had to be stretched across the two hollow ends.

The circumference of each skin was made larger than that of the drum so that they could be alternately threaded with cord which passed the length of the drum from one skin to another, through rings which had been inserted round the skins' circumference. The relatively loose retaining strings could then be firmly bound down across the ridges to achieve the optimum tautness. Resonance produced by such a ceramic body as this drum must indeed have been a pleasure to hear.

Lively musical performances including dancing to the rhythms of waisted drums similar to the one illustrated here can be seen in the murals of the Dunhuang and Yungang Buddhist cave temples painted in the period from the Northern Wei to the Tang dynasties. It appears that in the Northern Wei period the waisted drum was placed on a long table and beaten with both hands, but in Tang times it was placed across the knees of the performer, who either knelt or sat. The drummer, whose function was to lead the players by beating time, was usually placed at the front with a badge on her head-dress or sleeve. Interestingly, the drummer continues to occupy the same position in the orchestra of contemporary performances of traditional Chinese opera. There are also examples of performers dancing while playing the drum, which is slung across the chest recalling the 'long drum' dance still performed to this day in Korea. Among the musical

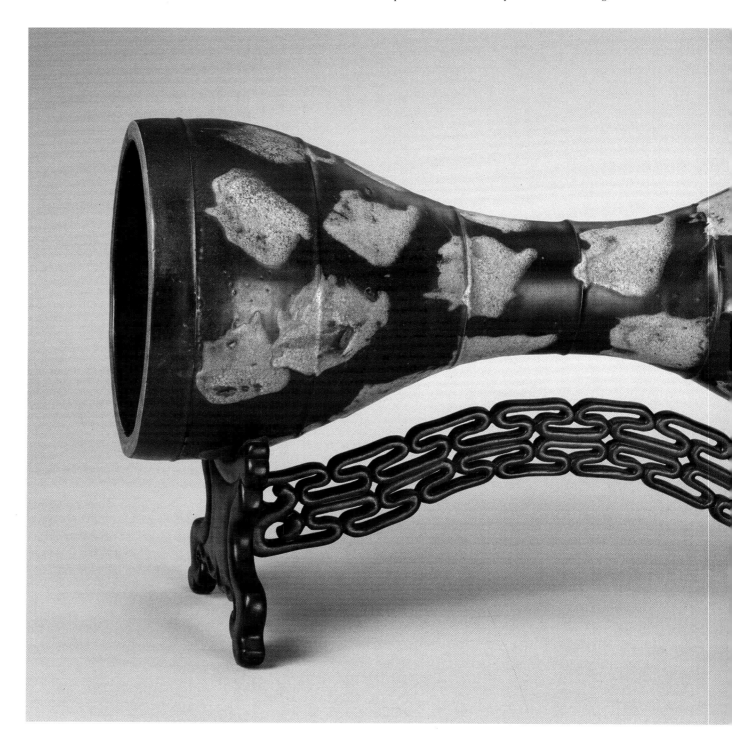

instruments used by some national minorities in Guangxi province, there can still be seen a drum similar to the porcelain waisted drum described.

The decoration on this drum demonstrates how Tang potters broke out of the confines previously placed on them by monochrome glazes. Advantage was taken of the inherent properties of the glaze in firing conditions which produced cloudy bluish-white to grey mottled effects where the black or dark brown glaze had been splashed.

On the strength of the colour of the glaze and the thin ridge lines encircling the body, current research has confirmed the validity of the statement concerning such drums made by Nan Zhuo of the Tang period who said in his *Jie gu lu, Records of Jie drums*: 'If this drum is not made of the ''stone powder'' of Qingzhou [northern Shandong], it must be of [the mottled type of] decorated ware of Lushan [central Shandong].'

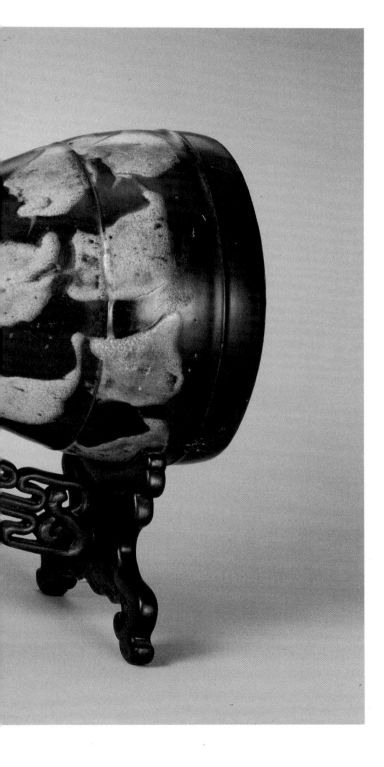

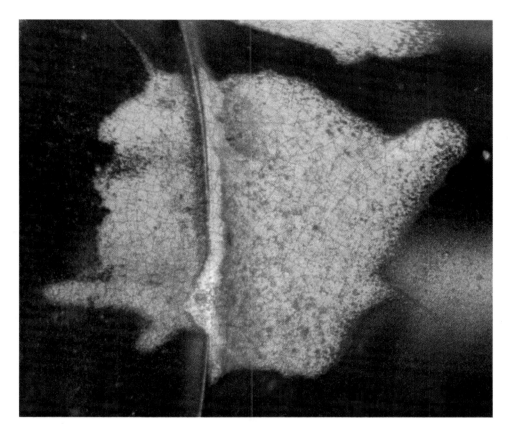

163

58. 定窯孩兒枕

DING WARE HEADREST IN
THE FORM OF A CHILD

height 18.3 cm.
length 30 cm.
width 11.8 cm.
Northern Song period

The Song was a period of great expansion in the ceramics industry when many famous wares, all different and with their own style and character, appeared in many different localities. Among them, the kiln producing Ding ware enjoyed the greatest reputation. For some time, it supplied items for use at the Northern Song court and its white wares, in particular, were to exercise a profound influence on later ceramics.

The ruins of the ancient Ding kiln are located in the area of Jianci cun and Yanshan cun in Quyang xian, Hebei province. Because Quyang xian was located within the region of Dingzhou during the Song period, the kiln acquired the name Ding.

Ding ware was first fired during the Tang period, reached its peak during the Five Dynasties' and the Northern Song periods, and ceased production some time during or just after the Yuan period. Besides its most famous white porcelains, the kiln also made purple or reddish-brown, black and green glazed wares, all of which are now extremely rare.

Decoration on the white wares is incised, carved, moulded or impressed under the glaze. In the first two cases, the work is executed free-hand with bamboo or bone tools round in shape with a bevelled face. The lines produced in the first two techniques betray a slanting inner face to the lines, as occurs when cutting into a material such as clay with a blade at an angle. Another similar method used was by means of combs, or implements with cutting points set equally apart. The use of such implements is immediately apparent in the regular sweeping and curving parallel incised lines which lend a graceful and lively air to the body surface.

Stamped impressions are often seen on the inner surface of bowls and dishes. They signify a technical progress which improved productivity and achieved uniformity in the application of patterns. The impressions were transferred from an intricately carved ceramic mould when the clay was still in its leather-hard (firm but not dry) state.

One of the most significant features of Ding ware lies in the method of glazing and firing. Dishes and bowls were fired upside down with the result that the glaze could not be allowed to run on to and past the rim otherwise it would have stuck the item to the surface on which it rested during firing. Referred to as *mang kou* 'rough mouth', the bare rim was subsequently bound with a copper, gold or silver band. Another characteristic technique of the kiln was to fire pieces using the *fu shao* method; that is, stacking bowls upside down one over the other. This was achieved by means of saggars, fireclay boxes which protected the ceramic wares during firing, the insides of which were stepped to receive the rims of bowls and to prevent their touching. In this way more items could be fired at once and production increased.

Among the fine examples of Ding ware which have been

passed down through the ages is this headrest in the form of an infant and it is the only piece of its kind still in existence. Stoneware headrests first appeared in the Sui period, their popularity increasing during the Tang and Song periods. The Southern Song poetess Li Qingzhao in her *Zui hua yin*, 'Drunk in the shade of flowers', wrote the line 'a jade headrest and a screen cupboard'. The 'jade headrest' refers to the jade-like qualities of *qing bai*, a bluish-green white porcelain.

The shapes of such headrests are many and varied, including rectangular, oval, ogival, heart-shaped, octagonal or silver-ingot shaped. Others are modelled in the round as dragons, babies and reclining girls. More than just an article for everyday use, the example shown here is a masterpiece of ceramic modelling and also incorporates all the external elements of first-rate sculpture.

Substantial in size, the pillow is completely covered in milky-white glaze. The plump child lies on his belly, his head inclined, resting on his folded arms, his right hand holding a piece of silk braid to which is attached an embroidered ball. He wears a gown under a sleeveless jacket, on which finely incised, circular floral patterns are just discernible. His legs are pulled up and crossed, and he wears soft shoes on his feet. His natural manner, twinkling eyes and smiling face convey a lovable innocence.

59. 青花釉裏紅蓋罐

COVERED JAR IN BLUE
AND WHITE WITH
UNDERGLAZE RED

overall height 42.3 cm.
mouth diameter 15.2 cm.
foot diameter 18.5 cm.
Yuan period

Blue and white porcelains rank amongst the greatest of China's traditional products. Those made at Jingdezhen, Jiangxi province, during the Yuan period were produced for the home market as well as for export to many other countries of East and especially Southeast Asia. At that time the technology of making such porcelains had already reached full maturity. New wares, such as underglaze red, red glaze and blue glaze, belong to the same category as blue and white wares, and their introduction paved the way for the development of polychrome porcelains and various other colour glazes in later times.

Yuan blue and white covered jars with underglaze red decoration are extremely rare. The jar presented in this album is one of the two excavated in 1964 in Baoding, Hebei province, together with another nine Yuan period pieces that had been preserved in an underground pit. Generally used as a storage jar, this piece has been made with such consummate skill that it may justifiably be considered as a work of art in its own right.

The colouring agent used for blue and white porcelains is the mineral cobalt. It is applied directly to the white body which is then completely covered with a transparent glaze and subsequently fired at an extremely high temperature. The finished product, having undergone only a single firing, is one of blue designs on a white ground, the fresh unchanging quality of which gives the vessel a reserved, timeless air.

In order to produce ceramics with a coloured glaze, as opposed to underglaze painted decoration, a substance such as copper oxide or cobalt, to produce a red or blue respectively, must be added to the glaze before applying it to the ceramic body and firing. Such substances are transformed into particular colours when they are subjected to the heat and atmospheric conditions in the kiln. Because copper red glazes are especially difficult to control during the firing process, fine examples of this type from the Yuan period are now extremely rare.

Yuan porcelains are generally large with thick, heavy bodies and therefore appear solid and powerful. This was a direct result of an improvement in the quality of the basic paste and the ability to achieve even higher kiln temperatures, which made it possible for the makers to reduce the rate of deformity after firing – a sign of progress in technology. This lidded jar is not only large, but the splendid decoration and glaze was also as perfect when recovered from the site as when it had first been made.

Perhaps the most pleasing aspects of this fine jar lie in its full, rounded appearance in combination with the carefully executed decoration. Four large ogival panels defined by a double string of pearls form the main decoration around the fullest part of the body. They enclose and emphasize the three-dimensional quality of the openwork pattern of the blue leaves and the red flowers and rocks from which they sprout. The two colours offset one another perfectly. Around the shoulder of the jar hang four cloud-collar motifs enclosing a design of full-blown lotus on a ground of stylized waves. The spaces between are filled with flower sprays and scrolls and the main area bounded above and below by classic scroll bands. Upright lotus panels form the lower register. Primary and secondary motifs are given equal attention and, while neither detracts from the other, both are brought within the harmonious scheme. The jar is appropriately finished by placing a crouching lion as a finial to the lid.

Yuan porcelains have been regularly discovered in the past three decades at such sites as the ruins of the great Mongol capital Dadu (Khanbaligh) on which Beijing was constructed, Baoding in Hebei province, Jintan xian in Jiangsu province, Gaoan in Jiangsu province, Changde in Hunan province, the imperial Yuan tombs in Boyang, Jiangxi province, and the tombs of the first Ming emperors in Nanjing. Besides the fine blue and white and underglaze red pieces retrieved from the Baoding hoard, the recent finds at Gaoan are of the highest quality.

Two jars similar to this one have ended up in collections outside China, one in the Percival David Foundation of Chinese Art (University of London) and the other in Japan. But as both lack a lid they cannot be compared with this one.

60. 青花壓手杯

BLUE AND WHITE *YA SHOU*
CUP

height 5.1 cm.
mouth diameter 9.1 cm.
foot diameter 3.9 cm.
illustration shows actual size
Ming period

Blue and white porcelains of the Yong le era of the Ming dynasty rarely bear reign period marks. However, in a few instances the inscription '*qing hua ya shou bei*', 'blue and white press hand cup', is written on the underside, as it is on the piece shown here. In all respects, the cup tallies with the description given by Gu Yingwu of the Ming period in the *Bo wu yao lan, Concise review of antiques*, which says: '*Ya shou* ['press hand'] cups were first made during the reign of Yong le. Such cups have flared mouths and steep sides cutting away at the waist and with a smooth base to the foot. At the bottom of the inner surface, in the centre, two lions are painted playing with a ball, on which are written six characters in seal script: *Da Ming Yong le nian zhi* ''the Great Ming Yong le years manufactured'', but in some cases there are only four characters, *Yong le nian zhi*, all as small as rice grains. Such cups are of the highest grade. The next in order are those carrying a central design of a pair of mandarin ducks; and the next, those bearing a central design of flowers. They are adorned outside with deep blue floral patterns and have wonderful shapes. Having survived for many many years, they are highly priced.'

As shown in the photograph, the present cup bears a design of two lions rolling a ball and four seal characters, *Yong le nian zhi*, and so, according to the description, is of top quality as well as extremely rare. There are two more cups of this kind in the collection of the Museum, both bearing a central design of flowers with four seal characters which coincide with the above descriptions.

Ya shou bei cups are sometimes called *yi shou bei*, but both mean that 'the mouth rim is splayed wide enough to be pressed on by the thumb'. With a wide mouth everted at the lip and a body contracting below the belly which stands on a ring foot, the cup has a thick wall. At the lip it is 1.5 millimetres, from which point the wall widens until it reaches a thickness of 5.5 millimetres at the centre of the bottom. The base of the foot is quite flat and smooth. In design, the cup is a model of perfection with its flared mouth and well-proportioned body.

In the past, the serving of tea existed in many forms, from the earlier *tuo*, 'shallow saucer', and many kinds of *wan*, 'bowl', and *zhan*, 'small cup', to the *gai wan*, 'lidded bowl', and *ming hu*, 'teapot', of the Qing period, all determined by the customs prevailing at different times. Tea drinking first became popular in the Tang period when, according to the *Cha jing Tea classic*, the six famous kilns of Yue (Zhejiang), Ding (Henen), Wu (Zhejiang), Yue (Henan), Shou (Anhui) and Hong (Jiangxi) were all engaged in the production of celadon bowls expressly intended for the drinking of tea.

In the Song dynasty *gao cha*, partially fermented tea, was a common drink and competitions were often held to see which kind of tea had better qualities. When tea dust was used instead of tea leaves, a foam would appear as the boiling water was added, and that would obscure the colour of the drink. Therefore, black glazed tea vessels such as *tu hao zhan*, small cups with hare-fur streaks, or *zhe qu ban*, the mottling on partridge feathers, were produced to show off the colour of the liquid more clearly so that its quality might be better judged.

In the Ming period, tea leaves were processed by the *chao qing* method, in which the newly plucked leaves are dried (*chao*) to prevent oxidization and thus preserve their greenness (*qing*). Only shoots or young tea leaves were used, and tea was drunk in much the same way as it is now. A drink made from good tea leaves should show a green colour. To bring out this colour, white glaze cups are often used. As the *ya shou bei* cup has a fine, white body, the glaze of which is lightly suffused with blue, it lends itself to its function perfectly and occupies the top position in its category.

The example shown is decorated on both the inner and outer surfaces with a rich blue, highlighted in places by additional touches which have produced a darker tone. A single painted line follows the outer line of the lip with a double line below it; the border between contains a pattern of twenty-six prunus flowers made up of small dots. The main design consists of eight interlocking lotuses. Another double line runs round the cup where the bowl and foot join. A 'honeysuckle' or classic scroll band encircles the foot. Inside the lip there is also a double-lined ring. The central circle containing the design of two lions playing, described above, has the ball as the focal point bearing the characters *Yong le nian zhi*, usually taking the form of a round flower with five petals surrounding the four characters in seal script. The inscription on this kind of cup marks the beginning of a tradition practised by imperial kilns in the Ming period of inscribing reign marks on the articles they produced.

By the reign of Wan li, blue and white *ya shou bei* had already become very rare and precious, and so imitations were constantly made throughout succeeding periods. But none was so finely made that it could be mistaken for the authentic original.

61. 成化鬥彩葡萄高足盃

STEM CUP WITH GRAPE
DESIGN IN *DOU CAI*
OVERGLAZE ENAMELS

height 6.7 cm.
mouth diameter 7.9 cm.
foot diameter 3.6 cm.
illustration shows actual size
Ming period

The crowning achievement of all the overglaze polychrome porcelains produced during the Ming period was porcelains made at the official kilns during the Cheng hua period. Traditionally, connoisseurs have put the porcelains of 'Cheng hua first, Xuan de second, Yong le third and Jia jing last but not least'. Of all the Cheng hua period types, *dou cai* wares are the most celebrated for their pure whiteness of body, translucent glaze, ingenious shaping and captivating colours.

The term *Cheng hua dou cai*' comes from contemporary Ming literature and refers to *wu cai* 'five colours' or polychrome enamels, and overglaze polychrome enamels filling the underglaze blue painted decorations on porcelain of the Cheng hua period. *Dou cai* as a name for these wares first occurs in the *Nan yao bi ji, Notes on kilns of the South*, published at some time between the Kang xi and Yong zheng reigns of the Qing dynasty.

There were several different methods of producing polychrome enamelled porcelains at this time. All but two involved painting directly on to the white body in cobalt blue, covering it with a clear glaze, firing it and then filling in the relevant outlines of the blue decoration showing through the glaze with such lead coloured glazes as red, yellow, aubergine purple and green. The underglaze blue and overglaze colours form a harmonious colour scheme in which the colours seem to vie with one another, giving rise to the name *dou cai*, 'contending colours'. Alternatively, *dou* also means 'to fit nicely together' and so the term may in addition refer to the 'fitting' or 'agreement' of the overglaze colour with the underglaze blue outlines.

Cheng hua *dou cai* wares are very delicately made and were highly prized during the Ming and the Qing periods. Examples which have been passed down through the generations consist mostly of small cups and bowls and, of those now in the collections of the Palace Museum, wine cups form the majority. According to the *Gao jiang cun ji, Collected writings of Gao jiang cun*, of the early Qing period, themes and decorations on *dou cai* wine cups included 'burning silver candles to highlight ladies' dresses', 'dragon boats', 'garden swings', 'virtuous scholars', 'children' and 'grapes', all of which except for the first three, are represented on cups in the Museum's collection. *Dou cai* wares include a type of stemmed cup. According to the palace archive records for the 7th year of the Yong zheng reign, the cups sent back from the famous Yuan ming yuan bore designs of 'parrots picking peaches', 'passion flowers', 'lotus flowers and leaves', and so on, all listed under the heading of Cheng hua polychromes,

and the shape is referred to as of 'high foot and rounded'. The stem cup with a design of vines illustrated here undoubtedly belongs to this category in both respects. It has a rounded body and a wide open mouth with a slightly everted lip. The hollow stem spreads outwards at the base. As the stem can be used to pick up the cup it has also sometimes been given the name *ba bei* 'grasp cup'.

In decorating the cup the craftsmen would first have outlined the grapevine, tendrils and leaves in cobalt blue directly on to the white paste of the body. Once the whole cup had been completely covered in a translucent glaze and fired at very high temperatures to achieve fusion between the porcelain and its glaze, purple glaze would have been carefully applied between the blue outlines of the grapes, showing from beneath the clear glaze, yellow for the tendrils and green for the leaves. After a second firing to fix the coloured overglaze enamels, the underglaze blue painted outlines are clearly visible through the glaze. The colours employed for the vine bring out the natural qualities of each element to the full. On the underside, the foot ring is left completely unglazed, but the characters '*Da Ming Cheng hua nian zhi*', 'Made in the Cheng hua period of the Great Ming dynasty', follow the inner glazed wall from right to left, in one of the typical Ming regular styles of writing.

The fame that authentic Cheng hua *dou cai* wares enjoyed at the time they were manufactured was a direct result of the exquisite craftsmanship lavished upon them. By the Jia jing and Wan li reigns they were already considered priceless. Although they were copied at much later periods, the best imitations were made during the late Ming. But in terms of the quality of the paste and colours of the enamels there was no comparison. In any event, the faked inscriptions are easily detected.

Introduced and developed on the basis laid by the acquired technique of successfully producing blue and white porcelain and then applying overglaze enamels during the Cheng hua reign, some sources maintain that the original concept was an extension of the *cloisonné* method of decoration, described elsewhere in this volume. The basic principle of containing the coloured glazes within the underglaze blue painting in *dou cai* wares is so similar to the *cloisonné* technique, of confining enamels that would otherwise run inside partitions of copper wire, that technical influence cannot be ruled out. Such interaction of method is not uncommon in other areas of the artistic world.

62. 五彩鏤空雲鳳紋瓶

POLYCHROME
RETICULATED VASE WITH
CLOUD AND PHOENIX
DESIGN

height 49.8 cm.
mouth diameter 15.2 cm.
foot diameter 17.2 cm.
Ming dynasty, reign of
Wan li

Ming painted porcelains opened a new chapter in the history of Chinese ceramics, and *wu cai* and *dou cai* of the Wan li and Cheng hua periods respectively are both well known abroad as well as in China.

Wares with painted decoration had made their mark during all the major periods from the Tang to the Yuan dynasties, and underglaze blue painting on porcelains had been successfully produced since the Yong le and Xuan de periods of the Ming. Splendid achievements in painted decorative techniques throughout the period – such as the underglaze copper red of the Hung wu reign, underglaze blue and copper red of the Xuan de period, Cheng hua *dou cai* and the Zheng de period *san cai* polychrome enamels painted on to a fired but unglazed body as well as the polychromes of the Jia jing and Wan li periods – all embody the spectacular progress made by potters of the Ming. The way had been paved for the future development of polychrome enamelled decoration under the Qing dynasty.

There used to be a saying that 'blue and white wares have a quiet elegance while *wu cai* polychromes possess a certain sumptuousness'. The Wan li *wu cai* polychromes fully concur with this latter description. Underglaze blue was combined with overglaze polychrome decoration in the most important pieces. At this time overglaze blue had not yet emerged, nevertheless the blue showed through the glaze and blended with the overglaze red, green, yellow, purple and brown to form a riot of colour.

The vase shown here was made for display in the imperial palaces. In addition to the use of colours, openwork skills were employed to enhance the three-dimensionality of the design, thus greatly increasing the artistic effect; it is therefore representative of the superb level of skill achieved at the Jingdezhen kilns.

This artefact is elaborately decorated all over with a tight intermingling of painted and reticulated elements confined to eight separate narrow and wide bands. Overglaze enamel colours used include red, yellow, green, aubergine purple, peacock or turquoise blue and browns, but it is the red which is the most eye-catching of all.

The fine reddish-brown outlines around parts of the decoration help to heighten the overall design and bright rich colours to radiate a warm, cheerful effect. Openwork, defining nine phoenixes which fly through variegated clouds, forms the theme of the main decorative register around the body of the vase. *Ru yi* decorative motifs form a band around the mouth in openwork, while a deeper line of blade-shaped plantain leaves topped with openwork butterflies and flowers encircles the upper part of the neck. Two lugs on opposite sides of the neck, modelled in the form of lions' heads, are placed between two small roundels of similar size bearing the stylized seal-script character *shou*, 'longevity', all on a regular but intricately patterned ground. Four cloud-collar devices are cut from the spreading lower neck decorated with the pierced copper-coin or trellis pattern and a swastika lozenge cut from the centre. Rosettes join these four main elements. Below, a narrower band contains small panels, self-contained compositions of birds on branches of pomegranates and other fruits, on a ground of the trellis pattern. The body is dominated by cloud and phoenix designs, below which are the eight precious things painted between a flower above and below against a trellis pattern ground. A broad painted line of red around the base completes and steadies the balance of the vase. The shape is of plain classical taste and the overall composition of the design is well integrated, the colours magnificent, and the openwork fine and meticulous.

The openwork vase vividly delineates the scene of phoenixes flying among auspicious clouds. The phoenix and dragon design has long been a traditional decorative motif in China and is commonly seen on ceramics, such as the phoenix-head ewers with a green-tinged glaze of the Tang period, jars of double phoenix design on Cizhou wares, and the pilgrim flasks with underglaze blue dragon and phoenix designs of the Yuan period. Excellent as these are, the present type of polychrome decoration such as that shown, which features this same theme in openwork, far outstrips them all.

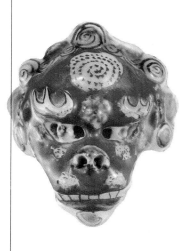

63. 達摩瓷塑立像

HE CHAOZONG: DEHUA
WHITE PORCELAIN
STANDING FIGURE OF
BODHIDHARMA

height 43 cm.
Ming period

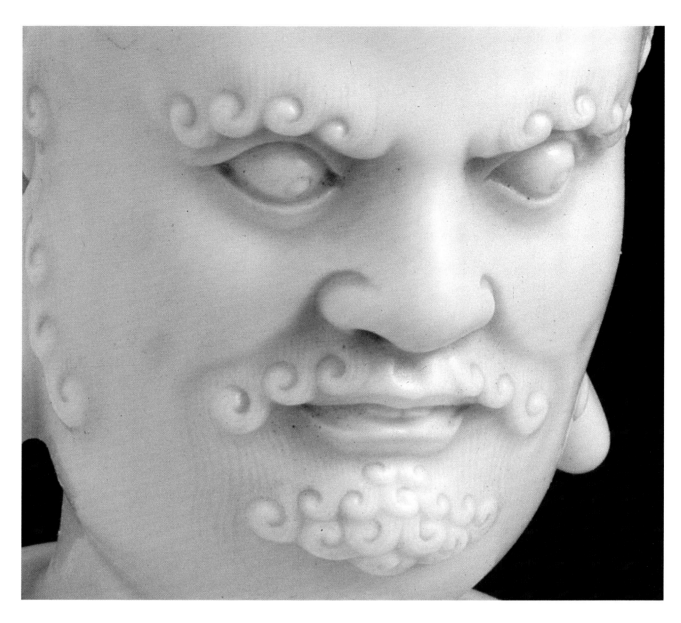

The superlatively fine white porcelains produced at the Dehua kilns in the Ming period are more than worthy of comparison with any previous wares of other famous kilns, whether in the quality of body or the clear glaze. Although produced as early as the Song, Dehua wares flourished mainly during the Ming period when a distinct group consisting of porcelain figures became the most notable part of its repertoire, especially works by He Chaozong which were held in special esteem.

His porcelain sculptures consist mainly of religious images, such as those of the historical buddha Sakyamuni, the bodhisattva Avalokitesvara or Guan yin in Chinese, Maitreya, Bodhidharma and Lü Dongbin, one of the eight Taoist immortals. The images of Guan yin form the vast majority of such works, while those of Bodhidharma are relatively few, making the statue of Guan yin (now housed in the Palace Museum and inscribed with the name of the maker) an even more rare and valuable piece.

Bodhidharma was born in southern India. He was invited to come to China in 520, the first year of the Pu tong era of the Liang dynasty. He arrived in present day Guangzhou by sea and then made his way to Jianyi (now Nanjing) where he met the emperor Wu di. Finding that his opinions were at variance with those of the emperor, he crossed the River Yangtze and went to Luoyang (Henan province), capital of the Northern Wei dynasty. Later, he settled at the Shaolin Monastery on Mount Song and proceeded to sit cross-legged in a cave on Mount Shaoshi facing the stone walls for nine years. During this time he acquired a disciple called Hui ke to whom he gave the following instructions: 'I came to this land to spread the tenets of Buddhism in order to save the people from going astray. Once the five-petalled flower has successfully blossomed, its fruit will form as a matter of course.' He also gave his disciple the four-volume *Leng jia scriptures*. Hui ke followed the instruction of his teacher and spread the teachings of the meditative Chan (Japanese, Zen) sect of Buddhism. Therefore the Chan sect was also called the Bodhidharma sect. In 528, the 2nd year of the reign of the Da tong emperor of the Liang dynasty, on the 5th day of the 10th lunar month, Bodhidharma passed away and his body was buried on Xiong'er shan, Bear's Ear Mountain, to the west of Luoyang.

173

64. 五彩鷺蓮尊

POLYCHROME VASE, *ZUN*,
WITH A DESIGN OF
EGRETS AND LOTUSES

height 45.4 cm.
mouth diameter 22.9 cm.
foot diameter 15 cm.
Qing dynasty, reign of
Kang xi

The three reign periods of Kang xi, Yong zheng and Qian long of the Qing dynasty marked a true high point in the history of China's ceramic technology, with Kang xi polychromes occupying the top and most illustrious position of all. Based on the achievements laid in the making of Ming polychromes, the Kang xi *wu cai* wares display innovations and improvements in the shape, application of colours, use of decoration and virtuosity in painted schemes.

A significant breakthrough was made in the controlled employment of overglaze blue, black and gold. Thenceforth blue painted on to the fired glaze surface took the place of underglaze blue, which had hitherto formed part of the colour scheme of the surface designs in the Jia jing and Wan li polychromes. Overglaze blue lent a more harmonious tone to the overall scheme and gave a dense richness surpassing anything that could be achieved in blue and white decoration.

The black colour appears dense – similar to calligrapher's and painter's ink – when applied to porcelains and as such became indispensable in the decoration of such wares. Gold had been used on the ceramic vessels of the Tang, Song and Yuan periods, but mostly in the form of gold leaf stuck on to the surface of the objects. Gold decoration on the Kang xi polychromes, however, was painted with a brush laden with gold powder which allowed an application more in keeping with the rest of the design. The unique decorative quality of the gold increases the effect of sumptuousness and marks a significant development in porcelain making.

The polychrome vase shown here is called a *zun* because of its similarity to the large archaic bronze wine vessel type with a broad body and flaring mouth. The diameter of the mouth and the widest part of the body are the same, and because the flaring shape resembles the two outward curling sweeps of a 'phoenix tail *zun*' it is graceful and dignified in shape with a wide everted lip, a long cylindrical neck, and ample, rounded shoulders curving inwards to a body which curves gently in and then slightly out until it reaches the base which is slightly splayed and rounded. The lines of the vase are gentle and full, the flowing and easy curves bringing a grace to the solid form.

Jars and vases of the Kang xi reign are of many kinds. Large vessels such as the 'phoenix tail' and 'mallet' types were all produced by the private kilns, as was this egret and lotus vase, its fine shape and resplendent colours so typical of the Kang xi polychromes.

As to decoration, the vase is painted all over with a scene of a lotus pond, with the lotus flowers and egrets as the main theme. The design is in two main parts, one covering the neck and the other the belly, both portraying the same theme. The two compositions – rich, imaginative and well integrated – are separated at the neck by a band of spiral meanders. Below and around the edges of the mouth as well as around the shoulder is a band of the wave pattern.

From these simple fringe decorations to the drawing of the water scene the painter's care is evident. Realistically drawn, perhaps from life or from a strong visual memory, the greens of the tender, young leaves and the old, worm-eaten leaves are cleverly distinguished. The red, purple and yellow lotus flowers and buds, none of which looks the same, stand up straight, like canopies. They are extremely rich in colour but not at all gaudy. Waterweeds and the roots of the arrowheads also grow thickly on the pond, with duckweed floating on the water. Coloured butterflies flit overhead and the birds perch on the curved lotus stalks as if keeping an eye on each other. One egret stands upright, its neck outstretched searching for food, while another is just flying up away from the pond's surface; both are vividly painted. The scene captures the idea of a stillness being suddenly broken by the quick movements of pondside creatures.

Lotus flowers have long been praised for their quality of being 'unsullied by the dross and mud out of which they grow' and 'standing erect and tall in full grace'. In the *Shi jing, Poetry classic,* is an ode to love wherein lotus flowers were extolled as the symbol of female beauty. It is, therefore, of no surprise that lotus flowers are commonly used as a decorative motif on painted porcelain. In terms of both the technical expertise involved in its production as well as the painterly skills employed in its decoration, this polychrome vase ranks among the best produced during the Kang xi era.

65. 五彩百蝶瓶

POLYCHROME VASE WITH
DESIGN OF ONE HUNDRED
BUTTERFLIES

height 44 cm.
mouth diameter 12 cm.
foot diameter 13 cm.
Qing dynasty, reign of
Kang xi

Kang xi *wu cai* polychromes possess a unique style and flavour among painted porcelains of the Qing period and justify epithets such as 'immensely wonderful' and 'strong, hard colours' by past Chinese writers. Rich and dense, their colours are fresh with an inherent translucence. The techniques of painting consist of the use of single outlines evenly filled with colours, producing an effect different from that of *fen cai* decorations – noted for its soft, gentle qualities – on Yong zheng porcelains on the later Yong zheng porcelains. Because they are fired at a higher temperature than *fen cai* enamelled wares, *wu cai* polychromes suggest a certain hardness, hence the reference to 'hard colours'. The *gu cai*, 'old colours', porcelains, a name given by the makers at Jingdezhen, are imitations of this kind of polychrome decoration.

In the Qing period wares for imperial use were supplied by the official ceramic workshops at Jingdezhen. This was managed in the following manner: most of the official wares were allocated to private kilns for firing where they were allotted the best firing positions in the furnaces so as to ensure the highest quality finished products. This became the established system after the 19th year of the Kang xi reign (1680). But, strangely, from a study of existing Kang xi polychrome, it is found that the products of the imperial kilns are inferior to those of the private kilns, for most of the imperial wares are small, such as dishes and bowls, while the jars and vases produced for private use are not only bigger in size but also more splendid in colour and more lively in design. The *Tao ya*,

On ceramics, contains the following comments on the making of Kang xi polychromes: 'Obviously they are produced in the imperial kilns, but the designs on them are uninteresting, while the unmistakable *ke hu* display meticulous and vigorous use of the brush.' *Ke hu* refers to products other than the official ones. Therefore connoisseurs judge a vessel of the Kang xi period on its own merit, and not according to whether it was from an imperial or private kiln.

Kang xi jars and vases come in a variety of shapes, including the 'phoenix tail vase', 'mallet vase', 'bottle vase', *yu hu chun ping* (spring jar), *mei ping*, 'prunus blossom vase', and Guan yin vase from the shape of the bulbous bodied, tall-necked vase usually carried by the bodhisattva, all of which are decorated in many colours. The vase shown here bears superbly executed painted designs on a beautifully shaped body, attesting to the maturity of the ceramic arts of this period.

This vessel has a slightly flaring mouth rising from a short neck and rounded shoulders. The body contracts slightly from below the shoulders and falls sharply to the rounded base which bears no reign mark or other inscription. The neck is decorated with two bands containing single cloud motifs on a diaper ground imitating textiles. The body is covered with colourful painted butterflies in flight accompanied by a few damsel and dragonflies. The artist has successfully and realistically concentrated a variety of butterfly species into a relatively small surface area.

Butterflies as decoration on porcelains had been seen on Yue ware as early as the Five Dynasties' period. Such a decorative motif was commonly seen along with other so-called 'one hundred' (multifarious) designs such as the 'one hundred sons', 'one hundred deer', 'one hundred flowers' and 'one hundred birds', all of which are symbols of auspiciousness, propitiousness and happiness. And one Song painting portrays a cat, butterflies and peonies to signify 'venerable old age, prosperity and nobility', expressing the desire for 'never ending wealth and worldly glory'.

The vase illustrated here depicts its subjects in an accomplished, painterly style using a pleasing array of colours which includes red, yellow, blue, brownish red, violet, black and green amongst others. Characteristic of the Kang xi polychromes are the watery light greens. Each butterfly is painted in exuberant colours; for instance, a shimmering yellow gold is used to dot the red spots on the patterned wings, black scales are used to embellish the green wings, and blue and white accentuated with enamels, or an elegant powder blue colour used to enhance the total effect of the blue butterflies, so that the multi-coloured brilliance of the whole picture is brought out to the full. A fine attention to detail combined with a broad sweep of the brush in the decorative qualities also brings out, in its naturalness, the qualities of the craftsman-artist.

Kang xi polychromes with added black colour and golden yellow are considered to be of first-class quality and the vase shown here demonstrates all that is best in polychrome porcelains of the period.

66. 琺瑯彩雉雞牡丹盌

FA LANG POLYCHROME
OVERGLAZE ENAMELLED
BOWL WITH DESIGN OF
PHEASANTS AND PEONIES

height 44 cm.
mouth diameter 14.5 cm.
foot diameter 6 cm.
illustration shows actual size
Qing dynasty, reign of Yong
zheng

Polychrome enamels of the *fa lang* group of porcelains, were first introduced into the decorative repertoire of porcelains during the very last years of the reign of Kang xi of the Qing dynasty. The most significant of the colours to be used was the opaque, rose-coloured enamel. Advances were made in the controlling of these enamels during the reign of the Yong zheng emperor, who took a personal interest in the enamelling technique, and it finally reached the summit of achievement during the Qian long era. During this period, palace porcelains were all placed in the Hall of Accomplishing Uprightness. According to records in the imperial archives, the collection amounted to more than 400 pieces, and the bowl illustrated is just one exquisite example taken from this store.

The process of producing these wares began with the making of plain white porcelains at Jingdezhen, their bodies so fine and translucent that they were referred to as 'bodiless'. They were then transported to Beijing. There, court painters created designs which would be particularly suitable for each shape which could be transferred by palace craftsmen to the bodies. A second, and by no means easy, firing produced the finished articles. During this period the palace enamelling workshop had recruited the most skilled craftsmen from all over China to produce everyday imperial wares as well as special items for the emperor's personal delectation and *fa lang* polychromes rated highly as one of the many types being produced. However, as indicated by the methodical way that they were listed in the Qing dynasty inventories as *ci tai hua fa lang*, '*fa lang* painted on the porcelain body', the name also carefully inscribed on their storage boxes, they were guarded with the utmost care. With such a complex process involved in achieving the intricate design and the precise, delicate colouring in the difficult firing process, very few pieces were actually produced. Not unexpectedly, these were reserved for the emperor and, very occasionally, were presented on important state occasions to such dignitaries as princes and the Dalai and Panchen Lamas of Mongolia and Tibet.

Fa lang enamels take the form of pigments made into a thick paste so that they stand very slightly above the surface when applied to the body. At first, these new materials had to be imported from abroad, but by the Yong zheng reign the Chinese mastered the complete art and their palette included more than twenty different colours. From the bowl shown alone, we can get some idea of the multiplicity of rich colours that were available as well as the matchless workmanship.

The body of this bowl is very thin, close to the very finest of the 'bodiless' porcelains produced in China. It is pure white and as unctuous as jade. The delicate colours include pink, mauve, pale pinkish-purple, pastel yellow, light, bright yellow, apricot, blue, green and umber. Meticulous drawing brings out the vivid scene of a pair of pheasants among blooming peonies. The reverse bears a couplet inscribed in black which reads: 'Tender stamens enveloped in powdered gold, full petalled corona sewn as billowing clouds', in a natural, flowing calligraphic style. Three seals accompany the calligraphy to complete the traditional appearance: to the right, *jia li*, 'beauty doubled', on the upper left, *jin cheng*, 'formed of gold' and on the lower left, *xu yin*, 'reflected brilliance of dawn sunlight'. All three seals are in relief. In the centre of the base of the bowl is the reign mark *Yong zheng nian zhi* within a doubled square frame.

The finest polychrome enamelled porcelains in existence were all produced during that particularly rich period covering the three reigns of Kang xi, Yong zheng and Qian long of the Qing dynasty. Thereafter, the porcelain industry went into decline. After 1911, in the years following the establishment of the Republic, some manufacturers of porcelain attempted to reproduce these fine wares, but their quality left a lot to be desired and there is no way in which the two can be compared.

67. 粉彩牡丹瓶

FEN CAI POLYCHROME
OVERGLAZE ENAMELLED
VASE WITH PEONY DESIGN

height 27.5 cm.
mouth diameter 6.3 cm.
foot diameter 8.6 cm.
Qing dynasty, reign of Yong
zheng

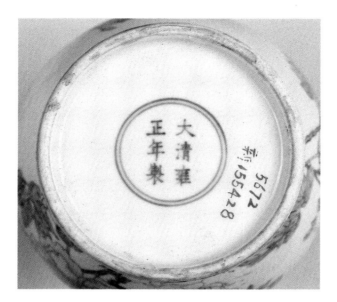

Among the polychrome porcelains of the Qing period, *fen cai*, often called *famille rose*, is another famous type of the Yong zheng reign, the making of which kind of vessels actually began at the very end of the Kang xi reign. Of all overglaze enamel decorations, it is renowned for its mild, quiet elegance.

The special feature of this type of polychrome porcelain lies in the addition of tin oxide to the opaque white powder on the parts that are to be decorated with coloured enamels, thus obtaining an artistic effect by means of the different grades of enamel used to achieve lighter and darker areas. Opaque white can also be mixed with pigments to make different shades and it can, of course, be used singly as a monochrome white in its own right. All this makes it possible for the decorator to exercise fully the expressive power of the various shades and tones, with anything up to twenty different hues being employed in some objects. Some of the enamel pastes contain powdered oxides which act as fluxes and as this lowers the temperature needed to fire them – compared with *wu cai* polychrome enamels, for example – the end product is softer in appearance; hence giving rise to another name for them – *ruan cai*, 'soft colours'.

As the compounds used for *fen cai* and *fa lang cai* enamels both contain arsenic it may be said that they are similar in quality, but *fen cai* is the product of the combined perfected skills of porcelain making and painting. It is first necessary to fire the body, which must be thin and translucent, making sure that no flaws appear on the pure white glazed surface. After the application of the mineral compounds they are fired to produce the final colours. There is a similarity, therefore, in the manufacturing stages and technological processes used to produce *fa lang cai* and *fen cai*.

That the production of these polychrome pieces was able to supersede production of all the other types of overglaze enamelled porcelains is because of the successful firing of home-produced *fa lang* coloured enamels in the 2nd lunar month of the 6th year of the Yong zheng reign. Thereafter, *fen cai* wares were not only produced by imperial kilns, but also by the private kilns at Jingdezhen in great quantities. The products of the private kilns were, however, made with less care and were inferior in shape, quality of clay, colours of the enamels and in the artistic skill of the painted decoration. In all respects they fall far short of the exquisite pieces from the imperial kilns.

The peony vase shown here is an exquisitely beautiful work of art. It has a graceful shape, a pure white body and a smooth, glazed surface. Its dished mouth sits atop a slender neck which curves outward into a bulbous body, the line of which continues and then flows out again to a base with a recessed ring foot. At the centre of the underside are six blue and white characters, *Da Qing Yong zheng nian zhi*, in regular script inside a double lined circle.

The design of the body is dominated by fully opened peonies in bright, attractive colours. The brushwork of the painting, the facility in the application of the enamels and the fine drawing and modelling in colour of the flowers are a testimony to the artistic talents employed. Particular artists were especially commissioned to furnish designs for these wares during the period and, since the right conditions prevailed to encourage them in their work, they were able to produce the ideas which are manifested in some delightfully simple compositions.

Other designs beside those done on a white ground include those executed against a coral red, light green, reddish-brown and ink black ground. Bark textured and gold tracery grounds were also sometimes employed. All these decorative techniques have individuality and attraction, but none quite matches those whose decoration is applied to the inherent or enhanced white of the porcelain, the effect of which is to embody the perfect interaction and harmony that can be achieved between porcelain and its painted decoration.

68. 粉彩鏤空轉心瓶

POLYCHROME ENAMELLED
VASE WITH
RETICULATION,
REVOLVING INTERIOR
AND 'ETERNAL'
CALENDAR

height 41.5 cm.
mouth diameter 19.5 cm.
foot diameter 21.2 cm.
Qing dynasty, reign of Qian
long

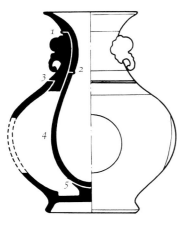

1. *Concealed fixed joint*
2. *Fixed joint*
3. *Movable opening*
4. *Inner vase*
5. *Support for inner vase*
Vertical section through vase showing structure and rotating parts

Porcelain making reached its zenith in the early period of the Qing dynasty during the reigns of Kang xi, Yong zheng and Qian long. The Qian long emperor himself took a personal interest in the production of high quality porcelains and because of this and the fact that the imperial kilns then possessed ample manpower, substantial materials and superior techniques, enormous numbers of new varieties and exquisite colours appeared in succession.

A vase with openwork decoration and revolving interior, such as the one illustrated here, was one of the types unique to the Qian long era. Owing to the difficulty of the manufacturing process, few such pieces were made and consequently still fewer have been handed down. This vase has a full and rounded body and is stately in shape, its neck and belly differing totally from the usual porcelains in that they can be revolved. The neck is adorned with two moulded elephant heads, the trunks of which stand out to form lug handles, and the body with four openwork roundels. Inside the body is fixed a revolving inner vase whose outside wall is painted with pictures of children at play. When the inner vase is rotated, different pictures can be seen through the openings in the outer vase. Another ingenious design lies in the revolvable neck and the shoulder of the fixed outer body: that is, both are marked with characters signifying characters for the Ten heavenly stems and the Twelve earthly branches respectively so that the neck may be turned until the upper symbol corresponds with the appropriate lower symbol. As the series of combinations is completed every sixty years, and then repeated *ad infinitum*, the vase could serve as a calendar, combining the stems and branches to designate the years, months and days in the traditional Chinese way, in theory, for ever.

The gilt decoration on the vase gives the appearance of real gold. Floral designs on a yellow ground cover the main outer body while similar scrolling leaves and flowers cover the deep pink upper and lower bands. The four roundels have cutwork flowers, plants, fruit, rocks and balustrades in garden scenes depicting the four seasons.

The stages of producing this vase involved first firing the neck, body and base of the outer vase and the body of the inner vase as four separate pieces. The inside part of the outer base, on which the whole rests, is formed as the 'socket' and the rounded base of the inner vase as the 'ball' to fit together and act as a free-moving ball and socket joint. While holding these two parts in position, the large outer wall was placed over and fixed to its base which only left the neck to be fitted at the top. At the crucial joints which had to remain fixed to achieve stability, and yet allow free rotation of other moving parts, a special adhesive paste was employed whose properties allowed subsequent adjustment and, when ready, scraping, polishing and decoration. Thus the illusion of a perfect and seamless vase could be achieved.

Such vases come in many shapes and sizes. During the design and construction stages it was essential to ensure that the exact and appropriate proportions between the sizes of the outer and inner vases had been meticulously worked out and that the openwork and decoration, especially around the outer movable parts, had been carefully executed. Another basic requirement was that the proportions of each separate part of the composite had to be calculated while the raw clay was being shaped so that relative changes in the firing process did not affect the dimensions of the finished pieces. Otherwise, the parts would not have fitted exactly. From this description, it may be seen that the level of technical expertise and artistic skill which must have been concentrated in the piece had to be of the highest order, not only in producing a reticulated polychrome enamelled vase, but also in the engineering problems arising from a design such as this one.

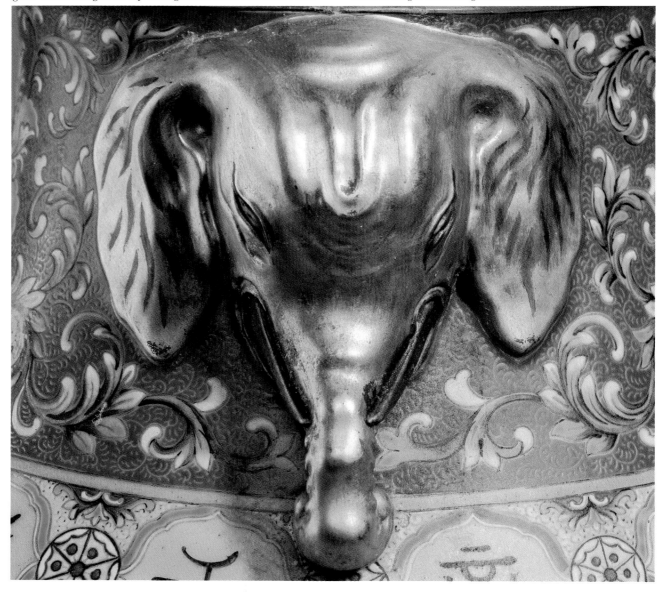

69. 仿古銅犧耳尊

CERAMIC VASE IN THE
FORM OF A BRONZE
VESSEL *ZUN*

height 22.2 cm.
mouth diameter 13.2 cm.
foot diameter 11.7 cm.
Qing dynasty, reign of Qian
long

The porcelain makers of the Qian long period, besides producing large quantities of polychrome and monochrome glazed ceramics, are also known for developing special techniques which could imitate the appearance and forms of other materials and artefacts. Archaistic bronzes, foreign porcelain, lacquerware, bamboo and wooden ware, ancient objects and vessels of coral, jade and so on, were all copied; there was nothing the craftsmen did not attempt. Such pieces not only reproduced exactly the outward appearance and feel of the original material used but so closely reproduced their shapes that it is often difficult to distinguish them from the original. The archaistic bronze copy shown here is one of the few extant pieces originally recorded in the *Tao cheng tu hua juan, Illustrations of objects made in clay*, by Tang Ying, who lived during the Qing period.

Officials who were installed in the imperial kilns as supervisors are known to have exerted great influence over the development of skills and techniques which led to the great innovations of the first century or so of Manchu rule in China. Supervisors of the imperial kiln at Jingdezhen during the Kang xi era included Zang Yingxuan, Lang Tingji and Liu Yuan and, in the Yong zheng period, Nian Xiyo. Therefore, the imperial kilns came to be distinguished by the names of the men who ran them: thus the Zang, Lang and Nian kilns. The famous 'Tang kiln' was named after Tang Ying, supervisor of the official kilns from the 2nd year to the 19th year of Qian long (1737–54), and the products made there were called Tang ware. Tang Ying went to Jingdezhen as an assistant in the 6th year of Yong zheng (1728). 'Tang wares' subsequently achieved originality both in the areas of imitating the ancient vessels and in the making of new varieties. The extant pieces from the Tang kiln are very precious and hard to come by. These splendid achievements derive of course from the experience of the past as well as the collective labour and accumulated wisdom of all who took part in the making of the articles. But as a manager of the imperial kiln, Tang Ying, by integrating theory with practice, did make an enormous contribution and was a prominent figure in the history of the Chinese porcelain industry. More than just an expert in porcelain, he was well versed in art and literature and was even capable of turning out his own designs. His writings published as *Tao ren xin yu, A potter's own experience, Tao cheng ji shi, Notes on the business of pottery making* and *Tao ye tu shuo, Illustrated explanations on firing ceramics*, are very important texts for the study of the history of ceramic technology.

This vase, representative of the so-called 'Tang wares' mentioned in *Illustrations of objects made in clay*, imitates a *zun* sacrificial bronze vessel inlaid with gold and silver of the period of the Warring States and reproduces perfectly the classical simplicity and elegance of shape. Perhaps most remarkable of all is the faithful imitation of the bronze colour and the turquoise, greenish and red patina of the corroded metal. The tea dust glaze used is the reincarnation of the colour of ancient bronzes. This glaze belongs to the category of ancient crystallized ferruginous glazes. The glazed surface of the vase has a semi-dull appearance, with the natural spots shining out from the sombre, greenish base colour.

Such glaze colours had already made an appearance during the Tang and Song periods and reappeared constantly throughout the Ming. During the Qing, glaze varieties such as 'snake skin green' and 'eel yellow' were produced on Tang kiln wares. These two were called 'crab-shell green' and 'tea dust' during the Yong zheng and Qian long periods, and were listed among the glazes monopolized by the imperial kilns. The illustrated archaistic *zun* is an excellent example of the use that such glazes could be put to in this area.

70. 各色釉大瓶

LARGE POLYCHROME
GLAZED VASE

height 86.4 cm.
mouth diameter 27.4 cm.
foot diameter 33 cm.
Qing dynasty, reign of Qian
long

A great variety of coloured glazes were used in the officially run imperial kilns of Jingdezhen in the Qing period. This multi-coloured vase brings together high-fired and low-fired glazes, as well as underglaze and overglaze polychrome decoration in a single piece and as such represents the combined skills acquired and mastered during this period.

This is one of the largest ceramic objects now on display in the Palace Museum; it is almost 90 centimetres in height, of imposing shape, with a rounded mouth rim, *kui* dragon handles and a stepped cylindrical body. Between the mouth and the base of the vessel are a dozen or so horizontal registers of decoration.

The mouth rim is decorated with a golden line. Below are two bands of *fa lang cai* enamels, one with a deep rose ground and the other with a turquoise green ground, both painted with floral designs. The next zone is a band imitating the glaze of Ru ware; that is, over the glazed surface can be seen small 'fish roe' crackles typical of this type. On the neck are blue and white floral patterns of interlacing flowers and plants. Two *kui* dragon handles adorned with gold are attached at either side.

The first band around the shoulder is covered with a cracked turquoise green glaze, followed by a band of imitation Jun ware glaze, a gorgeous crimson flush or *flambé* hue which results from changes in the glaze during firing. Below is a ring of *dou cai* patterns, followed by a light green glaze over a pattern of impressed florets.

Between the colour zones there is usually a ring of gold which contrasts with the bands and makes them stand out even more brilliantly to heighten the overall beauty. The belly of the vase has a ground of dark blue glaze with gold tracery, over which are twelve rectangular panels each framing a different coloured scene or flower pattern. These form the main decoration on the vase.

Underneath this is a band which imitates the glaze of Ge ware, and below that a second band of blue and white floral patterns and then a light green glaze with a line of hanging flower petals. Following on down is a band of lustrous brown glaze with spiral meanders in gold; the main convex foot surface reproduces a Guan ware glaze with the greyish-blue glazed surface decorated with crackles in the same colour. Round the edge of the foot is a ring of sheep-liver coloured glaze with golden classic scrolls. From top to bottom all these colour glazes and the paintings are absolutely faultless, reflecting the excellence and overall development of each of the skills of technique employed.

During the Qian long period, the techniques of underglaze

and overglaze decoration had reached an advanced state of maturity, and blue and white, *dou cai*, *fa lang cai*, *fen cai* and gold colouring overglaze enamelling had already reached a high degree of technical proficiency. The firing of high- or low-temperature glazes of all colours – light blue, turquoise green, azure blue, lustrous brown – were all firmly within the potters' grasp. In particular those colours produced in imitation of Ru, Guan, Ge and Jun ware glazes surpassed even the original products of the famous kilns of the Song period.

Ru, Guan and Ge wares all excel in glazed surface crackles, but the colours and crackle of each differ a great deal. For example, the crackles of Ru ware are highly fragmented; those of Guan ware are the same colour as that of the glaze itself; Ge crackles are a mixture of two kinds – thinly spread, deep-coloured crackles and densely light-coloured ones. There was actually no set technique for achieving a particular kind of crackled surface, but a master craftsman was able to imitate the distinguishing features of each famous kiln. This shows the sophistication of the art. When imitating the Jun ware glazes, the craftsmen were even able to show different *flambé* hues in any way they liked. Such superb objects could never have been fired with any success without the mastery of all the required techniques in the making of the clay paste body, the mixing and use of glaze materials, the painting and the firing.

The pictures on the panels are skilfully executed; they are based on the traditional store of phrases which employ written characters with one meaning which share the same sound as other symbols with different but always auspicious meanings. A good example is the first shown below left which takes the homophone phrase *san yang kai tai* which means 'the opening of nature in spring bringing prosperity'. An alternative translation, embodied in pictorial form, might be 'three rams bringing peace (and prosperity)' or 'three rams heralding spring'. The remaining panels utilize the play on sounds and meanings: *ji qing you yu*, 'auspicious blessings in excess', portrayed as a boy striking *qing* stone chimes with another boiling water for tea; *dan feng chao yang*, 'the red phoenix facing the sun', shown as peonies and the male and female phoenix; *tai ping you xiang* (shown as the front panel on the vase) drawn as elephants with precious vases on their backs, homophones for 'universal peace'; a traditional garden scene; and the one hundred antiquities. Six more panels placed alternately with the former group also incorporate symbols of good fortune, longevity and the *ling zhi* fungus of immortality combined with floral designs reproducing silk embroidery and textiles.

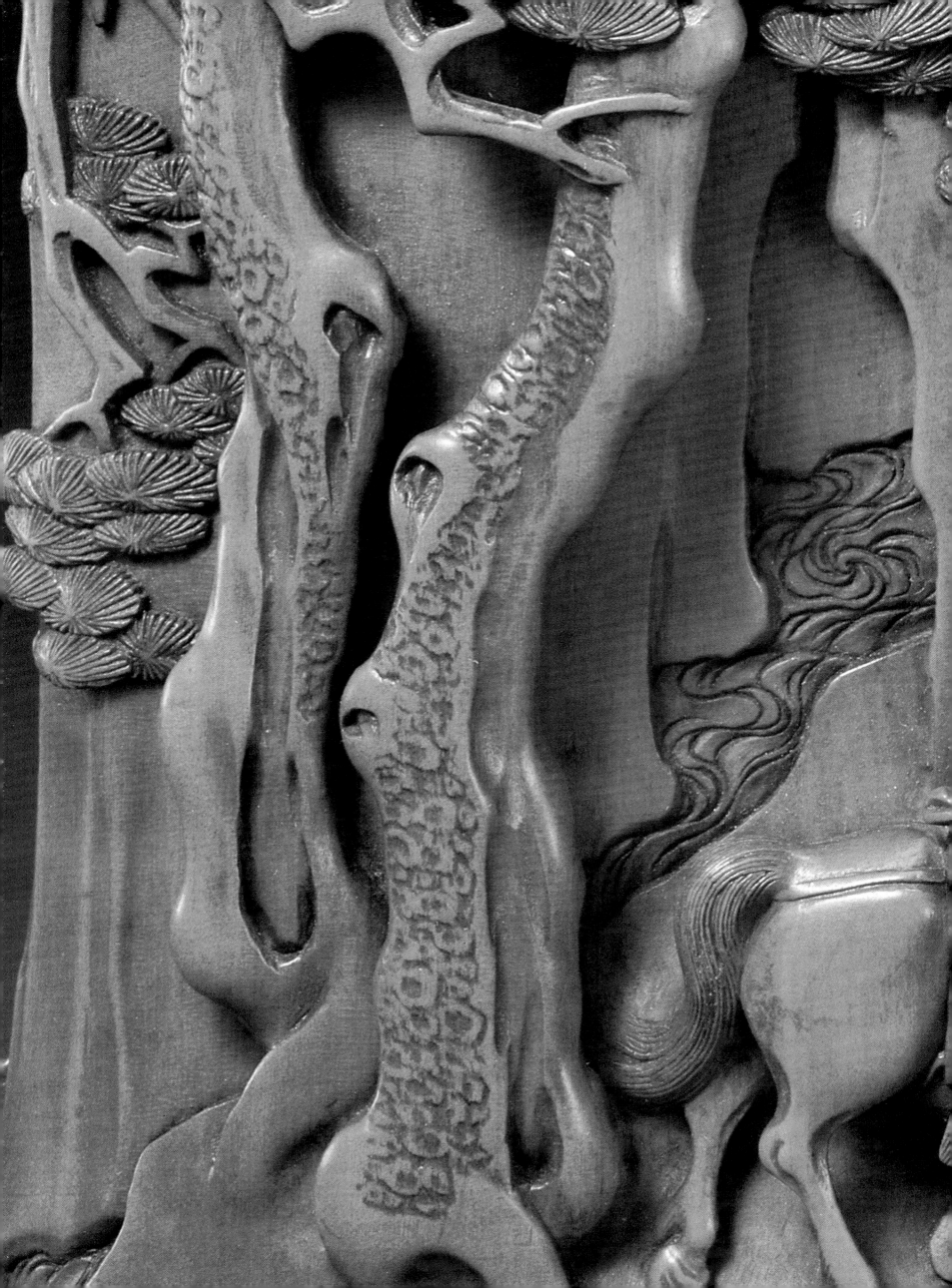

MINOR ARTS

Minor and handicraft arts occurred as needs arose in everyday life and then developed from the simple to the complex. This first happened as early as the neolithic period when, apart from the immediate demands for the functional requirements, people sought to enhance the appearance of their utensils. Thus quality became the main criterion in the choice of raw materials, and beautiful shapes and shining surfaces embellished with decorative designs were required of the finished products. This gave rise to the handicraft arts. The division of labour in the production of tools and utensils gradually evolved alongside the increasing need for food, clothing, shelter and travel. Contemporary and later historical records show that in the Shang and Zhou periods agencies or guilds were established on a countrywide basis to supervise various trades such as construction, metal processing, carpentry, the weaving of vegetable fibres, masonry and tanning.

In keeping with these systems, successive dynasties following the Shang and Zhou maintained their own huge official workshops specializing in specific products and, from objects either passed down throughout history or excavated, it is apparent that the products of each dynasty possess individual and distinctive styles of manufacture. One example of this system were the many workshops attached to the Yang xin dian, Hall of Mental Cultivation, of the Qing dynasty. From the Han down to the Qing dynasties, besides government-operated workshops, there were also folk workshops and independent artisans as well as amateur producers of the minor arts who have left behind an abundance of fine pieces. However, that is not to say that there was not a great deal of interaction and mutual influence between these different craftsmen. For example, Zhang Cheng, the maker of the round 'Red lacquer tray carved with Cape jasmine' reproduced in this volume, was originally a non-official lacquerer of the Yuan period. Following in his footsteps, his son Zhang Degang rose to fame and his works became well known as far afield as Japan and the Ryūkyū Islands during the reign of Yong le, of the Ming, so much so that he was called to the court to supervise the palace studio. From extant works bearing his signature and other works bearing the reign marks of Yong le and Xuan de, we can see that carved lacquer objects of this period followed in the tradition of Zhang Cheng. Like the tray illustrated, the thick lacquer is carved with a fluid facility, and with more attention given to polishing with abrasives, producing glossy surfaces of gentle rather than harsh cut lines. During the same period there was also an increase in the numbers of items produced as well as the repertoire of techniques employed.

Cloisonné, from the French *cloison* meaning 'partition', describes the method of baking coloured enamels on to an object made of a metal such as brass or copper. The enamels are prevented from running into each other during firing by these partitions, which are constructed from copper or brass filigree and stuck on to the surface. In the early part of the Ming period *cloisonné* objects were generally made by the craftsmen from Yunnan province, but during the Jing tai reign the *cloisonné* ware made in Beijing displayed a marked improvement both in quantity and quality. The enamels used were strong, durable and fresh in colour, while the cells of wire, or partitions (*cloisons* in French) which separated and prevented the enamels from running into each other became more intricate and smoothly arranged. Such was the progression from previous efforts that the name *Jing tai lan*, 'Jing tai blue', refer-

ring to this period of achievement, evolved as the technical standard by which later *cloisonné* was judged.

Another illustrated piece from the Ming period which is worthy of attention is the long, black lacquer side table inlaid with mother-of-pearl, made under the auspices of the Yu yong jian, the official office of the Ming dynasty which oversaw the production of utensils and objects for imperial use. The design of five dragons on the surface and mark of the reign period Wan li on the underside are two distinguishing features which are characteristic of items produced by this imperial workshop. Thus it can be seen that the general trend in the development of Ming craftsmanship is marked by the interplay of ideas and influences between the court-hired artisans and private craftsmen. In addition to these two types of professional craftsmen, there were also enthusiastic amateurs like Zhu Bishan of the Yuan period, who excelled in the making of silverware, and You Tong of the late Ming and early Qing, who was skilled in the carving of rhinoceros horn. The unique characteristic shared by these men was the way in which they blended practical technical skills with scholarly cultural pursuits in an enthusiastic approach to their artistry. This combination led directly to innovations which exerted a great influence over other craftsmen.

Wu Zhifan was a craftsman of the Qing period who did not hold an official position, famous for his carving in bamboo, an example of which is the bamboo container for holding brushes illustrated here. He was a recipient of the traditions first introduced by the highly influential Jiading group of bamboo carvers. The ivory brush-holder by Huang Zhenxiao, also illustrated, depicting the life of fishermen, is subject to the same tradition. Although he hailed from Guangdong province his style is completely divorced from that of other Guangdong ivory craftsmen. Carving in this area was a flourishing industry characterized by pagodas, dragon boats and the intricate reticulated balls carved from a single piece of ivory, one inside another and all movable. It was just such men from Guangdong who were responsible for ivory carvings marked *ya zuo* executed in the Yang xin dian Qing imperial workshop. In 1731 the famous carver of bamboo, Feng Shiqi, was enlisted into the service of the court. His ivory carvings helped to set up a new, fresh and elegant style conspicuously devoid of such artefacts as dragon boats or ivory balls. Again, at the beginning of the Qian long era, he was ordered to experiment in the production of new kinds of carved lacquerware. Carved lacquer of this period is characterized by its distinctive cut edges, with the craftsman using the knife as if he were wielding a writing brush, and ground edges are rarely seen.

During the reign of the Yong zheng emperor, artisans drafted into the palace jade-carving studio included Hu Decheng, Zou Xuewen, Bao Youxin, Wang Bin, Chen Yijia, Yao Hanwen and Yao Zongjiang. All these were southerners and they formed the backbone of the studio. It is also worth noting that, apart from being master carvers, both Zou Xuewen and Yao Zongjiang were connoisseurs of ancient jades and that Yao's family had produced at least three generations of skilled carvers – his grandfather, his father and himself. It is no surprise that, as Suzhou had become a centre which had attracted skilled jade carvers since the Ming, the chief artisans of the jade-carving studio during the Qian long period – Ni Bingnan, Zhang Xiangxian, Zhang Junguan, Jia Wenyun, Zhang Deshao, Jiang Junde, Gu Guanguang and Jin Zhenhuan, for example – had all been recruited there. However, they only undertook everyday carving and restoration. When it came to large-scale projects demanding more hands, such as the 'Jade mountain depicting Yu the Great regulating watercourses', included in this album, it was first roughed out by the palace craftsmen and then handed over to an official in Yangzhou who had it carefully carved by craftsmen drafted locally from Suzhou and Yangzhou.

Because it was the job of the enamelling section of the imperial workshop to apply decorative enamels to ready-made items, such as copper, porcelain, glass and Yixing pottery wares, it had to work in close cooperation with other specialist craftsmen. Some, like Song Qige and Deng Bage, were responsible for the preparation of enamel pastes and completing the firing process; others, such as Hu Dayou, were responsible for the blowing of the glazes on to large vessels, while still others supervised the transfer of designs to the body of the object. These included the porcelain painters from the ceramic centre of Jiangxi province – Song Sanji, Zhou Yue and Wu Shiqi – and the painters in enamels from Guangdong – Zhang Qi and Kuang Li'nan. Lin Zhaokai, a pupil of Lang Shining (the Italian missionary Giuseppe Castiglione), had come from Guangdong as well as artists of the imperial academy of painting like He Jinkun, Tang Zhenji, Dai Heng, Zou Wenyu, Zhang Weiqi and Lang Shining; all were required to take part. Responsible for writing the signatures of the makers on the objects was Xu Tongzheng, the scribe of the correspondence department of the palace, attached to the Wu ying dian, Hall of Military Eminence. The famous calligrapher Dai Lin, attached to the same office, brushed verses which were to be included in the decoration. The paper-thin eggshell porcelains that were used were made by the government-run Jiangxi kiln under the supervision of Nian Xiyao, while stoneware bodies to be enamelled were made in Yixing. The glass objects came from the palace glass works. Thus it can be seen that each piece of finished enamel was only achieved by means of the joint efforts of a host of skilled craftsmen and talented artists. In the same way, the products turned out by the other twenty-four court workshops or studios were to some extent the result of similar cooperation and this brief account goes some way in relating the typical interaction which took place between four of them.

71. 大聖遺音琴

QIN. MUSICAL
INSTRUMENT

length 120 cm.
width at shoulder 20.5 cm.
width at end 13.4 cm.
thickness 5 cm.
thickness of underpart 1 cm.
Tang period: inscribed *Zhi
de bing jia*, equivalent to
756.

This musical instrument, called a *qin*, is made from wood of the Tong tree, the chestnut-brown colour of which is offset by streaks of black and the small patches of red lacquer with which it has been restored. Jade stops are inlaid on the front, and jade pegs, a gold emblem, and two sounding holes, one round, one oblate, set into the back. The inscription, large square seal and name of the instrument at the top, *Da sheng yi yin qin*, were carved at the time of its manufacture, which according to the date written in red lacquer beside the round hole was during the Zhi de era. The cyclical characters which follow fix the date at 756, the year when, having led his rebellion against the dynasty, An Lushan had forced the emperor to flee to Shu, now Sichuan province. When the new emperor ascended the throne he had changed the name of the region to Zhi de.

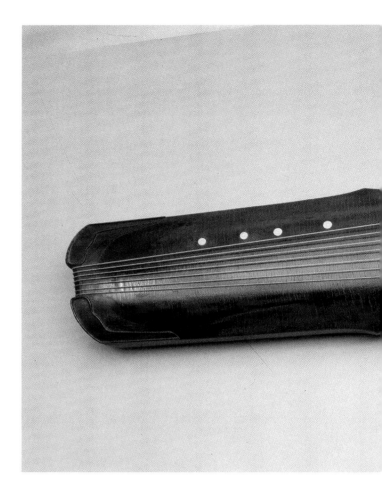

During the Qing period the *qin* was stored in the South Repository, the storehouse of precious objects, attached to the Yang xin dian, Hall of Mental Cultivation, the private apartments of the emperors, which demonstrates the value placed upon it. However, by the time that the committee responsible for putting in order the affairs of the toppled imperial household entered it, they found that the building had been long neglected. Muddy rain water had trickled through the leaking roof over a long period directly on to the face of the instrument, forming a thick layer of hard encrustation. Consequently, the wood had lost its colour, appeared grey and was in a state of complete disrepair. It was then decided that the instrument should be removed to another warehouse, in its existing condition, for safekeeping. Not until 1947 was it identified by Wang Shixiang, an expert of the Palace Museum, as an object of the Tang period. In 1949, with the permission of the then director Ma Heng, the Museum employed a well-known specialist *qin* player, Guan Pinghu, to undertake the restoration. After months of painstaking work he succeeded in clearing away the dirt and unexpectedly found the lacquer surface to be still intact. That the instrument has been passed down over a period of 1,000 years and that the lacquer covering has been able to withstand long years of exposure to the elements is a testimony to the great skills that were employed in its manufacture.

When played by Guan the newly restored instrument was found to produce a sound which was both clear and delicate. According to the music books of the Ming and Qing dynasties, there are nine qualities of sound which the ancients thought an excellent instrument should possess, namely *ai* 'rarity', *tou* 'penetration', *run* 'mellowness', *jing* 'tranquillity', *jun* 'evenness', *yuan* 'roundness', *qing* 'clarity' and *fang* 'sweetness'. These were called the 'nine virtues'. They believed that it was unusual to find all these qualities in a single instrument, but according to Zheng Mingzhong, a contemporary player of the classical *qin*, this instrument possesses all those qualities. There are altogether five *qin* in existence from the Tang period, three of which, including this one, are housed in the Palace Museum.

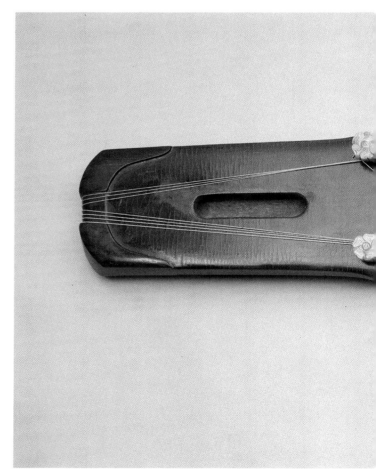

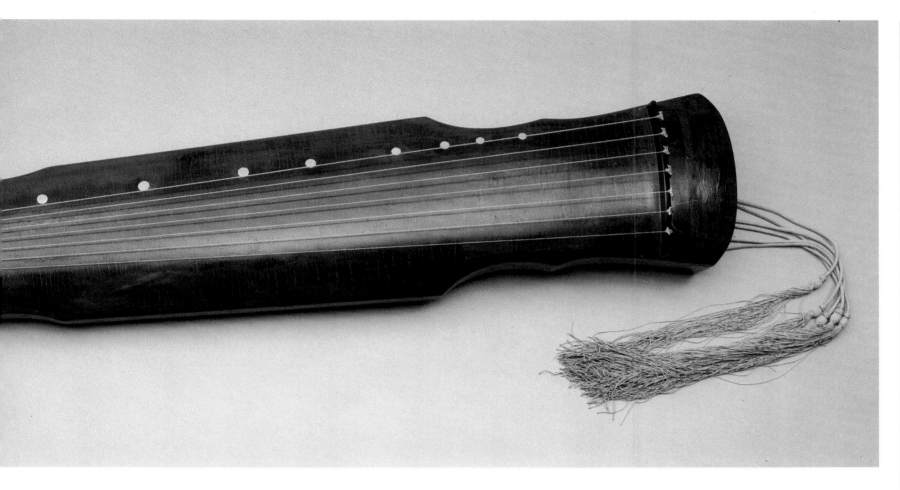

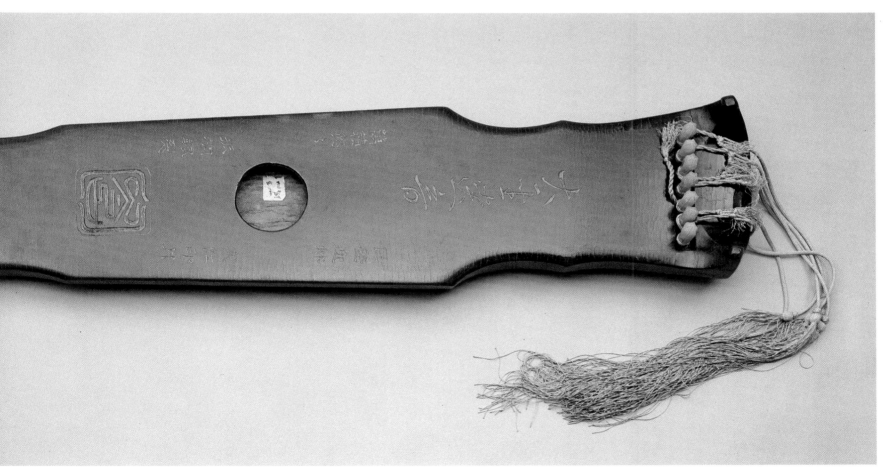

72.剔紅梔子花圓盤　73.剔紅觀瀑圖八方盤

ZHANG CHENG: CIRCULAR
RED LACQUER TRAY
CARVED WITH CAPE
JASMINE

diameter 16.5 cm.
height 2.8 cm.
Yuan period

YANG MAO: OCTAGONAL
RED LACQUER TRAY
CARVED WITH SCENERY
AND FLOWERS

diameter 17.8 cm.
height 2.6 cm.
Yuan period

'Carved red', *ti hong*, is a term used to describe a particular kind of lacquerware. It is manufactured by covering a base, called the core, with a layer of the transparent lacquer that has been mixed with cinnabar (red mercuric sulphide) to produce the familiar red colour. As the lacquer dries, subsequent layers are added and allowed to dry until the desired thickness is reached. The article is then ready for carving. Articles thus made are called carved red lacquerware. It is recorded in the literature concerning lacquerware that both the patterns and the ground of one type of Tang carved red lacquerware are red in colour and on the same plane; that is, the designs are incised into the surface. Another kind is said to have patterns standing in relief against a yellow ground, referred to as 'carved red [lacquer]ware on a sunken yellow ground'. In carved red lacquerwares of the Song and Yuan periods the use of a sharp blade is not immediately apparent as carved edges tend to be smooth and rounded.

No pieces of carved red lacquerware from the Tang and Song periods survive. However, as the literature states that Song and Yuan carved red lacquer differ very little, the two Yuan trays shown here may also be regarded as generally representative of Song lacquer as well.

The design on the circular tray carved by Zhang Cheng consists entirely of the double-flower of Cape jasmine in full bloom at the centre, surrounded by leaves and four buds with no further decoration added on the ground. The sturdy yet freely carved forms possess such a natural strength and grace that it would be difficult to conceive of the carver as only having copied from flower paintings or other carved lacquer designs. Rather, he must have observed his subject closely in its natural state. Combined with a seasoned facility in the techniques of his craft and thorough knowledge of the intractable properties of the lacquer medium, he was able to translate the freshness of elements of the natural world and concentrate them into the confines of such small articles as the tray shown here.

The octagonal carved red lacquer tray was produced by Yang Mao. Within the border of leaves and the alternately raised and lowered heads of flowers lies a scene of a pavilion surrounded by pines. To the right an old man approaches the balustrade and gazes towards a waterfall which cascades into a stream from the mountain opposite. Two boys stand separately, one inside the building, the other on the terrace. Three different patterns carved into the sunken ground are used to denote the sky, the terrace and the water. Both trays have a black ground. The inscriptions 'Made by Zhang Cheng' and 'Made by Yang Mao' respectively are to be found incised into the underside of each article.

During the Yuan and early Ming periods, lacquerwares were densely carved with flowers such as the Cape jasmine, chrysanthemums, peonies and plantain lilies but without a fine-patterned ground. Only landscapes were carved against

roughly patterned grounds. Generally speaking, ground patterns of the Jia jing era were more delicate than those of the Yong le and Xuan de periods, but those of Wan li period were even finer. Patterned grounds were at that time provided for all kinds of carvings – landscapes, figures or animals – and gradually patterned ground became finer and finer as the Ming period progressed.

Artists of the Yong le and Xuan de reign periods not only inherited such traditions as represented by Zhang Cheng and Yang Mao, but greatly increased the variety of carved lacquerwork. The colour and lustre of their objects are highly attractive and the quality of the lacquer itself so high as to allow the carving of lively, realistic subjects. From the time of Chang and Yang up to the early Ming, the technique employed is, characteristically, a quick and neat handling of the knife with greater amount of attention paid to the final grinding and polishing of edges. Although the reign eras of Yong le and Xuan de technically belong to the same period, some of the works of the latter began to develop a style of their own, with the coating of lacquer getting thinner and the ground becoming more spacious. Yet no further changes took place until the reign of Jia jing. Lacquerwares of this period make no attempt to conceal the sharp cut edges but by the Wan li era another, quite different change occurred when lacquer artists sought to represent compact scenes with extremely complicated and fine lines.

So far, reference has only been made to the lacquerware produced by official workshops. There was, however, another somewhat cruder type with distinct edges which suggest a quick fluid action of the blade in carving. They bear no reign marks and their designs have a popular, folk quality. Though less elegant and refined than the official or imperial lacquerwares the artistry of its simple and uninhibited style is of no less value.

In the Qing period greater importance was attached to the carving than the grinding or polishing of lacquer. With the reign of Qian long, carved lacquerware became even more refined. Today, carved red lacquerwares are still being produced in Beijing and Yangzhou, generally reproducing the style prevalent in the Qian long period of many-layered pieces with finely cut designs. They do not incorporate the finer aspects of Yuan and Ming lacquerwares, such as are shown here.

74. 銀槎盃

ZHU BISHAN
(1271–1368): SILVER
WINE VESSEL, *CHA BEI*

height 18 cm.
length 20 cm.
Yuan period

Zhu Bishan, who lived more than six hundred years ago in Jiaxing, Zhejiang province, is well known for the exquisite silverwares he created with such masterly skill during his life. Famous men such as Ke Jiusi, the celebrated landscape painter of the Yuan period, commissioned Zhu to make silverwares for them or composed verses for his works. He was also eulogized in poetry throughout the Ming and Qing periods.

The oldest extant vessel made in silver is the sauce-boat shaped *yi* made in the state of Chu during the period of the Warring States, now kept in the Palace Museum. The existence of silver wine vessels was also recorded during the period of the Northern and Southern dynasties. By the late Tang period, silverwares had increased both in quantity and variety and wine cups engraved with patterns came into use. So-called 'canoe-shaped' wine vessels did not exist before the Song but gained in popularity during the Yuan and Ming periods.

According to old records, silver pieces made by Zhu Bishan were numerous in quantity and varied in design. The canoe-shaped wine vessel shown here was originally exhibited in the Palace of Doubled Glory inside the Forbidden City. It was used as a wine container during the Yuan period but was regarded as a treasured object of art during the Qing.

This wine pourer was first cast and subsequently engraved with details. Although the head, the hands and shoes of the immortal were welded on to the body at a later stage, the process has been completed with such skill and care that there are no traces of a join and appear as if cast in one mould. The container part of the object is made to resemble a section of an old tree that has been cut down, with the immortal holding a book sitting on it. Two characters, *long cha*, 'dragon canoe',

are engraved at the tail end of the craft. Below the mouth of the cup is neatly inscribed in running script the couplet: 'To hold good wine for your own enjoyment, to float over the Milky Way and go on high. Written by Du Ben.' On the inside bottom of the canoe a poem in regular script is beautifully engraved:

> Being unrestrained, Li Bai could drink a
> hundred cups,
> And Old Liu Ling was ever seeking his
> intoxication;
> Only those who know the joy of wine
> Remain immortalized in this world when they
> die.

On the underside another inscription in regular script reads: 'the year *yi you* of the Zhi zheng era [equivalent to 1335] made by Zhu Bishan of Wei tang at the Hall of Everlasting Spring in Zhejiang for my children to keep'. Below is the seal of the maker.

Zhu Bishan drew his inspiration for the subject of this vessel from the legend of a celestial being who had flown to heaven in a canoe. Others have mistakenly interpreted it as relating to the story of Zhang Qian's search for the source of the Yellow River during the Han period, saying that Zhang had also flown to heaven in such a canoe.

This masterpiece in silver incorporates many elements of traditional Chinese painting as well as sculpture, and not only offers us an insight into Zhu Bishan's personal artistic achievements but also reflects the high standard of silver casting in the Yuan period.

75.銅招絲琺瑯番蓮花大碗　76.銅招絲琺瑯纏枝蓮觚

CLOISONNÉ ENAMEL
BOWL WITH GILT COPPER
FILIGREE AND LOTUS
PATTERN

mouth diameter 26.6 cm.
height 13.7 cm.
base diameter 13 cm.
illustration shows actual size
Ming dynasty, reign of
Xuan de

CLOISONNÉ ENAMEL GU
GOBLET WITH GILT
COPPER FILIGREE AND
INTERTWINING LOTUS
SPRAY PATTERN

actual size
mouth diameter 7.9 cm.
height 14.5 cm.
Ming dynasty, reign of Jing
tai

Although *cloisonné* wares were produced in great quantities during the Jing tai era of the Ming, giving rise to another common name for them, *Jing tai lan*, 'Jing tai blue', the craft can be traced back beyond this to the Yuan period. A poem entitled *Da shi ping*, 'On an Arabian vase', by the Yuan poet Wu Yuanying (died 1341) describes the material quality, size, colour, pattern as well as the bright, glossy and durable surface of the vase which is immediately recognizable as *cloisonné*. The poem also clearly states that the bowl came from Persia, demonstrating that the making of *cloisonné* was still a novelty in China at that time. Again, at the beginning of the Ming period, in his work *Ge gu yao lun*, *Criteria for judging antiquities*, Cao Minzhong described an 'Arabian vase' as having a body made of copper rendered polychromatic in the firing process after being coated with 'powders' or minerals in the section discussing the different kilns for firing porcelains. Craftsmen from Yunnan province who lived in Nanjing, he wrote, made a trade of this, producing items such as bottles, boxes, incense-burners and wine cups but that utensils produced in the imperial palace looked more refined and attractive. No *cloisonné* object still in existence bears a reign mark which precedes the Xuan de period. Thus it appears that some 100 years elapsed, between the date that Wu Yuanying wrote his poem and the Xuan de era of the Ming, before the technique reached its full maturity.

The Palace Museum possesses in its collections a number of *cloisonné* articles which bear the reign mark of Xuan de and the gilt decoration accords with that found on pieces produced during that period. They take the form of braziers, vases, boxes, bowls and so on. Most of them have a blue-glazed ground with red, yellow, white or green decorations within the spaces enclosed by the metal partition patterns. Some have white as the main colour, such as the bowl illustrated here, with red, yellow, blue and green flowers. A remarkable work of art of the Xuan de period, the fresh, bright colours, flowers in full bloom, and the vigorous pattern of leaves and tendrils comprise a simple yet powerful overall design. In the main, products of this period consisted of goblets and wine vessels and the like in imitation of ancient bronzes as well as porcelain bowls. The larger ones, more than a foot high, have strong, glazed surfaces inlaid with thick, smooth, gilded metal with a brilliant sheen.

The craft reached even greater heights of accomplishment during the Jing tai period. Among the products produced were archaistic wine vessels, pots, jars, tripods of up to one metre in height, and some *gu*, goblets, were even as tall as a man. At the same time new designs appeared on an ever increasing variety of objects such as flower vases, charcoal braziers, basins, flower pots, lamps, candlesticks and boxes. Although, in the main, Jing tai artefacts share the same colour schemes as Xuan de objects – light blue, sapphire blue, red, light grass-green, dark green, and white – yet Jing tai objects are more lustrous. On the other hand, new colours were added to the repertoire such as a glassy grape purple, rose pink and a kingfisher blue, somewhere between azure and sapphire blue, but brighter than the two. A good example which demonstrates such strong, firm colours as these is the goblet illustrated, which bears the mark of the Jing tai era. Small but heavy, with a finely polished surface and evenly and precisely laid metalwork, this goblet testifies to the progress made since the Xuan de period, and indicates the reasons why Jing tai *cloisonné* wares earned such a reputation.

Only a few objects bearing authenticated reign marks which are later than Jing tai are still in existence. Of those in the Palace Museum there is a tray with a Jia jing reign mark, and a four-footed incense burner in the shape of a *ding* tripod vessel with a polychrome design of dragons on a sapphire blue ground bearing the inscription 'made in the Wan li period of the great Ming'. The burner has an openwork enamel lid instead of the usual openwork, gilt copper lid which was an innovation of the period. There are also candleholders with red, white and yellow bud patterns on a pale green ground and burners with red, white and reddish-brown butterfly patterns. These patterns, as well as the pale green and reddish-brown colours mentioned above, were also innovations of the time.

Many quite outstanding Ming pieces bearing no reign marks at all were produced after the Jing tai period. To give one example, the Palace Museum possesses a pumpkin-shaped lampstand which is approximately life-size. The legs are wrought in gilt copper in the shape of a trailing stem and several pumpkin leaves similarly made in gilt copper serve as a lampholder on top. The colour of this artificial pumpkin is between yellowish-green and green, with yellow mottled leaves so vividly done that they might have been executed with an artist's brush. So far, no Jing tai object has been found which could boast such a comparable design. Some of the archaistic bronzes too bear anachronistic designs of flowers and birds which were also hitherto unseen. Others, also products of the Ming, have thin bodies and dull glazed surfaces.

In the early Qing period, a *cloisonné* studio was set up in the palace as a part of the Hall of Military Eminence and later incorporated into the Hall of Mental Cultivation. From the objects in the Museum, no great advances appear to have been made during the Kang xi period with respect to *cloisonné* enamel artefacts with copper filigree, but their thick, strong bodies and firm but rather lacklustre enamels put them on a pair with the products of official workshops of the Ming period. In fact, few objects with a Kang xi reign mark are found today. With the advent of the Qian long period, however, the craft reached its zenith alongside lacquer carving, silk weaving and embroidery as well as the art of the inlaying of semi-precious stones. First, the scope of the products was greatly increased. Apart from the traditional types, large-size objects such as screens, desks and chairs, beds and couches, along with smaller articles like brushholders, wine vessels, inkstone cases, book markers and caps for the rollers of scroll painting mounts, appeared as a vast array of domestic items for use or ornament.

Over and above these, pagodas and religious constructions of room height were made, and still stand in the temples of the Forbidden City and the Summer Palace resort in Chengde in the hills north of Beijing. As far as techniques were concerned, pink and black glazes had now come into use, though the grape purple glaze that had looked like translucent amethyst in the Ming period had turned to a greyish-purple. The mineral white had also become rather grey, and other colours had lost their glassy appearance. On the other hand, the bodies were just as thick and strong as previously, further progress is discernible in the technique of gilding and the finely wrought and densely distributed metal strip partitions now gave an impressive appearance to the objects.

77. 紫檀荷式大椅

RED SANDALWOOD
ARMCHAIR CARVED IN THE
FORM OF A LOTUS

height 115 cm.
width 84 cm.
Ming period

There appears to have been a complete absence of chairs in ancient China. A type of bed is known to have been used for the dual purposes of sleeping and sitting, otherwise people sat on mats on the ground. From the painting 'Night entertainment given by Han Xizai' by Gu Hong zhong (illustrated elsewhere in this volume) it can be seen that chairs and embroidered cushions were in existence during the period of the Five Dynasties. It is known that by the Song period they had come into general use, as exemplified by the number of terms referring to them, such as 'gold folding chair', 'silver folding chair', 'imperial whitewood armchair', 'sandalwood chair', 'bamboo chair', 'yellow silk armchair decorated with pearls'.

Though chairs were common in the early Southern Song period, they probably formed only part of the furniture arranged in reception rooms in the houses of great officials for entertaining visitors. When relaxing in the inner chambers even the highest official would as a rule sit on couches or beds. Although many types of chair existed during the Song and Yuan, none was made of red sandalwood, as this particular timber did not come into popular use before the Ming period. Red sandalwood chairs can be subdivided into several different types. The chair illustrated here may tentatively be termed a 'couch chair'; it is not one of a pair, as is common, but has been made as an individual item. When placed in the centre of a room in a palace, it could be partially enclosed by a screen and fans to act as a grand seat for the emperor. In ordinary houses or gardens it could be placed either behind a long writing table for a scholar or near the window to face the view outside. Armchairs like this occupied permanent places and could not easily be removed. They were also called 'celestial chairs' or 'meditation chairs' in the Ming period because, due to the width of the seat, the legs of the sitter could be drawn up so that he might sit, with ankles crossed, in a calm and composed attitude. Such chairs included a horizontal headrest at the top of the backrest to cushion the head, all of which is similar to the chair shown here. The red sandalwood armchair shown is covered with lotus flowers, leaves and stalks, except for the seat, which is left smooth. The headrest, ingeniously and unobtrusively carved in the form of a lotus leaf, is of superbly fine workmanship. Although the carving of lotus patterns on to furniture is usually of a high standard, this is an exceptional example in that the leaves, flowers, stems and roots are all executed so naturally that the chair itself almost becomes a lotus plant to which one ascends by means of a huge, flat lotus pad at the front. It resembles the technique of lacquer carving in the Yuan and Ming periods.

Apart from such sculptural and decorative qualities, this chair may be singled out from others which have come down to us from the Ming period for its other qualities. The timber selected is particularly strong and durable. Also, as a piece of furniture, it is well designed and, in terms of comfort, admirably fulfils the function for which it was conceived.

78. 黑光漆嵌螺鈿大案　79. 黑光漆嵌螺鈿盒

The earliest example of lacquer inlaid with mother-of-pearl to have been discovered to date is a red and black lacquer tray, excavated in 1964 from a tomb of the Western Zhou period at Pangjiagou, Luoyang, Henan province. A mirror of the Tang period, its back inlaid with mother-of-pearl, represents a step forward in the development of this art, but it was not until the early Yuan period that the technique was to be completely mastered. There is an example of the skill possessed by craftsmen of this time excavated from a site of the old Yuan capital in Beijing, in a fragment of a piece depicting the Guanghan Palace, which employs the technique of embedding thin slivers of mother-of-pearl into the lacquer. The use of thinner pieces of inlay represents an innovation derived from the practice of using thick pieces during the Tang and Song periods. The thick mother-of-pearl chips are either a jade or ivory white, while the thin slivers are an iridiscent blue with green, pale blue tinged with red or dark green tinged with blue. Of the two items illustrated, the long table utilizes thick (also called 'hard' due to their consistency) pieces of mother-of-pearl, while the box is inlaid with thin (similarly, also called 'soft') slivers.

In keeping with the most popular style during the Ming period, the four legs of the long black lacquer table are fixed at some distance in from the ends rather than at the four corners. Iridiscent mother-of-pearl inlays form five scale-covered dragons on the top, main surface. On the underside of the table top is the inscription *Da Ming Wan li nian zhi*, 'Made in the Wan li reign of the Great Ming dynasty'. Of all the tables in the Palace Museum this product of the palace workshop is the only one that bears the Wan li reign mark.

The lid of the rectangular black lacquer box illustrated is inlaid with thin mother-of-pearl to depict a scene of the paying of tribute, with some elements traced in gold. A three-arched bridge in the lower part of the picture is formed by different coloured mother-of-pearl pieces to give the appearance of being built with 'tiger-skin colour stones', examples of which are to be seen in the Forbidden City. Crossing the bridge a total of some twenty-seven men bear along their tribute gifts. Some drive an elephant, some lead a lion, some drag along a reluctant camel; two of them bear up a large wooden cage; others hold coral and pearls in their hands. It is also possible to discern the hook-nosed and bushy-bearded men in high hats from foreign tribute states. At the far end of the bridge the balustrade disappears and re-emerges back diagonally across the scene taking many more tribute-bearers to a hall outside which seventeen people, flanked by attendants, are lying prostrate on the ground, paying homage. Behind the hall are row upon row of palace buildings. In the sky above are swirling cloud patterns, delineated in gold, with three dragon heads made of mother-of-pearl appearing through them. The top of the picture is occupied by clumps of trees showing between mountains, the peaks of which are modelled with contour lines in cut powdered gold, leaving the black lacquer lines in reserve to describe the outlines. Other crags and rocks are built from mother-of-pearl either in piece or ground form, while some consist of slightly raised patches of reddish-brown lacquer, their tops defined in gold. Judging by the quality of the lacquer, the shape and compositional elements, the box is a product of the Kang xi reign of the Qing dynasty. The combination of 'soft' mother-of-pearl and gold produces a rich brilliance which is hard to match even in landscapes painted in the meticulous gold and green style.

height 6.8 cm.
length 40 cm.
width 34.1 cm.
Ming dynasty, reign of
Wan li
Qing period

80. 匏製瓶

BOTTLE GOURD WITH
GARLIC HEAD AND
DESIGNS OF CLOUD AND
LOTUS

height 23.8 cm.
mouth diameter 4.3 cm.
base diameter 6.8 cm.
illustration shows actual size
Qing dynasty, reign of
Kang xi

Pao qi, or 'bottle gourd ware', often called *hu lu qi*, is a uniquely Chinese art produced through the combined effort of nature and man. It is made by placing a mould over the young gourd and allowing it to grow into the desired shape. Although the final article may suggest otherwise, there is not even the smallest amount of carving involved in any part of its manufacture. Indeed, the natural growth surpasses anything that could be achieved in the medium by artifice or skill.

The art of *pao qi* has long been practised in China. A bottle gourd in the shape of a covered jar bearing a design of three groups of men, called the 'Eight ministers of the Tang gourd', is known to have been brought from China and deposited in the Hōryūji Temple, Japan. Also it is recorded that during the Ming period, bottle gourds decorated with patterns or written characters were popular as folk-art objects.

In the Qing period the official manufacture of gourd ware in the palace began during the reign of Kang xi. So far none of the gourds in the Museum has been found to possess a reign mark which predates this. In the 12th year of his reign (1747) the Qian long emperor composed a poem entitled 'Ode to a vase-gourd', *Yong hu lu qi*, relating how during the reign of Kang xi an order was issued to grow gourds. It said that *pao qi* could be produced by putting moulds over the young gourds which would mature into whatever shape was desired – a bowl, a jar, a plate or a box. Another poem by the Qian long emperor was written in praise of the gourd bowl produced by the Kang xi emperor himself. The poem describes how the latter had once grown gourds in his experimental plots for cultivating improved strains of rice in the Imperial West Gardens just outside the Forbidden City and that the gourd bowl, bearing on the bottom the inscription 'Made by the Kang xi emperor', now a century old (up to the year when Qian long wrote the poem), bore the venerable patina of age. Despite the relative simplicity of the method involved, very few gourds come out in perfect condition. For this reason they have always been highly prized.

A good many gourd dishes and bowls of the Kang xi reign period with their insides painted with black lacquer bear nothing more than bow-string patterns, that is, lines in ridged relief running down the contoured lines of the body, and the inscription 'For the appreciation of the Kang xi emperor' on the base. These were probably initial prototypes experimentally produced from simple test moulds. Known examples of later date – such as the lobed 'six-petalled bowl-gourd', a box with the Chinese character *shou*, 'longevity' and interlocking sprays of lotuses and an octagonal rushholder bearing a Tang poem – present quite a different appearance. They are beautiful both in shape and decoration. Illustrative of this type is the gourd-bottle shown here. The body is of the 'garlic bulb' type, in that the sectional lobing resembles the corms and the whole shape of the bulb with the top cut off. Lappets form the upper decoration with pendant scrollwork and the main design of stylized lotuses and scrolls on the body below. The embossed appearance of the decoration, combined with the recessed lines produced by the lobing, contrasts simply with the burnished chestnut brown of the smooth surface to produce an object of great rarity and beauty.

YOU TONG: RHINOCEROS
HORN *CHA BEI* WINE
VESSEL CARVED IN THE
FORM OF AN IMMORTAL
SITTING IN A HOLLOW
TREE TRUNK

length 27 cm.
width 11.7 cm.
Qing period

Ever since the period of the Song dynasty it had become common practice to collect small ornaments made from ivory, horn, bamboo, wood, gold or semi-precious stones for display on a desk, together with the implements of the scholar known as the 'four treasures of the study', which consisted of the writing brushes, inkcakes, paper and inkslab. During the Yuan and Ming such artefacts constantly appeared in ever more dazzling variety. The Qing period saw the emergence of a great many skilled men who distinguished themselves in while a group of maid-servants stand looking on. To make the figurines, trees and rockery stand out in keeping with a selected perspective, some parts are carved in deeper relief than others in a technique invented by the Three Zhus, referred to above, wherein the medium is divided into imaginary layers receding towards the centre of the object. Close elements, such as the players and stone table, are carved almost in the round, or three dimensions, while distant elements are left much lower, and carved deeper into the material. An additional device employed is the utilization of the diagonal of Xie An's arm as it points to the game board as if inquiring about an impending victory, backed up by the intensity of gaze on his and his friend's faces. Travelling up and back, the hands over the board and Xie An's arm add to the illusion of depth. Horsemen gallop out of the trees on the reverse side, one bearing the red flag of victory. The group of maids talking amongst themselves therefore unites the two scenes into one complete composition and story which is full of vigour and movement.

Huang Zhenxiao was a master craftsman from Guandong province. He was summoned into imperial service on the recommendation of the provincial governor. The brushholder bears the inscription 'Respectfully made by Huang [Zhenxiao], His Majesty's humble servant', and the period mark shows that it was made in the third year of the Qian long era, equivalent to 1738. As he began regular service in the *ya zuo*, 'ivory studio', in the fourth year of the Qian long era, 1739, the brushholder must have been executed as a sample submitted for the emperor's inspection shortly after he started his period of probation. Though Huang was a native of Guangdong province, his style bears no relation to the style currently prevalent there. Instead he adopted the technique of high relief, pioneered by the Jiading group.

The subject of the brushholder is the carefree life of fishermen living at the foot of a hill at the water's edge. The composition is built around the cylindrical body carved at the lowest level in the form of a precipitous cliff which acts as a backdrop to three main scenes. One of these consists of a boat sailing out of the reeds on the lake with a poem personally written by the Qian long emperor carved as if on to the cliff face; another represents five fishermen drinking wine under the pine trees. Huang's signature can be found on the lower part of this slope. Executed in high relief, using several imaginary layers of depth to achieve an effect close to three-dimensional sculpture by undercutting the nearer elements, the brushholder is close to perfection in its use of material. elaborate works. Typical of the period are the three containers shown here.

Traditionally held as a precious element in the Chinese pharmocopoeia, rhinoceros horn became all the more valuable after treatment by a master carver. You Tong, creator of this

horn cup, was born towards the end of the Ming period in the city of Wuxi, not far from Hangzhou. Good at carving rhinoceros horn, ivory and semi-precious stones, when he was a child his father borrowed a much treasured rhinoceros horn cup from a close relative so that he could appreciate its beauty for a time. It so happened that the You family had just acquired a new rhinoceros horn which You Tong took and immediately set about making an exact copy of the cup his father so admired. When finished there was no difference between the two except in the colour. In order to reproduce the colour of the original, the boy dyed the replica with the juice of the crushed blossoms of the garden balsam in the same way as fingernails used to be painted. When he put the cups before his relative, the owner was unable to distinguish the new from the old one. As a consequence of his early abilities and achievements he was subsequently nicknamed 'Rhinoceros Cup You'. During the reign of Kang xi he was enlisted as a craftsman to serve in the palace. After he returned home in his old age, he told others that he had carved the prose-poem verse *Chi bi fu*, 'The red cliff', on a pearl smaller than a longan, which demonstrates how much further his skills had progressed in his later years.

The *cha bei*, 'canoe' or 'raft cup' vessel for wine drinking shown is one of You Tong's masterpieces. It may be compared with Zhu Bishan's silver vessel (illustrated elsewhere in this volume) in choice of subject and the use of such elements as the immortal sitting on an old gnarled tree trunk which acts as a boat, but there the similarity ends.

The maker of the 'Boxwood brushholder', Wu Zhifan, also called Luzhen, was a renowned bamboo carver of the Qing period. Before the Ming, no craftsmen had gained a professional reputation solely from their bamboo carving. It was not until after the middle period of the Ming that Zhu Sanglin, Zhu Xiaosong and Zhu Sansong, known as the Three Zhus, from Jiading xian and Li Yao and Pu Cheng from Jinling (now Nanjing) respectively, came to the fore as master bamboo carvers. They formed the Jiading and Jinling groups of craftsmen, with Wu Zhifan remembered as the greatest of the Jiading group after the death of Zhu Sansong. Most of his bamboo carvings bear the reign marks of the early Kang xi period, when he was at the height of his creative activity. The brushholder shown here is carved from boxwood, the technique used being the same as that employed for bamboo. The techniques of bamboo carving fall into two general categories: one is surface carving, such as used for brushholders, folding fan ribs, arm rests and the like; the other is sculpting in the round in order to produce three-dimensional figures as well as the adaptation of the natural shapes of bamboo roots. The first category consists of incised carving and relief carving, both of which comprise a great many particular techniques. This brushholder belongs to the type which uses high relief. The scene shown at close range depicts Xie An, an assistant grand tutor of the Jin period, playing *wei qi*, a board game, with a friend. Someone sits at Xie An's shoulder watching the progress of play, with the visitor who has come to play *wei qi*,

HUANG ZHENXIAO: IVORY
BRUSHHOLDER SHOWING
THE HAPPY LIFE OF
FISHERMEN

height 12 cm.
mouth diameter 9.9 cm.
Qing dynasty, 3rd year of
the Qian long reign,
equivalent to 1738

84.大禹治水圖玉山

CARVED JADE MOUNTAIN
DEPICTING THE STORY OF
YU THE GREAT
REGULATING RIVERS AND
WATERCOURSES

height 224 cm.
width 96 cm.
approximate weight 5,330 kg
Qing dynasty, 52nd year of
the Qian long reign period,
equivalent to 1787

This monumental sculpture in green and white jade, hewn from deposits in Xinjiang in west China, rests upon a mountain-shaped pedestal cast in bronze that has been given an old, patinated finish and inlaid with gold filigree. With this backdrop of venerable crags, ancient trees and thickets and streams issuing forth from deep crevices and gullies, Yu the Great himself is seen half way up the mountain undertaking the great task at hand while his men work with hammers, spades and levers in an attempt to chisel out a course for the water to flow down and away. The lively scene illustrating the astounding feats of Yu the Great was carved out of the stone, taking into account and utilizing to the full its natural shape which involved a great deal of artistic ingenuity and effort.

Its back is inscribed with a poem composed by the Qian long emperor in the first lunar month of the 53nd year of his reign, equivalent to 1788. The poem, which eulogizes the feats of Yu the Great in regulating the rivers and waters, describes how, in order to bring the catastrophic floods under control, he travelled the length and breadth of the country, tunnelling through mountains and dredging rivers so that there would be no repetition of such disasters and his beneficence would live through all eternity. The emperor continues that to have split such a magnificent stone open for carving into such petty objects as wine vessels and the like would have been a piteous waste. On the other hand, to translate a famous painting of Yu the Great controlling the floods, by a Song artist and in the imperial collection, into a carved jade sculpture would be to construct an indestructable monument. And an inscription by no one but the Son of Heaven himself (the title assumed by Chinese emperors) would be worthy of such a monolith. Including the quarrying, the stone took ten years to complete with the expenditure of vast amounts of manpower and materials. The poem also warns posterity against similar extravagance to gratify its passion for treasures and riches. We are also told in this eulogy about the ways and means involved in its manufacture. According to old records, in order to transport huge blocks of stone from Xinjiang to Beijing it was necessary to build a specially designed gigantic wagon with a shaft 35 feet long. The wagon was drawn by one hundred-odd horses assisted by one thousand labourers who pushed the vehicle from behind. On the way, paths had to be cut through mountains and bridges built across rivers. In winter, water was splashed over the road which froze, so that the stone could be easily slid over the icy surface. In this way it was possible to cover five or six *li* a day. Based on this it has been calculated that it must have taken at least three years to cover the distance of nearly 11,100 *li* (approximately 5,520 km.) between Hotian, in Xinjiang, and Beijing. Once the stone had reached Beijing, the Qian long emperor selected the painting of Yu the Great from the *Shi qu catalogue* as the one on which the carving should be based. He handed the picture to Shu Wen, the minister in charge of the imperial household, bidding him to charge Jia Quan with the task of transforming the picture into three dimensions. In the 2nd lunar month of the 46th year of his reign (1781) a wax model of the jade mountain and four scale drawings of each side of the jade mountain were produced. Having been approved by the emperor in the 5th lunar month of the same year, the huge stone was shipped along the Grand Canal to Yangzhou where an official responsible for the production and distribution of salt was empowered to select qualified jade carvers to copy the models provided. Further wooden models were subsequently made for fear that the wax ones might melt in the heat of the southern summers. Work started in the 9th lunar month of the 46th year and was completed in the 6th lunar month of the 52nd year of the Qian long reign period (1787), a total of seven years and eight months. That same year the jade mountain was transported by the route it had come back to Beijing and was installed in the Palace of Tranquil Longevity in the Forbidden City. In the first lunar month of the next year an order was issued to carve the emperor's poem on the back.

No reliable or accurate data concerning the man-hours and money spent on this jade mountain are now available, but from the expenses involved in the manufacture of another jade mountain, 'Travelling in autumn mountains', a rough esti-mate can be made. The Yu the Great mountain was four times the size of this other. Thus, the final expenditure on the former can be calculated at about 150,000 working days and the cost in excess of 15,000 *taels* (1 *tael* = 50 gm) of silver. The figures only take account of the actual manufacturing process, but exclude the inscribing of the poem, quarrying and transportation. Payment would have been made in the form of grain which amounts to 16,000–17,000 *dan* (1 *dan* = approximately 60 kg) of rice calculated at current price levels. Total expenditure for this one jade carving would be several times these figures if the excluded items of transportation and so on were taken into account. As a unique feat in the history of the art of jade working, the manufacture of this jade mountain is without doubt a tribute to the great talent of the various Chinese nationalities who were involved.

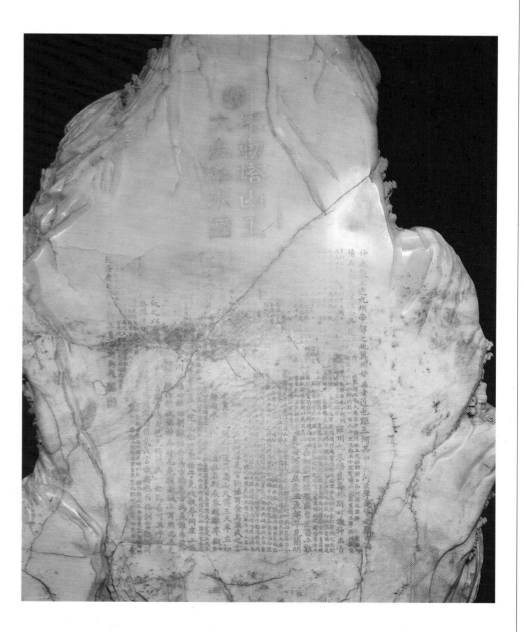

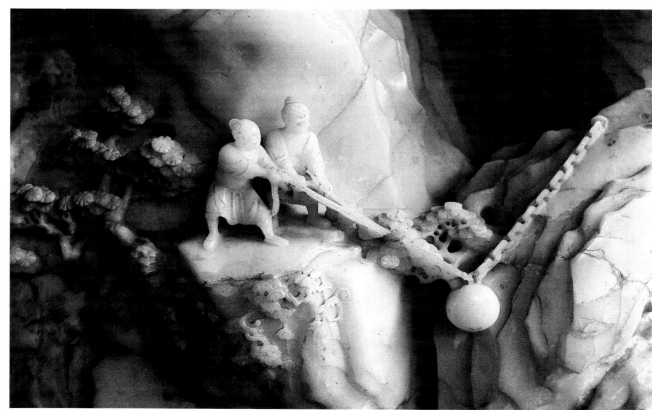

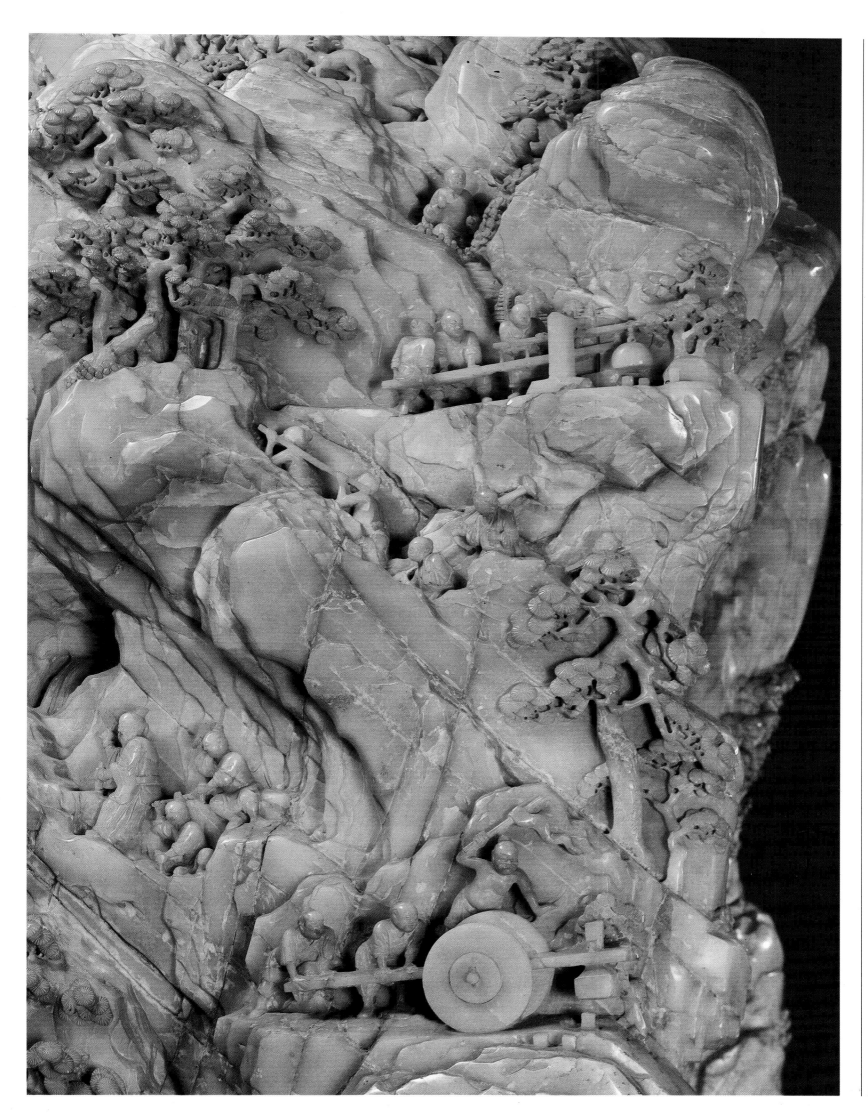

85. 白玉桐陰仕女圖　86. 翠竹盆景

JADE GARDEN SCENE

height 15.5 cm.
length 25 cm.
width 10.8 cm.
Qing period

This composition, showing two sides of a garden gate, is carved from a lump of jade by making optimum use of its natural shape. The underside is inscribed with a poem and note by the Qian long emperor to the effect that it was carved from what was left of a piece of jade after the body of a bowl had been cut out of it, and that it was thanks to the superior quality of the jade that the carvers decided to make good use of it by having it elaborately designed and carved into a beautiful object. In the centre is a circular entrance surrounding two folding doors, the middle section being left ajar. Two girls face each other, one standing outside the entrance with flowers in her hand, the other standing inside holding a box. The reddish-brown surface of the jade is carved as Tong trees, the broad leaves of the banana plantain and rocks, and the inner white part, on the reverse side, into tables and stools.

During the Qing dynasty the palace studios worked together to produce *pen jing*, miniature potted landscapes, using a combination of materials, many of which are of the highest order in terms of design, materials used and manufacture. They began to specialize in this kind of product after the reign of Yong zheng. Hai wang, who became minister in charge of the imperial household, was the chief planning officer with many other designers as well as carvers below him to carry out the actual work. Such miniature landscapes or artificial flower arrangements in vases are constructed with particular categories of painting in mind – that is, 'bamboo and rocks' and 'vases of flowers' – and make use of the natural colours present in the materials, usually semi-precious stones. For example, when a *pen jing* of garden balsam was being made, ox horn was usually the material employed, as its natural translucent, veined appearance, as if full of water, reproduced exactly the characteristic stems of this plant. The craftsman most well known for miniature landscapes was She Tianzhang, a talented jade carver from Suzhou.

A jointly made product, the miniature potted landscape illustrated here, is set into a gilt brass bowl decorated with prunus flowers on a ground of cracked ice. It represents old bamboos with their tops cut off and tender leaves shooting forth from their stems. The well-arranged sturdy stems show to the full the fine qualities of the jadeite. Set off by the foliated metal bowl, the miniature landscape is a colourful and unusual desk ornament.

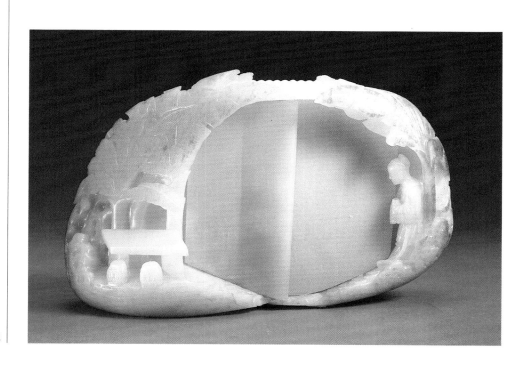

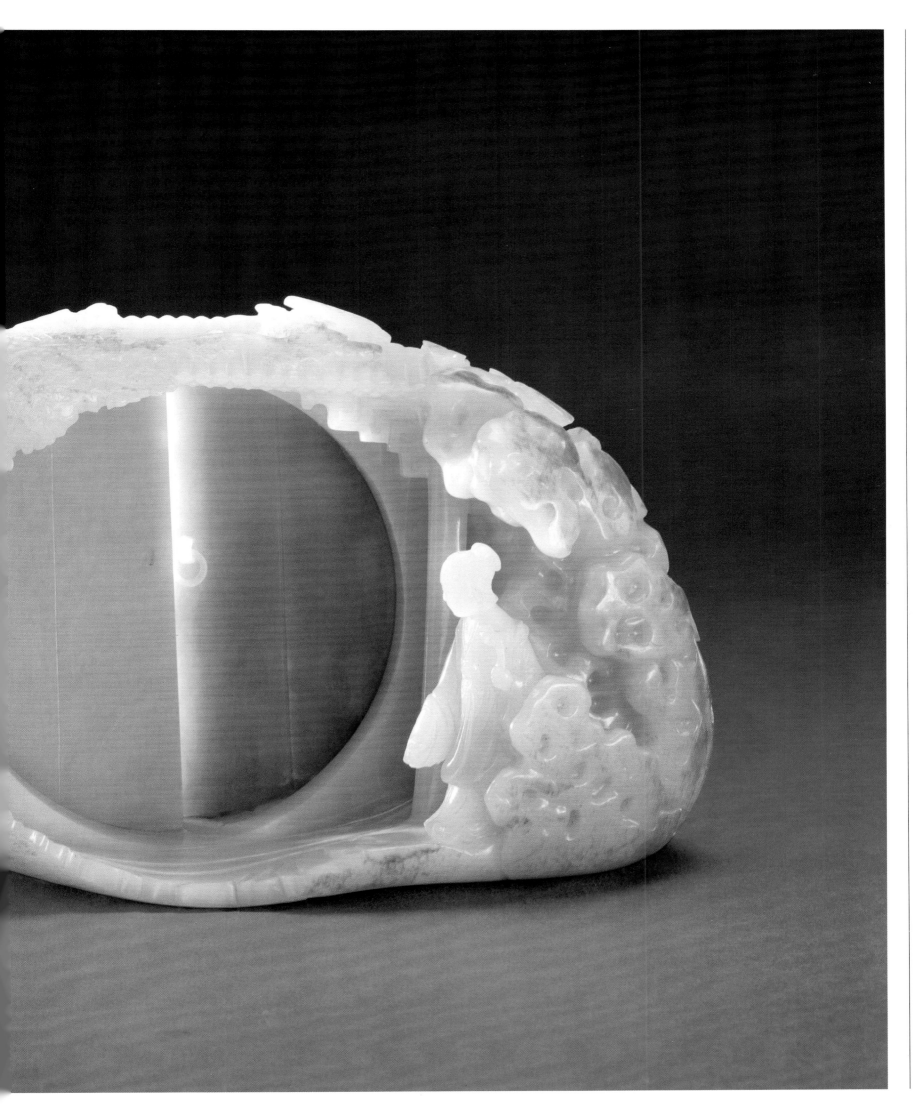

PEN JING MINIATURE
POTTED LANDSCAPE WITH
JADE BAMBOO AND
ROCKERY IN A COPPER
FILIGREE BOWL
total height 25 cm.
bowl height 6 cm.
Qing period

87. 碧玉仿古觥

DARK GREEN NEPHRITE
VESSEL IN THE FORM OF
AN ARCHAISTIC BRONZE
VESSEL, *GUANG*

height 18.7 cm.
base 7.7 × 4.2 cm.
Qing dynasty, reign of
Qiang long

During the Qing period the jade workshop, *yu zuo*, of the imperial manufacturing department attached to the Yang xin dian, Hall of Mental Cultivation, not only used jade as its main material but any hard stone which needed the specialist skills it encompassed, such as agate, tourmaline and Burma jadeite, for example, as well as naturally occurring minerals, and manufactured glass of every description. At that time many places boasted skilled jade carvers, especially around Suzhou, Yangzhou and other areas inhabited by the Hui (Moslem) people, in which there was a high concentration of expertise. Their products fetched high prices in the marketplaces where there was great rivalry among the jade carvers to produce increasingly unusual pieces in response to the sharp commercial competition spurred by the high prices offered by the rich salt merchants. It was during the reign of Qian long that a particularly thriving market in elaborately reticulated, or pierced, jade objects grew up in Yangzhou.

The authorities in charge of the production of salt and textiles once met with a rebuke sent down by the Qian long emperor when they presented some of this kind of carved jade to him. On the 14th day of the 8th lunar month of the 59th year of his reign (1794), an imperial edict was issued to them, prohibiting the manufacture of such wasteful carvings on the grounds that reticulated jade vessels were of no use as utensils for practical use; it was further added that other jade carvings with over-abundant openwork deprived the jade of its natural beauty, and that much jade had already been wasted as a result of the widespread copying of this practice even as far as the more remote Hui areas.

The criticism of current abuses in the art of jade carving struck home and the production by the imperial workshop of such articles as the nephrite vessel shown here went some way in restoring more basic styles in direct response to the edict. Carved in the form of an archaistic bronze, *guang*, wine vessel, bearing a design which includes the *tao tie*, glutton, monster mask, the mottled green jade imitates the much-admired patina produced by the exposure of the constituent metals of authentic ancient bronzes to oxidizing conditions. As the artisans, handsomely remunerated by the palace workshop, were specially selected from all parts of the country and guided by expert designers, the products they turned out were of the highest quality and occupy an important place in the history of the decorative and minor arts.

88. 銅胎畫琺瑯花鳥瓶

CLOISONNÉ VASE WITH
DECORATION OF BIRDS
AND FLOWERS

height 21.8 cm.
mouth diameter 3.5 cm.
belly diameter 13.3 cm.
base diameter 7.9 cm.
Qing dynasty, reign of Qian
long

The art of *cloisonné* enamelling reached unprecedented heights during the reigns of Kang xi, Yong zheng and Qian long of the Qing dynasty. During the reign of Yong zheng, the palace workshop succeeded in developing nine new coloured enamels entirely different from those which had originally been imported and adopted for use from the West. Subsequently a further nine were introduced, bringing the grand total to thirty-six.

At that time *cloisonné* was produced in Guangdong, Yangzhou and Beijing, but Beijing boasted no privately run workshops besides the one established and run by the court, called *fa lang zuo*, during the three reigns mentioned above. The imperial studio recruited not only the best artisans from Guangdong province and Jiangnan area but also potters from Jiangxi province and painters from the imperial art academy. Consequently *cloisonné* production flourished during these three reigns.

Articles bearing a Kang xi reign mark are distinguished not by their lustre, but by their smoothness and detail. Among the products are, for example, small vases decorated with finely delineated birds and flowers on a white ground, dishes, bowls, flower bowls and the like artistically decorated with flower patterns. Apart from the traditional vases, jars, dishes and bowls, new products appeared during the reign of Yong zheng such as hat stands and snuff bottles; and new designs included a black ground, the theme of one hundred flowers and circular patterns. During the reign of Qian long the range was greatly extended to include large palace furnishings and large objects for practical use, such as screens, to the smallest objects such as smoking sets, for example. There seemed to be no item which did not lend itself to this technique. In addition to traditional decoration, those found on porcelain, lacquerware and textiles and bronzes were absorbed to produce innovative designs. Figures, landscape or flowers set off by a fine-patterned ground found a place alongside more traditional schemes. Landscapes painted in blue or red on a white ground were not uncommon and the amalgamation and overlapping of different decorative elements on one piece were also popular. Some of the coloured glazes are somewhat flat and dull while others have a glassy appearance. The rocks, bird and flowers shine magnificently through the hard shiny surface of the body, a perfect balance to its solid, imposing shape.

89.百寶嵌花果紫檀盒　90.百寶嵌花卉漆掛屏

BAI BAO QIAN RED
SANDALWOOD CARVED
BOX INLAID WITH
SEMI-PRECIOUS STONES
AND OTHER RARE
MATERIALS

6 × 22 × 27.5 cm.
Qing dynasty, reign of Qian
long

The art of *bai bao qian* has a long history in China. According to written records, it can be traced back to the Han period. The three *bai bao qian* articles shown here, however, were made according to methods which originated from the Ming dynasty. Basic materials used include semi-precious stones, pearls, coral, nephrite, Burma jadeite, rock crystal, agate, hawksbill turtle shell, lapis lazuli, turquoise, mother-of-pearl, ivory, beeswax and agaloch eaglewood which are cut into shapes and set into a suitable medium such as sandalwood or lacquer to form decorative compositions. Articles constructed using these two common materials – wood and lacquer in particular – such as screens, tables, chairs, window frames, bookshelves, pen-racks, inkstone cases and bookcases, presented surfaces suitable for this type of decoration. This process began with Zhou Zhu during the reign of Jia jing in the Ming dynasty which gave rise to the name by which it is known, the 'Zhou method of manufacture', *Zhou zhi*, a synonym for the art of *bai bao qian*. During the Qing, Wang Guochen and Lu Yingzhi were regarded as the most gifted exponents of the art.

The inlays of *bai bao qian* may be flush with or raised above the main surface or in low relief. The lacquer hanging screens and carved sandalwood box shown here are excellent pieces belonging to the first type and were made during the reign of Qian long. The frames of the pair of hanging screens are decorated with a border of inlaid ivory and their blue lacquer surfaces inlaid with a design of prunus, or plum, trees and blossom, one white the other pink. The stump, branches and twigs are carved from a kind of wood whose natural texture and grain bears a close resemblance to gnarled tree bark. The white prunus blossoms are cut from white jade and the pink ones from tourmaline. A red camellia gleaming against the white prunus has flowers made of carnelian and leaves made of dark green nephrite. Orchids with leaves made of green nephrite have flowers of light coloured jade and ruby centres. The rocky ground of both compositions is made of malachite and the rock protruding below the white prunus of streaked grey jade. Of all the materials used, tourmaline was the most

costly, each square inch costing nearly one thousand *taels* of silver at the time. Although the two compositions are constructed according to painting techniques, the effect is quite different and the use to which they are put underlines the fact. In a heavily decorated Qing period room, or hall, the effect of a traditional ink painting would be quite lost, whereas the relatively more powerful decorative effect of hanging screens, such as the two in question, would be entirely in keeping with their surroundings.

The rectangular and round-cornered red sandalwood carved box is made of red sandalwood of the best quality. The design inlaid on the lid consists of a root and a seedpod of the lotus, a white and yellow chrysanthemum, cotton rose hibiscus, orchids, grapes, haws and bamboo leaves. As with the screens, the composition once again is based on another type of painting category and similarly provides a contrast to brush, ink and colours. The excellence of the craftsmanship involved is demonstrated in the choice of materials to depict the lotus root. Although the main body is made mostly of white jade, the depth and space of the holes is perfectly described by the use of mother-of-pearl. Despite their both being white in colour the subtle contrast between their reflective qualities brings out the difference between the flesh of the root and its moist, glistening surface. Similarly, the contrasting greens of the seedpod and the leaves of the chrysanthemum are represented with interesting effect by nephrite and malachite. The use of green jade for the orchids and carnelian for the haws bring out the natural qualities of both.

BAI BAO QIAN LACQUER
HANGING SCREENS
INLAID WITH
SEMI-PRECIOUS STONES
AND OTHER RARE
MATERIALS

64.5 × 98 cm.
Qing dynasty, reign of Qian
long

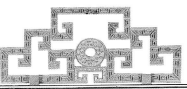

SILK
TEXTILES 織繡

SILK TEXTILES

China is the birthplace of silk. The use of silk thread obtained from cocoons dates back to primitive times more than 5,000 years ago. Chinese archaeologists have discovered cocoons and artefacts made of pottery, stone and bone bearing designs of silkworms and chrysalises at neolithic sites in Shanxi, Hebei, Henan, Liaoning, Jiangsu, and Yuyao in Zhejiang. In 1958 archaeologists unearthed in the neolithic sites at Qianshanyang near Wuxing in Zhejiang province a kind of thin silk with as many as forty-eight threads to the square centimetre. All this testifies to the long history of Chinese silk making.

That figured silk weaving had already entered its first phase in the Shang period is proven by a bronze halberd of Shang date which shows the imprinted 'ghost' of some silk textile with a spiral decorative pattern, unearthed at Anyang, Henan province, the site of the last Shang capital. It is now in the collection of the Museum of Far Eastern Antiquities, Stockholm. Further proof is to be found in a green nephrite *ge* halberd bearing traces of silk with the rectilinear spirals of the *lei wen* 'thunder' pattern, now in the Palace Museum. By the time of the Zhou dynasty, when silk weaving and embroidery had become quite highly developed crafts, the court commissioned special officials and established specialist workshops to oversee the management and production of silk. Throughout the period of the Warring States, when varieties of silk products increased, each boasted its own special silk products. High quality silks became indispensable gifts when feudal princes paid tribute to the Son of Heaven, the king or prince who assumed a divine mandate to rule, or on other formal occasions between themselves. Of the embroidered brocades excavated from the tombs of the state of Chu at the Martyrs' Park and at Zuojiatang in Changsha, Hunan province, at Changtaiguan in Xinyang, Henan province, and in the Baling Mountains in Jingzhou, Hubei province, some of the silk textiles were found glued to the surfaces of the inner coffins as decoration. Some were used as clothing and bedding, and many as funerary objects buried underground in complete bolts. The woven brocade of the Warring States' period unearthed at Jingzhou is of extremely fine texture with an elegant blending of colours, its beautiful surface being covered with alternating and overlapping designs of dragons and phoenixes. The brocades excavated in Zuojiatang, Changsha, are rich in their variety of weave patterns.

Several special techniques which were to become widespread were already in use. The designs embroidered on the silk products discovered at Changsha and Jingzhou display a stunning array of flying dragons, dancing phoenixes, fierce looking tigers and animals symbolic of good fortune amidst the intertwined design of branches, flowers and grasses. The forms and themes of these patterns resemble the phoenixes or birds embroidered on the surface of a saddle blanket made of Chinese silk that was discovered in the 1960s at Pazyryk in the Altai region of Southern Siberia in a fifth-century tomb of the chieftain of a nomadic tribe. During the early Qin period Chinese silk was transported northward and exchanged for battle horses with the nomadic tribes there. Chinese silk and embroideries excavated in Siberia provide sufficient evidence that Chinese silk and embroideries were shipped to Europe by way of the Central Asian steppes and the grasslands in the North as early as the fifth century BC. When in 138 BC Zhang Qian, envoy of the Western Han emperor Wu di, set out to explore the regions to the west of the empire he opened up two great and significant routes. One travelled north and the other south of the Tarim Basin but they were interconnected and linked China with her western neighbours and beyond. Thereafter, Chinese silk began to flow into Europe in a continuous stream, contributing enormously to the commercial and cultural exchanges between the East and the West. China came to be known as the 'Silk Country', the Chinese being called *seres* or *serices* by the Romans. The route leading from the northwest of China to the West came to be known as the 'Silk Route'.

From the Han to the Tang periods and thereafter, as Chinese silk products increased in variety improvements in techniques continued unabated. For example, one type of Han brocade bore raised velvet-like patterns formed out of the warp brocades which were capable of forming highly complex but richly coloured designs of mountains, clouds and animals. Craftsmen of the Tang period also created new varieties of silk textiles such as those which made use of different coloured warp threads. Perhaps the most outstanding were the woven silk tapestries, *ke si*, which were characterized by ingenious pictorial designs and brilliant colours.

In the Song period the technique of brocade weaving was further improved in the separation of patterned areas away from the basic material. The application of a new technique of using tiny bobbins to partially weave colourful designs in certain areas succeeded in throwing the patterns up from their brocade ground. As a result, the designs became more distinct and their colours more beautiful. This period also marked the introduction of Song brocades with their naturalistic and realistic motifs and designs. The best known kinds of brocade belonging to this category were those with *ru yi* and peony patterns, day lilies and one hundred flowers chasing the dragon, peacocks among flowers and stylized written characters with auspicious meanings. All these classical examples of the Song period are renowned for their realistic and lively depiction of nature. Also celebrated for their elegance and beauty, they were eagerly copied in later generations. In fact, the popular brocade referred to as 'Song-style brocade', produced in Suzhou during the Ming and Qing periods, evolved from it. The arts of *ke si* woven silk tapestry and embroidery had been so polished during the Song that they were not only able to imitate the meticulous style practised by court painters to perfection, but also surpass the original with their realism and sheen. *Ke si* is a uniquely Chinese method of weaving in areas of silk colour after the construction of the warp and lent itself particularly to the reproduction of Chinese paintings. Historical records show that Song embroidery employed a wide variety of stitches and used silk threads thinner than a human hair. Artists like Zhu Kerou, Shen Zifan and Wu Xu emerged as masters in the art of *ke si*.

The period of the Yuan dynasty is considered to have been the time that saw the height of the development in the use of gold and silver thread. The *na shi shi* which the Yuan rulers were so fond of was in fact brocade woven with gold threads, which had patterns of unusual beauty. In the Ming and Qing periods, the three major silk manufacturing centres of Nanjing (Nanking), Suzhou and Hangzhou produced a rich variety of sumptuous and high quality silk products including the various brocades with gold thread and Song-style brocade as well as satins decorated with gold and incorporating peacock feathers. Their varieties were innumerable.

Satin was a new silk product that emerged during the Song and Yuan periods. It continued to be made throughout the Ming and Qing periods in a great number of varieties which served utilitarian as well as decorative purposes. Satins with flowered designs were used for clothing, upholstery and curtains. When gold, silver or peacock feathers were incorporated into its decoration, satin became an even more sumptuous and costly textile.

During the Ming and Qing periods large-scale pictures of great complexity and intricacy were constantly produced by means of the *ke si* method and while the craftsmanship remained superb there were bold developments in the usage of colours. In order to intensify the artistic effects of painting, details were added, in embroidery and, in some cases, a brush and pigments were used. Such embroidered pictures began to make an appearance as commodities for sale in the large cities during the Ming period. During the Chong zhen reign of the Ming dynasty, Han Ximeng, who lived in Shanghai, successfully reproduced paintings and calligraphy by famous artists in embroidery. Known as 'Gu embroidery', from her husband's family name which was Gu, her works were celebrated for their exquisite appearance and extraordinary craftsmanship. The twisted silk Lu embroidery produced in Shandong province, which formed a sharp contrast to the Gu embroidery generally used coloured double-thread to embroider designs on satin with damask patterning, producing an impression of decorum and simplicity. In the north of China twisted silk was also popularly used to stitch designs all over thin gauze grounds. Large quantities of silk textiles with embroidery using this and the wrapped gold and silver thread methods were discovered in Ding ling, tomb of the Wan li emperor and his two empresses, one of the Ming tombs situated in the hills outside Beijing.

During the Qing period, most of the embroidered items used by the court were designed by the court artists of the Ru yi guan and then made up according to the specifications supplied to the workshops of the three southern textile centres administered by the court. The works thus produced were a combination of beauty and skill. At the same time, many centres for local embroidery sprang up, where items were produced by private individuals with the aim of earning some money for themselves. The most famous of these included the 'capital', or Peking, embroidery centred on Beijing, 'Suzhou embroidery', 'Shu embroidery', 'Yue embroidery' and 'Xiang embroidery', centred around Chengdu, Sichuan province, Guangzhou, Guangdong province, and Changsha, Hunan province, each characterized by its special local features. They were subsequently called 'the four most famous embroideries in China'.

'Suzhou embroidery' developed the inherited traditions of the embroidered pictures of the Song period picture, as it still does to this day, in which the needle is substituted for the brush, greatly expanding the possibilities and repertoire of needlework. Skills in this area were brought to such a standard that the stitches themselves are not apparent at all and their arrangement so natural as to produce a smooth, even surface. The method of shading is employed in blending colours which involves the use of similar colours or pastel shades to achieve a colour scheme that is both elegant and tranquil. In addition, an innovative technique peculiar to this area was introduced called 'double sided', or reversible, in which identical designs are produced on both sides of the textile and, indeed, further to that, the front and back of objects, with stitches concealed, as they would appear in life are the pride of embroidery institutes there today.

'Shu embroidery', practised in Sichuan province, became one of the most famous commercially produced silk embroideries by assimilating the best points of 'Gu embroidery' of the Ming period. These privately produced items are known for their rich and meticulous designs, brilliant colours and highly decorative stitches.

'Yue embroidery', also called 'Guang embroidery', from the names of Guangdong and Guangxi provinces, has well thought out designs and vivid images. The simple and precisely executed stitches cause the threads to overlap one another and stand out from the ground. Its lively designs feature sumptuous and fresh colour schemes and lustrous surfaces. Peacock feather and twisted gold threads are frequently used to enhance the effect.

'Xiang embroidery', produced around Changsha in Hunan, uses especially thin silk thread, which is rubbed clean with bamboo paper after being steamed in a solution made from legume kernels in order to prevent the silk from becoming hairy. As a result, the silk thread is finer, more lustrous and smoother than human hair and that is why embroidered works of this kind were once called *yang mao xi xiu*, 'threads as fine as a single sheeps' hair'. 'Xiang embroidery' aims to reproduce exactly the original and natural colours of the subjects it depicts. In technique, its stitches embody some of the features of 'Suzhou embroidery', in which the different light effects produced by the sheen of the threads reproduces the light and dark and modelled areas of a painting.

The long history of Chinese woven and embroidered textiles reflects the brilliance of the arts and civilizations of East Asia. Especially rich in textiles of every description, the ten outstanding examples from the Museum's collections have been selected as representing a particular variety or as a work which embodies rare skills to be found nowhere else in the world.

91.毬路雙鳥紋錦袷袍

LINED POLYCHROME
BROCADE ROBE, *JIA PAO*

Polychrome figured weave
length 138 cm.
width across shoulders, cuff
to cuff, 194 cm.
width of cuff 15 cm.
hem 81 cm.
Northern Song period

Brocade is one of China's most celebrated traditional woven silk textiles; it can be traced as far back as the Western Zhou period, over 2,500 years ago. According to archaeological findings, the designs of brocades prior to the Tang dynasty were produced by the warps, which led to the name warp-faced pattern brocade. From the early Tang, however, designs began to be produced using the wefts. So-called 'weft brocade' gradually replaced 'warp brocade'.

This lined robe made of 'weft brocade' was excavated from a tomb along the ancient Silk Route in Xiangjiang in the far west of China. A wide panel wraps over the opposite side down the front. The sleeves are comparatively narrow and there is an opening up the seam at the back. The surface is covered with the *qiu lu* pattern surrounding twin bird motifs while the lining is made of plain silk. The edging of the coat is of brocade with a design of mandarin ducks in circles of flowers; the cuffs, however, have a pattern of repeated twin sparrows on balustrades, also in brocade. All these borders were originally edged with sheepskin but this had all but disappeared by the time the robe was excavated.

The warp threads of the material are yellow and the wefts light yellow, black, yellowish green and white. The surface pattern is formed by the wefts as they float over three warp threads, producing the familiar diagonal of the twill weave. A basic pattern of large, interconnected, repeated rings or circles was among the most popular during the Song and known as *qiu lu*, 'circular paths'; within each of these decorated circles are two birds, standing back to back, with upstretched heads and outstretched wings, pointing backwards, as if about to fly. A stylized flowering tree stands erect behind them. Each large ring is filled with a 'coin' pattern bordered on either side with 'strings of pearls' deriving from Persia. At the tangent of each circle are smaller, overlapping roundels containing a design of alternately four leaves and four birds edged by the same strings of beads. Persian influence, also evident in the latter, blends with Chinese elements to produce a harmonious, uniquely Chinese style. Mandarin ducks fly in and out of the scrolls of flowers within circles which decorate the brocade-bound edging of the collar, and down the front and round the bottom edges of the garment, while symmetrical flowers and leaves fill the ground of these outer circles. This was also a popular style during the Tang and Song periods. Designs of a pair of birds on balustrades covering the wide cuff attached to the sleeves were also popular decorative themes after the Tang.

When unearthed, this brocade robe was found on a male mummy of what was assumed to be a Cossack general, 1.9 metres tall, whose head was wrapped in plain white silk. The robe is 62 centimetres shorter than the overall height of the mummy. This corresponds with the relative height to length of garments on a figurine discovered of a person from China's borderlands, as fixed by the dress regulations observed since Tang. In 'The imperial sedan', by the Tang painter Yan Liben, illustrated elsewhere in this volume, the garment worn by the Tibetan envoy bears a close resemblance to the present coat both in style and decorative themes and motifs.

Silks produced in China specially for export to countries to the west often adopted designs customarily used by the people there. For example, a brocade known as *Hu wang jin* excavated in Turfan, also in Xinjiang, of the period of the Northern dynasties, has designs of a foreign king leading a camel within a pattern of strings of pearls. Designs showing two tribesmen from this region drinking wine, again surrounded by the same bead patterns on a woven textile called the 'Drunkards' brocade', all of which belongs to this group of textiles. The western arts also exerted their influence on the Chinese arts through commerce and the double-layered brocade robe shown is a very good example of the economic and cultural exchanges which took place between China and her western neighbours. Very few examples of Song garments woven in brocade have been preserved as well as the one illustrated. It is therefore an invaluable primary source for the study of the techniques of brocade weaving and the decorative patterns of the Song period as well as for the dress, fashions and styles of the national minorities in China.

92. 青碧山水圖軸

SHEN ZIFAN: *KE SI*
WOVEN SILK TAPESTRY.
LANDSCAPE IN THE BLUE
AND GREEN STYLE

Hanging scroll
88.5 × 37 cm.
Southern Song period

Ke si refers to a particular kind of silk tapestry-woven textile, completely different in its processing manufacture from brocades and embroidered textiles. In the case of the latter, silk thread is sewn into a ready-made piece of silk fabric to produce designs and motifs which stand up above the main surface. However, the designs of *ke si* remain flush with their background. Although both *ke si* and brocade have designs produced by the interweaving of warps and wefts, the patterns on brocade are woven through complicated and varying arrangements. Threads floated over its surface produce a clearly delineated design but the reverse shows the loose warps as they travel to the next area where they will surface to form the design, thus forming an incoherent mass on this other side of the textile. *Ke si*, on the other hand, is plain-woven and all the elements including texture, designs and colours on both sides are completely identical. The designs appear as if cut into the fabric, and it is perhaps this which gave rise to one of the several written characters used for the technique *ke si*, in this case meaning 'cut silk'. *Ke si* and brocade designs, themes and forms, are used in response to different requirements. Brocade, as a rule, serves some practical purpose such as for the making of clothes and consequently tends to employ all-over, repeated patterns, generally spread in four directions from one central group or unit with designs on some of the brocades arranged according to the shape and cut of the finished product. Pieces bearing identical designs may then be joined to form a connecting overall design (as seen in the case of the garment shown in the previous example) of the brocade excavated in Xinjiang. Before weaving, the craftsman first works out a 'master', or template consisting of a perforated card to control warp-lifting, in accordance with the designed pattern and then transfers it to the drawboy. A second person sits at the loom and begins to operate the warps in proper sequence. At the same time, a third works in conjunction with the other two passing the shuttle through the different combinations of warps, automatically producing the design. But *ke si* weaving requires no such pattern card. The weaver simply uses both his hands to weave out the designs as required on a very simple loom, adhering closely to the composition placed before him or her. This method can be used to reproduce calligraphy and painting, and is used to make hanging tapestry panels, folding screens, garments, cushion covers, upholstery, court fans and small ornamental purses, regardless of size or complexity.

Ke si is made by using an ordinary, plain-weave, wooden loom. The process begins with the fixing of the warps and the positioning of the heddle – a mounted set of cords placed across the warps and used to keep them separate – and the bamboo implement, or 'reeds', used to push the wefts down. The design to be copied is placed below the warps through which the weaver can see clearly the shape and colours of the design. The outline is then 'traced' on to the warps with a brush. According to the outline produced small bobbins are used to hold and carry different coloured silks and threads to weave out the plain-woven design in various areas of the fabric. Unlike the usual woven fabrics which are made by using relatively large shuttles that carry the weft threads from one selvage to another without a break, *ke si* weaving requires the weaver to change bobbins from time to time according to the outline of the design and the borders separating different colours. It is therefore a skill which can only be carried out by a weaver who is not only an accomplished craftsman but who also possesses an artistic sensibility. And because the wefts do not run uninterrupted in direction from side to side this technique is often termed *tong jing duan wei* or 'halting [the direction of] the wefts while interconnecting all the warps'. This particular use of the wefts to weave both colour and line, as well as the basic material, produces a unique decorative effect similar to inlaying or the edges of pictorial elements which have been cut with a knife.

Excavations in Xinjiang have disclosed wool textiles from the periods of the Han and Northern and Southern dynasties which have been shown to have been made by this method, and some woven silk textiles from the Tang are of the *ke si* type. By the Northern Song period, aristocratic women were wearing clothing and using bed covers made in *ke si*.

In this landscape executed in the archaic blue and green style by Shen Zifan, the artist has made use of a variety of methods. One method of rendering the transition of colours from dark to light is called dovetailed tapestry, *shen he qiang*, in which they encroach irregularly upon each other horizontally. This is also effectively used for vertical transitions by building up the colours horizontally one above the other with the wefts. Examples of both these can be seen in the mountains of the landscape. A more subtle way of achieving a blend of colours is called *chang duan qiang*, in which wefts of colours from adjacent areas are irregularly extended and reduced (*chang duan*) in length and interwoven where they overlap, producing a shaded effect akin to painting methods. *Gou ke* refers to the method of using the woven lines of darker, contrasting colours to delineate and emphasize the shapes and contours of different elements, also in evidence in the present textile. *Ping ke* is used for the flat, monochrome areas of colour. *Zi mu jing*, 'mother and son', or composite weft working, is used for the written characters and seals. In this case, from top to bottom, Zifan is the given name of the weaver, followed by *zhi*, 'made by'.

By employing these and other methods – such as the careful placing and arrangement of light colours, the proper perspective, shading and modelling of rocks, trees and mountains – the composition is endowed with a sense of depth. No less attention is paid to the details which are portrayed with equal vigour and power. Consideration of all these combine to invoke a feeling of great spaciousness and tranquillity such as may be found in areas south of the River Yangtze. While successfully substituting the shuttle for the brush to reproduce all elements required to produce a fine landscape painting the textile version goes further in creating aesthetic qualities which a painting could not hope to achieve. As such the present *ke si* landscape is a rare work of art that is a testimony to the talents and skills of Shen Zifan.

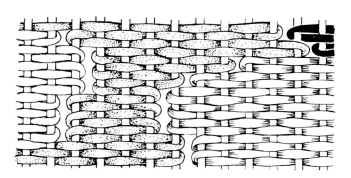

Example of warp (vertical) and weft arrangements for ke si tapestry weaving

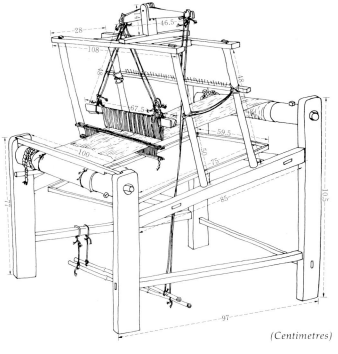

(Centimetres)

Loom for ke si weaving.

235

93. 東方朔偸桃圖軸

KE SI WOVEN SILK
TAPESTRY: DONGFANG
SUO STEALING THE
PEACHES

Polychrome silk
58.5 × 33.5 cm.
Yuan period

This *ke si* silk tapestry is copied from a painting of the Song period. The character portrayed is Dongfang Suo, a writer known for his wit and humour, who lived in the reign of the emperor Wu di of the Han dynasty. After he had become an immortal, he intruded upon the lavish feast of the peaches of immortality, which ripen only once every 6,000 years, given by Xi Wangmu, the Heavenly Queen Mother of the West. He audaciously stole one of the reserved fruits but was caught in the act by guards who marched him before the queen for punishment. However, Dongfang Suo so delighted her with his wit that she rewarded him with nectar and dew wine of which Dongfang drank deep. Due to its associations with a long life and good fortune as well as its theatrically humorous content, this myth became a favourite subject for artists and craftsmen alike.

Branches heavily laden with the peaches show through the multi-coloured clouds, suggestive of the orchard of the heavenly palace where the story takes place. From the rocks below grow a *ling zhi*, fungus, narcissus and bamboo, each associated with longevity or immortality and thus conveying a theme of good luck. In the centre Dongfang Suo flees, looking over his shoulder anxiously, the psychological moment of having been caught in the act ingeniously captured.

The usual *ke si* methods of 'painting with textiles' are employed, such as the careful usage of coloured threads, outlining and emphasizing by means of woven darker threads and the interweaving of lighter colours to produce shading and areas of interest. The overall colour scheme, which is fresh and light, consists of shades of blue and green from very dark to extremely light. Additional water-based colours are applied, bringing the whole scheme into complete harmony. The use of a combination of twisted green and light tan threads for weaving the stem of the fungus is an innovation. Generally, colours are woven in a straightforward manner to depict large, flat areas but when the method whereby both encroach horizontally in a vertical 'zig-zag' is used, it succeeds in achieving a more gentle and natural transition between the two. This entailed the alternate use of tiny bobbins carrying different coloured threads. The chief way in the actual blending of colours is the 'varied length method', *chang duan qiang*, in which darker weft threads are interwoven with light-coloured weft threads, producing a wash effect which helps achieve a spatial harmony between different compositional elements. Dark blue threads both delineate and separate certain parts as well as complete the tonal range, thus bringing an overall harmony to the composition. The effect of this method of weft weaving is to lend a sense of strength combined with a striking decorative effect.

Few embroidered or woven textiles have come down to us from the Yuan period and those portraying human figures as part of a story as the main theme are even rarer. Its further value lies in the fact that it is recorded in the *Mi dian zhu lin, The court collection of masterpieces*. The seals it bears also record the high value placed upon it. Two are the Qing emperor Qian long's personal seals and another records its inclusion in the San xi tang, Room of the Three Rarities' collection, in the Forbidden City. However, such fine extant examples seem to underline the high standards of craftsmanship achieved in this area during the Yuan period. On the mounting are the following seals: 'A treasure for the enjoyment of His Majesty the Emperor Qian long', 'Appreciated by His Majesty the Emperor Qian long', 'The court collection of masterpieces', 'Appraised by the Hall of Three Rarities', and 'Beneficial to posterity'.

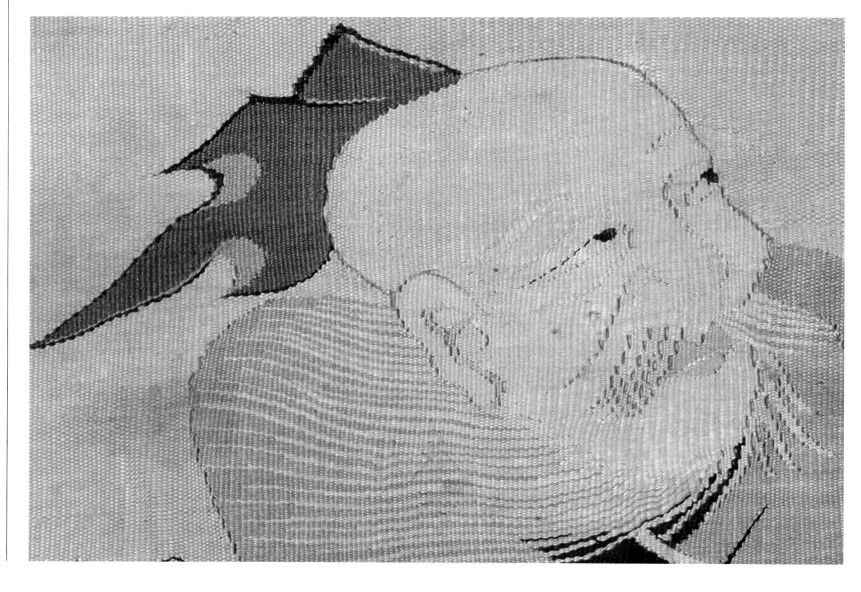

94. 芙蓉鴛鴦圖軸

SATIN VERTICAL SCROLL
EMBROIDERED WITH
MANDARIN DUCKS,
FLOWERS AND GRASSES

Polychrome embroidery
with double-thread on satin
140 × 51 cm.
Ming period

This decorative vertical scroll embroidered with a pair of mandarin ducks and hibiscus was produced in Shandong province in the northwest, the home of some of the finest embroidery products. An area that used to be under the control of the state of Lu, it is known to have been green with mulberry trees, the staple diet of the silkworm, and a renowned centre of silk production as early as the fifth century BC. The local women, who were deft with their hands, embroidered exquisite silk articles which went by the name of 'Lu embroidery'. During the Yuan and Ming periods, Lu embroidery thread was made by twisting two threads together, known as *yi* thread or 'clothing' thread. The works done with such threads are sometimes called '*yi* thread embroidery'. Lu embroidery, known for its durability, not infrequently employs satin with damask patterning as the ground material and is characterized by relatively thick thread, long stitches, sparsely set arrangements of threads, and a simple yet firm and uninhibited style. The choice of heavily symbolic subject-matter would seem to indicate that the scroll was either used as a decoration at a wedding ceremony or presented as a gift to the bride and groom. A mandarin duck and drake symbolize conjugal fidelity and happiness while the hibiscus was regarded as the embodiment of purity and virtue.

The scene depicts the male and female ducks floating happily side by side below the sprays of hibiscus flowers. Red knotweeds, reeds and begonias arch gracefully from left to right while the rocks at the base anchor the composition. Lotus flowers and waterweeds suggestive of autumn complete the scene. The absence of a large number of elements has led to the economical use of embroidery silks, imparting a sense of spaciousness, liveliness and richness.

The basic material used for the scroll is a light cream satin with damask patterning of alternate lines of cut blooms, peonies and Chinese roses, which form a contrasting ground against which the rich, vigorous designs are embroidered in double twisted threads. Overlaid in this way, a three-dimensional quality enhances the composition. Greenish-blue, greyish-green, greyish-blue, a muted red and creamy white, all firm yet reserved colours, are chosen for the embroidery and lend it a simple yet vigorous quality. This forms a sharp contrast with the works done with light-coloured, fine threads characteristic of the embroidery of the South and is representative of the characteristic simplicity and strength of the folk embroidery made in the north and northeast of China.

The success of the present work lies in its application of different stitches which are in keeping with the different designs and shapes. For example, the hibiscus flowers, leaves, rocks and mandarin ducks are done in *sou he* stitch, a type of satin in which there is an uneven arrangement of stitches of irregular lengths. *Da zi* or seed stitches which use the thread coiled into raised 'granules' are admirably suited to the clustered spikes of the red knotweed flowers. Following the outlines precisely and therefore defining them, with parallel stitches of irregular lengths, the *chan* stitches are the perfect method of describing the smooth yet crinkled faces and edges of the grass-like leaves of reeds and knotweed. *Bian zi gu* stitches, some 3 centimetres in length, describe the reeds, short grasses and other leaves. In this diverse use of types of satin stitch as well as the arrangement of silk threads a realistic quality is given to the images, which makes them appear more lifelike and vivid. The three dimensionality thus created by the objects embroidered in slight relief offers something more than painting in its two-dimensional format can and demonstrates the unique decorative qualities of the art of embroidery.

95. 宋元名蹟冊之一──洗馬圖

HAN XIMENG:
EMBROIDERY: WASHING A
HORSE

One of a series from *Song
Yuan ming ji ce, Album of
famous Song and Yuan
masterpieces.*
'Gu embroidery'
polychrome embroidery on
white silk ground
33.4 × 24.5 cm.
Ming period

Embroidery reaches far back into China's past. Historical records traditionally maintained that it originated in the time of the emperor Shun, a legendary figure. Archaeologists have discovered embroidered works from the Western Zhou period. Large sized embroideries showing Buddhist images and subjects emerged during the period of the Northern and Southern dynasties. During the Song period, embroiderers became adept in the art of reproducing famous paintings and calligraphy, opening up new possibilities in this specialist area of craftsmanship. So-called 'Gu embroidery', which was developed in the mid-Ming, was evolved from such Song embroidered compositions based on paintings.

Han Ximeng was a renowned embroiderer of the mid-seventeenth century. Her husband's family, named Gu, had long been noted for the embroidery produced by the women members. Because their place of residence was called Luxiang yuan, their embroidery is called 'Luxiang yuan Gu embroidery', or simply Gu embroidery. Gu embroidery was initiated by the wife of Gu Huihai, eldest son of Gu Mingshi, who acquired his *jin shi* degree in the Jiajing period of the Ming dynasty. But the embroideries by Han Ximeng, the wife of Gu Mingshi's grandson, are considered the best and most valuable works. At first these embroideries produced by the family were kept as part of the family's private collection or given as gifts to relatives and friends. After the death of Gu Mingshi the family's affairs fell into decline and it began increasingly to rely on the needlework of its women members, thus marking the transition from a purely pleasurable pastime to works produced for commercial gain. The already established fame of 'Gu embroidery' enabled it to find a relatively quick and ready market. By the end of the Qing period most of the embroidery stores in Suzhou and Shanghai advertised their goods as Gu embroidery, or put the name 'Gu embroidery shop' on their sign boards, resulting in a confusion of 'Gu' with 'Suzhou embroidery'. In fact the two techniques are easily discernible.

The *Album of famous Song and Yuan masterpieces*, a collection of embroideries by Han Ximeng, is representative of the kind of work carried out by the Gu family. Dong Qichang, the famous Ming critic and painter, graced the album with a colophon in praise of its work and Gu Shouqian, Han's husband, added his own inscription. The album consists of eight works, 'Washing a horse', shown here, being the first of the set.

'Washing a horse' is embroidered with extremely fine silk thread – finer than a human hair – using the thinnest needles possible. Different objects in the picture are depicted in various colours, and a variety of stitches are used faithfully to convey the spirit of the original painting while, at the same time, making the objects appear more realistic. The dominant technique used is the *sou he* stitch, characterized by an uneven arrangement of stitches of irregular lengths tightly knit in formation and providing a smooth surface. Not a single thread is misplaced. In addition Han Ximeng has ingeniously supplemented the stitching with faint dots of colour wash on the river banks, giving a more resonant feeling which is in keeping with painting techniques. After the commercialization of Gu embroidery this became one of its special features and is the reason why it was also called 'painted embroidery'. Naturally, the art of painting is different from embroidery, for in painting ink and brush are used to draw pictures on mounted silk or paper, while in embroidery the realistic quality of the objects is depicted through the colours of the silk threads, the density of the stitches and the arrangement and direction of silk threads. So besides its ability to imitate faithfully the poetic touch of brushwork, embroidery enjoys additional advantages of its own.

The most outstanding characteristic of Gu embroidery is its substitution of threads for brushwork and its extraordinary ability to duplicate paintings faithfully. Historical records show that Han Ximeng had spent many years in the making of this album. It was also said that she would stop embroidering in cloudy, windy or rainy weather and only worked when the sun was shining, when the birds sang merrily and flowers were in full bloom, because only under such circumstances could she embroider the scene and atmosphere into her works. The renowned artist Dong Qichang admired her works enormously, remarking upon her almost superhuman ability.

96. 盤條四季花卉宋式錦

SONG-STYLE BROCADE,
WITH A DESIGN OF
FLOWERS

140 × 32 cm.
Ming period

Suzhou was a famous silk-producing centre in Jiangnan, the area south of the River Yangtze, during the Ming period. The Song-style brocades produced there, based on the patterns and colours prevalent during the period of the Song dynasty, were amongst the most sumptuous and beautiful.

Pan tiao is the name given to a geometrical floral pattern of large or medium size. A variety of silk with *pan tiao* patterns known as *liao ling* was produced during the Tang period. This very thin *ling* silk bearing such a pattern was considered to be very precious. The piece of Song-style brocade shown here, with a design of various flowers of the four seasons made in the Ming period, evolved from the Tang and Song traditional patterns of filling a geometrical framework with designs based on flowers. The framework of the patterns is formed by imaginary intersecting concentric circles, the actual shapes composed of six lobed brackets which may also be seen as chains with two lobed brackets forming each link. The interstices are filled with diamonds or lozenges, key-fret patterns and the like, all of which carry an implied auspicious meaning. All were traditionally found on textiles since the Tang and Song periods. The centre of each concentric circle, itself a flower shape, is separately decorated with stylized plum flowers, narcissi and peonies, also popular decorative patterns since the Song. The combination of the stylized shapes of the flowers with abstract geometrical patterns creates an ingeniously conceived overall design which, while appearing complex, is at once integrated and simple. Red, dark green, bright yellow and light blue designs are set off against a ground dominated by orange. The method of coloration consists in the alternation of light colours and the use of golden

outlines. This involves a light-coloured edging around every motif, and the addition of a golden-coloured fringe on the outside, so that contrasts between different colours is softened and the motif emphasized to attain an effect of splendid harmony.

Woven brocades are the best of all silk products. Of the written Chinese characters used for brocade throughout history each has incorporated the element meaning gold to show that it equals gold in value because of the cost of labour involved in production. Since the eighth century BC brocade has been woven after carrying out a lengthy set of procedures consisting of first refining the silk strands pulled from the cocoons; second, dying the refined skeins of silk; and finally weaving it on a loom. Historically there were two kinds of brocade: those with designs produced by the warps or warp-faced patterns, and brocades with designs produced by the wefts. The former was the earliest type and was usually plain-woven, while the second type, the more recent, was a twill devised during the early Tang period. The surface designs of this piece of Song-style brocade are created by the diagonals produced in taking the weft threads over three then under the three warps with the ground produced in the same way and number of units, but by means of the warp. Of the warps, one set was specially set aside for the ground pattern called 'ground warps', or *di jing*, while another set, the 'special warps', *te jing*, was used in forming patterns with the weft threads. A device called a *zong huang*, or '[warp] thread controller', may be used to control the lifting of the ground warps while the movement of the special warps can be controlled by the 'pattern plate'. In this way the patterns are automatically reproduced, thus improving productivity as well as making the surface designs stand out more prominently. This represented considerable advances in silk weaving in Suzhou during the Ming. Six shuttles were needed in the weaving of the colours and designs into this piece of brocade, with three of them weaving the full width of the weft, generally incorporating the geometrical framework of the ground patterns, the stems of the flowers, and the outlines of the patterns. The other three shuttles, having travelled a distance of about three to four centimetres, are replaced by another three shuttles carrying threads of different colours. In fact, six shuttles are used to weave patterns in sixteen different colours, without causing the brocade to become too thick. The three shuttles that cover only short distances and are constantly replaced by another set of shuttles carrying threads of different colours are called *duan pao suo*, or 'short distance shuttles'. They are used to weave the main motifs against the ground of the brocade. The method of changing colours by *duan pao suo* is called *huo se*, or 'moving colours'. This technique is still used in contemporary silk production.

The designs of this piece of Song-style brocade, with its harmonious colour scheme and auspicious symbolism, remain perfectly intact. It is so soft and durable as to be suitable for the making of clothes, curtains, bed covers and upholstery; but, above all, it is indicative of the high standards of silk weaving in Suzhou during the Ming period.

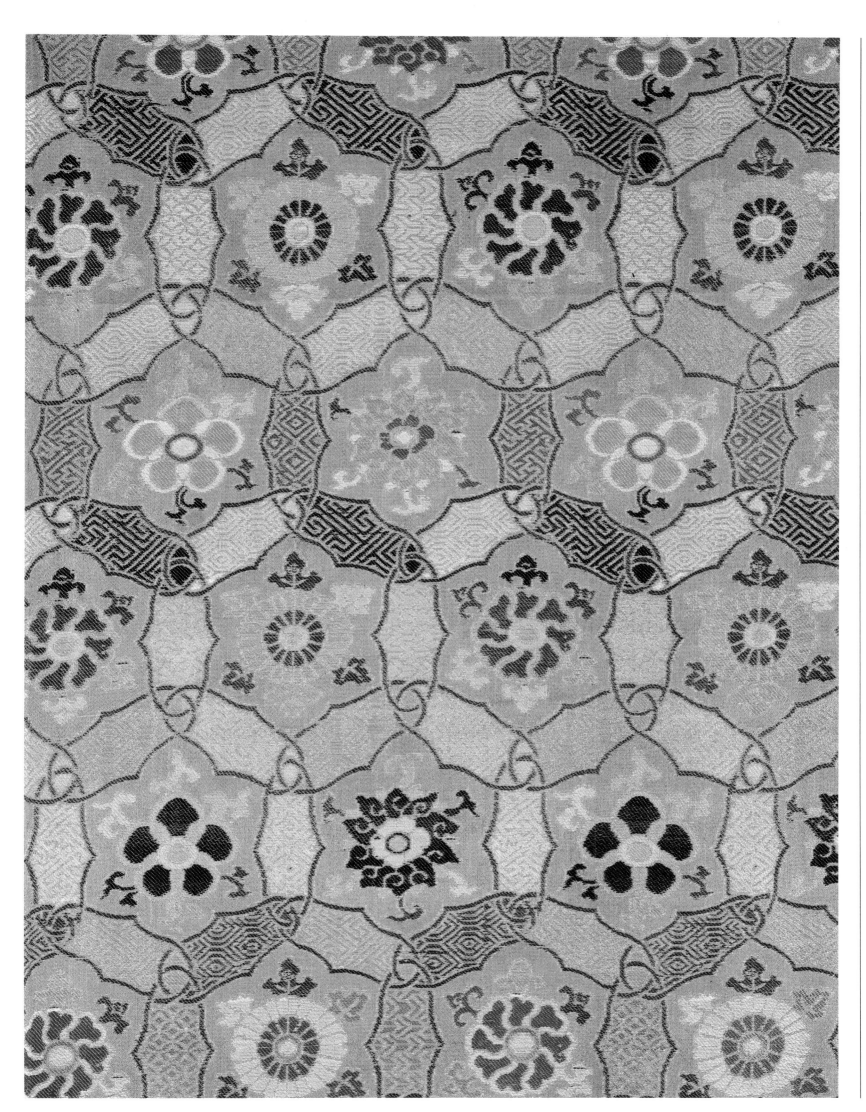

97. 極樂世界圖軸

SILK WEAVING DEPICTING
THE PURE LAND OF THE
WESTERN PARADISE

Polychrome satin tapestry
448 × 196.5 cm.
Qing dynasty, reign of Qian
long

Based on an account of the Buddhist 'Pure Land of the Western Paradise', this silk tapestry is woven with multi-coloured silk threads.

Many of the murals in the Mogao Buddhist cave temples at Dunhuang, Gansu province, draw their subjects from scenes of the Pure Land of the Western Paradise. These include cave no. 220 of the early Tang period, nos 172 and 217 from the height of the Tang, no. 112 from the middle Tang, no. 154 late Tang, and no. 25 in the Thousand Buddha caves at Yulin. The silk weaving shown here similarly portrays the same subject in an imaginative and vivid way. Like other similar representations executed since the Tang period, the composition is symmetrically placed about the buddha Amitabha at the centre, presiding over the Pure Land. Just in front of and slightly below the buddha sit two bodhissatvas, saviours of mankind, to the left and right. The three figures serve to balance the picture from the central focal point. Around these three images are symmetrically woven many other lokapālas or guardian kings of the Four Quarters, gods, lohans or followers, bhiksus or monks. Other conventional elements including trees, rocks, exotic flowers and birds and a total of 278 divinities, each possessing their own distinctive facial features, are woven into this grandiose, palatial scene amidst the swirling, auspicious and coloured clouds. The lower part of the picture consists of the Pool of the Seven precious things of Buddhism, in which grow lotus leaves and their flowers, thrones on which believers will be reborn into this paradise.

The original painting on which this silk tapestry is based was the work of Ding Guanpeng, an artist of the Qian long era. Specializing in painting figures and landscape, Ding was an artist of consummate skill, capable of painting extremely complex scenes. Inheriting the traditional technique of the religious paintings accumulated since the Tang period, this work represents the grandiose, solemn, prosperous and magnificent scenes which were the embodiment of the idealized Pure Land.

The complete format, including borders, was woven in one section with a total of nineteen different coloured weft silk threads. Red, blue, green, orange, cerise, ochre and cream are the predominant colours which form a striking contrast to the basic sombre blues and blacks of the ground. Where contrasting colours meet many methods are employed to achieve a smooth transition and harmonious integration of the whole tonal composition. Light colours separate darker areas, sometimes black lines define the outlines and three or four layers of graduated tones of the same colour achieve the gradual transition required: for example, from a pale pink through to a pinkish-red and finally a muted cerise. Also, a pure white is followed by a creamy white and then a dark blue. Wrapped gold and silk threads are used to highlight certain features of the figures' faces and the decorated parts of buildings. The colourful and brilliant major decorative designs combine with the mysterious tranquillity conveyed by the background to build up a picture in which real life is interwoven with fantasy, thus reflecting the reality of daily life as well as human spiritual aspirations.

Enormously complex skills and techniques were involved in the weaving of this huge tapestry, combining as it does such a rich variety of images and colours into an extraordinarily detailed structure. In the first place, it required a craftsman well acquainted in the principles of painting to make a 'pattern plate' from the original. Next, another technician had to set up figure harnesses – a warp- and weft-lifting device – on a special loom. Workers responsible for the operation of these different loom parts began to work in close collaboration with the weavers. The textile is so wide that it would have required more than one weaver, so several weavers must have sat side by side to relay the shuttles. According to historical records, similarly large works were being woven in Suzhou as early as the Xuan de period of the Ming dynasty. Judging from its special features, this silk tapestry must have been produced by only the very best artisans employed by a controlled silk factory in Suzhou.

The silk weaving was originally housed in the Palace of Heavenly Purity in the Qing period and bears the impressions of eight imperial seals. The work is also included in the supplement to the *Mi dian zhu lin*, *The court collection of treasures*. Retained in the collections of the Museum, it is the only extant work of its kind.

98. 九陽消寒圖軸

KE SI WOVEN SILK
TAPESTRY WITH
ADDITIONAL
EMBROIDERY: NINE SUNS
DRIVING AWAY THE COLD

Polychrome silk
213 × 119 cm.
Qing dynasty, reign of Qian
long

This *ke si* woven silk tapestry would have been hung as a decoration on one of the palace walls during the Qing period at some time during the 1st month of the lunar year. According to the traditional calendar the period between the second day following the winter solstice and the eighty-first day thereafter was the coldest time of year. Eighty-one is the product of the most perfect digit, that is nine squared. Being also an uneven number, it is further strengthened by belonging to *yang*, the male and positive of the two controlling *yin–yang* forces in the universe. The nine rams around which the composition is built are also pronounced *yang* in Chinese. Thus a pun is produced, drawn from the traditional collection of usually four-character phrases that always incorporate symbols of prosperity or good fortune. Here, the main pun relies on the homophone *yang* and, in accordance with custom, 'nine rams driving away the severe cold' symbolizing harbingers of spring, the symbol of fresh hope for a primarily agriculturally based society. Other elements and motifs, their Chinese names sometimes stretching out beyond the original words of the phrase, are included in this scene to encompass as much auspicious symbolism as possible. *Yang* occurs in the word for sun, *tai yang*, and the playing princes, male offspring always being the most treasured of children and therefore of the *yang* principle, are pronounced *tai zi*. *Tai*, meaning 'peace', is often included with rams, *yang*, in another of these phrases, *San yang kai tai*, 'three rams heralding peace', discussed elsewhere in this volume. Also, the green pine, representing long life, and the white prunus blossoms and camellias mark the death of winter. The Qian long emperor has written a poem concerning this very subject on the mount.

The background and subordinate elements of the scenery are woven in *ke si* tapestry while the most important images, such as the princes and animals, are embroidered. On the upper part of the scroll the bright blue of the sky sets off the multi-coloured clouds of good fortune, the green pine tree, the plum trees, and the rocks. The banks and the surface of the water are woven in a creamy white, thereby bringing out the images of the nine rams, the three princes, the flowers and the trees. An azure sky above and the bright coloured ground below gives the impression of a sunny spring day. Colouring to obtain the desired effect is achieved in several

ways. The dominant method uses large, flat areas of colour. These areas are often bordered by four bands of colour of different tones when making the transition to another area of flat colour, a common device in *ke si* work. Traditional Suzhou satin stitches are used to achieve an effect of shading on the flowers. Some of the tree trunks are touched in with a brush in addition to the ground weave or embroidery to emphasize the natural quality and texture of the bark, while the river banks and rocks are fringed with bands of eight different colours, imparting a lyrical quality which also unites the composition.

Suzhou embroidery is characterized by the rich variety of stitches at its disposal. But in their selection for inclusion the basic principle is the same: that is, the shape and structure of the designs decide the suitability of particular stitches with a view to bringing out the realistic quality of the objects, by means of the arrangement of the silk threads, their density, length, linear shape and distribution. The use of ink and water colour and painting techniques to supplement the range of visual effects is an innovation of the Qing period.

This work, listed in the third volume of the *Shi qu catalogue*, and bearing a seal to that effect, was kept in the Palace of Tranquil Longevity. It bears many other imperial seal impressions as well as an inscription by the Qian long emperor.

99. 孔雀羽彩繡袍

DRAGON ROBE OF
EMBROIDERED SATIN

length 143 cm.
width across shoulders
including sleeves 216 cm.
chest 134 cm.
hem 124 cm.
cuff 18 cm.

This robe has a round collar, a right-facing overlapping panel, broad front, horse-hoof cuffs, and straight slits on right and left sides. The surface material is blue satin with embroidered designs covering the robe which incorporate such valuable materials as peacock feathers, strings of white pearls and coral beads, and gold and silver threads. Tightly packed motifs form an all-over integrated design consisting of forward facing imperial dragons, which always have five claws, on the centre of the chest and back as well as on both shoulders. Five more writhing dragons are distributed around the middle and bottom of the garment, bringing the total to nine. Dragons of this type were strictly reserved for use as decorative and symbolic motifs by the Qing emperors and their immediate family. According to rigorously enforced published regulations governing status and the wearing of clothing, this robe probably fell into the *ji fu*, 'auspicious garments', subdivision of the imperial category. The number nine, discussed elsewhere, was the most perfect and therefore symbolized the lofty position of the imperial family. The so-called 'three balances and nine similarities' are emphasized in depicting the dragons. The 'three balances' meant that the neck, tail and waist should be slender and curving. The 'nine similarities' were that the horns should be similar to those of a deer, the head to that of a camel, the eyes to those of a demon, the neck to that of a snake, the belly to that of a clam, the scales to those of a fish, the claws to those of an eagle, the feet to those of a tiger, and the ears to those of a bull. In addition, one smaller forward facing dragon is embroidered on each cuff and two on the upper sleeves and four other twisting dragons. Auspicious symbols are inserted between these main decorative motifs, such as stylized clouds and bats.

Other eclectic symbols to be found on the robe include the eight Buddhist and eight Taoist emblems. Of the Buddhist set the *chakra*, or wheel, conch shell, parasol, canopy, lotus, vase, pair of fish and entrails or endless knot are included. The eight Taoist emblems shown are the attributes of eight Taoist immortals who are symbolized in the following way: Li

Tieguai, Li 'iron crutch', representing the sick, carries a crutch and gourd; Zhongli Quan, a military man, by a fan; Lan Caihe, a flower basket, representing florists and gardeners; Zhang Guolao, a bamboo tube-drum containing iron rods or sticks; He Xiangu shown with the lotus, emblem of purity; Lü Dongbin with his precious sword or fly-whisk, a scholar-warrior, associated with scholars and barbers; Han Xiangzi, a flute, patron deity of musicians; and Cao Guoqin with castanets or a jade tablet, the latter a symbol of admission to court, patron of actors. All symbolic of good fortune and happiness, these objects sometimes vary. Branches bearing peaches, pomegranates and the fruit called Buddha's hand, *fo shou*, or the fingered citron, which are also to be found, stand for longevity, posterity and prosperity respectively. The *ling zhi*, fungus of immortality (*Ganoderma lucidum*), crane and bamboo are representative of long life also. Making up the deep band around the base of the robe serried rows of embroidered lines, some undulating, others straighter, represent the waves of the sea. Combined with the stylized rocks, also symbols of perpetuity, the whole takes on a cosmic significance with the ethereal sky, full of dragons and clouds, above. In this lower portion are also scattered the eight precious things, *ba bao*: the jewel, the cash which is a coin with a square cut from the centre, the open lozenge with ribbons, the solid lozenge, the musical stone, the pair of books and the pair of rhinoceros horns. Bats and lotuses fill other spaces. Each one of the dragons, cranes and bats is decorated with hundreds of tiny pearls and coral beads, while the outlines, including underbellies, horns, scales, fins, claws, tails and manes of the dragons are sewn with a special stitch which, on a smaller scale, imitates the granular quality of the pearls and coral. Gold and silver thread is used for their whiskers. Individual filaments stripped from peacock feathers and twisted into usable form are sewn into the spaces between all the decorative motifs producing a gem-like green and blue base. An amalgamation of this sombre, ethereal background, in which float brilliant symbols and flashing colour, marks the robe's formal and majestic function. But compared with those vestments bearing the twelve cosmic symbols, reserved by regulation for the emperor alone, it would appear to have been allowed a certain latitude in originality in its design.

Many of these embroidery techniques can be traced back through China's history. As early as the period of the Northern and Southern dynasties, there exist records of peacock feathers being used in textile decoration. Excavations at Ding ling, the tomb of the Ming emperor Wan li, just outside Beijing, yielded dragon or imperial robes with peacock feather threads. Another example is to be found in the famous novel *Hong lou meng, Dream of the Red Chamber*, written by Cao Xueqin during the Qing period, when Qiu Wen, a maid-servant, mends a fur coat decorated with gold and peacock feathers for her young master Jia Baoyu. The dragon robe illustrated represents a development in the use of peacock feathers whereby the individual filaments are worked across the whole surface of the ground called 'spreading blue-green'.

Strung pearls are also historically to be found as decorative elements on slippers, clothing and beaded curtains. Literature tells us of multi-coloured embroidered skirts with fringes of red cords strung with pearls. Similarly, the *Ming gong shi, Chronicles of the Ming imperial palace*, relates the imprisonment of innocent people as a result of the discovery of a missing pearl-decorated robe in 1596, indicating both the existence of such garments during the Wan li era and the high value that was placed on them.

It is not just the use of exotic precious and semi-precious materials in the embellishment of this robe but also the incorporation of the many types of embroidery stitch, practical, decorative and textural, that makes it a representative synthesis of the Chinese textile handicrafts. Furthermore, the unique use of bright, striking colours against a stately and mysterious ground in reserved, darker colours, heightens its courtly aspect. Not least, the silver and gold thread outlines bring a sumptuousness which crowns the work as being amongst the best produced in the classical, imperial style in Suzhou during the Qing period.

100. 三羊開泰圖

GUANGDONG
EMBROIDERY ON
CREAM-COLOURED
SATIN: THREE RAMS
HERALDING SPRING

Polychrome embroidery
67 × 52 cm.
Late Qing period

Guangdong embroidery is considered to have been one of the four best kinds to have been produced during the Qing period, alongside Sichuan, Suzhou and Xiang embroideries. Its history dates far back to the Tang period as exemplified by a certain Lu Meiniang, who lived in Nanhai during this period and was renowned for her skill in the art. In Guangdong embroidery, the stitches are extremely fine and hair taken from the tails of horses is mixed with wool to form strong threads which, when used around the outlines of animals, for example, produce a naturalistic yet neat appearance. The colours used are also extraordinarily brilliant and attractive. Chief amongst the subjects selected for inclusion in this region's needlework are birds, animals, flowers and antiques, and themes taken from auspicious phrases such as 'A hundred birds worshipping the phoenix' and the present subject are favoured.

As discussed elsewhere in this volume, the compositions portraying the puns associated with the auspicious phrase *San yang kai tai*, 'three rams heralding spring', always include the sun and three rams. The atmosphere of awakening spring is enhanced by exotic birds, trees, rocks, flowers, grass and butterflies which form lively groups around the central theme. A springlike crispness is fully underlined by the use of fresh, bright colours against a luminescent cream satin background. Dark brown, bronze, light tan and light ochre are the dominant colours employed to embroider the rocks and rams. Light blue, azure, light green, yellowish-green, grey, white and scarlet are used to embellish the scene, achieving a jewel-like effect that enlivens the scene.

Nine different types of embroidery stitch are employed, serving different functions, which are mainly concerned with textural representation and modelling. The *bian zi gu*, with its textural coiling up technique, is used to describe the curly and shaggy coats of the rams in a most realistic way. Colours combine with stitches of uneven length to describe the flat faces and shaded crevices of rocks, bringing out their three-dimensional qualities in fawn, ochre, grey, pale green and pale yellow. A hard, dark line of thread around their contours gives them added solidity and clarity. Such great care is exercised in conveying the nature of each subject that even the smallest of birds employs six and more different stitches to distinguish their beaks, legs and different plumage. The luminosity of the sun, different hues, qualities and textures of small grasses as opposed to pine needles or the broad leaves of the banana plantain are all painstakingly described by means of different stitches, colours and types of thread.

Every skill available to the embroiderer, from the basic rise and fall of a silk thread or a needle to the careful placing of silk threads and their directions, is used to give the embroidered objects a feel of reality. In this way the potentially expressive qualities of needle and thread are exploited to the full, achieving results and effects that cannot be produced in other forms of the applied or fine arts.

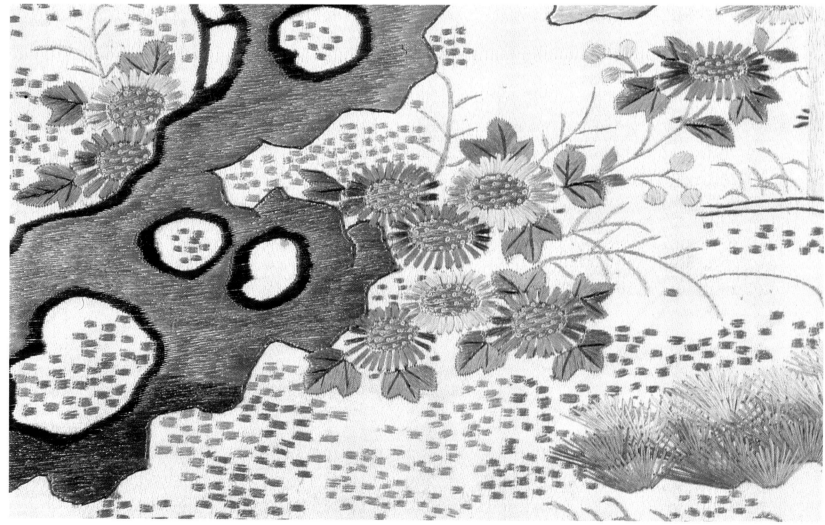

FURTHER READING

Although the following titles are divided according to the sections as presented in this volume, many will be found to cover several areas of Chinese art. They are intended as a basic guide only to other works available in this wide subject area. For an index of books and articles published between 1920 and 1965 see *Vanderstappen* below.

GENERAL

Hansford, S. Howard, *A Glossary of Chinese Art and Archaeology* (London: China Society, 1954).

Hucker, Charles O., *China's Imperial Past* (London: Duckworth, 1980).

Lawton, Thomas, *et al. The Freer Gallery of Art. 1. China* (Tokyo: Kodansha, n.d.).

Lee, Sherman E., *A History of Far Eastern Art* (London: Thames and Hudson, 1964).

MacFarquhar, Roderick, *et al.*, *The Forbidden City* (London and New York: Reader's Digest/Newark, 1972).

Medley, Margaret, *A Handbook of Chinese Art* (London: Bell, 1964; reprint paperback 1973).

Qian Hao, *Out of China's Earth. Archaeological Discoveries in the Peoples' Republic of China.* (London and Beijing: Frederick Muller/China Pictorial, 1981).

Sirén, Osvald, *The Imperial Palaces of Peking*, 3 vols (Paris and Brussels: Libraire Nationale d'Art et d'Histoire, 1926).

Sirén, Osvald, *The Walls and Gates of Peking* (London: John Lane, Bodley Head, 1924).

Sullivan, Michael, *Chinese Art. Recent Discoveries* (London: Thames and Hudson, 1973).

Tregear, Mary, *Chinese Art* (London: Thames and Hudson, 1980).

Vanderstappen, Harrie A. (ed.), *The T. L. Yuan Bibliography of Western Writing on Chinese Art and Archaeology* (London: Mansell, 1975).

Watson, William, *China before the Han Dynasty* (London: Thames and Hudson, 1966).

Watson, William, *The Genius of China* (London: Times Newspapers, 1973).

Watson, William, *Art of Dynastic China* (London: Thames and Hudson, 1981).

Weng, Wan-go, *The Palace Museum, Peking* (London: Orbis, 1982).

Yu Zhuoyun (ed.), *Palaces of the Forbidden City* (London and New York: Allen Lane/Viking, 1984).

BRONZES

Kuwayama, G., *Ancient Ritual Bronzes of China* (Los Angeles: Los Angeles County Museum of Art, 1976).

Loehr, Max, *Ritual Bronzes of Ancient China* (New York: The Asia Society, 1968).

Pope, J. A., *et al.*, *The Freer Chinese Bronzes*, 2 vols. *Catalogue* (Washington D. C.: Freer Gallery of Art, 1969).

Rawson, Jessica, *Ancient China. Art and Archaeology* (London: British Museum Publications, 1980).

Watson, William, *Ancient Chinese Bronzes* (London: Faber, 1962).

Watson, William, *Handbook to the Collections of Early Chinese Antiquities* (London: British Museum Publications, 1962).

Wen Fong (ed.), *The Great Bronze Age of China* (exbn cat.) (New York: Metropolitan Museum of Art, 1980).

PAINTING AND CALLIGRAPHY

Cohn, William, *Chinese Painting* (London: Phaidon, 1948).

Kuo Hsi (trans. Sakanishi, S.), *An Essay on Landscape Painting (Lin ch'üan kao chih by Kuo Hsi)* (London: John Murray, 1935).

Lai, T. C., *Chinese Calligraphy* (Washington: University of Washington Press, 1973).

Lee, Sherman E., *A History of Far Eastern Art* (London: Thames and Hudson, 1964).

Loehr, Max, *The Great Painters of China* (Oxford: Phaidon, 1980).

Sickman, Laurence and Soper, Alexander, *The Art and Architecture of China* (Harmondsworth: Penguin Books, 1968).

Sirén, Osvald, *The Chinese on the Art of Painting* (Peiping: Henri Vetch, 1936).

Speiser, Werner, *et al.*, *Chinese Art. The Calligraphic Arts* (London: Oldbourne Press, 1964).

Tregear, Mary, *Chinese Art* (London: Thames and Hudson, 1980).

Willetts, William, *Foundations of Chinese Art* (London: Thames and Hudson, 1965).

CERAMICS

Ayers, J. G., *The Bauer Collection, Geneva: Chinese Ceramics* (four vols) (Genève: Collections Bauer, 1968–74).

Ayers, J. G., *Far Eastern Ceramics in the Victoria and Albert Museum* (London and New York: Sotheby Parke Bernet, 1980).

Donelly, P. J., *Blanc de Chine* (London: Faber, 1969).

Garner, Sir Harry, *Oriental Blue and White* (London: Faber, 1954).

Kerr, Rose, Chinese Ceramics in the Victoria and Albert Museum (Series) 1. *Chinese Porcelains of the Qing Dynasty* (London: Victoria and Albert Museum, forthcoming).

Kerr, Rose and Hughes-Stanton, P., *Kiln Sites of Ancient China* (exbn cat.) (London: Oriental Ceramic Society, 1980).

Medley, Margaret, *Tang Pottery and Porcelain* (London: Faber, 1981).

Medley, Margaret, *Yüan Porcelain and Stoneware* (London: Faber, 1974).

Medley, Margaret, *The Chinese Potter. A Practical History of Chinese Ceramics* (Oxford: Phaidon, 1976).

Tregear, Mary, *Catalogue of Chinese Greenware in the Ashmolean Museum* (Oxford: Ashmolean Museum, 1976).

Tregear, Mary, *Song Ceramics* (London: Thames and Hudson, 1982).

Watson, William, *Tang and Liao Ceramics* (London: Thames and Hudson, 1984).

Valenstein, Suzanne, G., *A Handbook of Chinese Ceramics* (New York: Metropolitan Museum of Art, 1975).

van Oort, H. A., *Chinese Porcelains of the 19th and 20th Centuries* (Lochem: Uitgeversmaatschappij de Tijdsroom, 1977).

MINOR ARTS

Ayers, J. G. and Rawson, Jessica, *Chinese Jade throughout the Ages* (exbn. cat.) (London: Oriental Ceramic Society, 1976).

Beurdeley, Michel (K. Watson, trans.) *Chinese Furniture* (Tokyo: Kodansha International, 1979).

Chu, Arthur and Grace, *A Collector's Book of Jade* (New York: Crown Publishers, 1978).

Crosby Forbes, H. A., *et al.*, *Chinese Export Silver 1785–1885* (Milton, Mass.: Museum of the American China Trade, 1975).

Ecke, Gustav, *Chinese Domestic Furniture* (Rutland and Hongkong: Charles E. Tuttle/Hongkong University Press, 1962).

Ellsworth, Robert Hatfield, *Chinese Furniture* (London: Collins, 1970).

Feddersen, Martin, *Chinese Decorative Arts. A Handbook for Collectors and Connoisseurs* (London, Faber, 1961).

Garner, Sir Harry, *Chinese and Japanese Cloisonné Enamels* (London: Faber, 1962).

Garner, Sir Harry, *Chinese Lacquer* (London: Faber, 1979).

Hansford, S. Howard, *Chinese Carved Jades* (London: Faber, 1968).

Ip, Yee and Tam, Laurence, C. S., *Chinese Bamboo Carving* (Hongkong: Hongkong Museum of Art, 1978, 1982, 2 vols).

Jenyns, Soame and Watson, William (W. Watson rev. and ed.) *Chinese Art. Textiles. Glass. Ivory. Snuff Bottles. Carving* (Oxford: Phaidon, 1981, 2nd edn).

Jones, R. and Forsyth, A., *Wood from the Scholar's Table* (Hongkong: Artfield Gallery, 1984).

Lacquer. An International History (London: Crowood Press, 1984).

Loehr, Max, *Ancient Chinese Jades* (Cambridge, Mass.: Fogg Art Museum, 1975).

Singer, Paul, *Early Chinese Gold and Silver* (exbn cat.) (New York: China House Gallery, 1977).

Wan Shixiang and Weng Wan-go, *Bamboo Carving of China* (New York: China House Gallery, 1983).

Watson, William (ed.), *Chinese Ivories from the Shang to the Qing* (exbn cat.) (London: Oriental Ceramic Society, 1984).

Watson, William (ed.), *Lacquerwork in Asia and beyond* (series. Colloquies on art and archaeology in Asia, no. 11) (London: Percival David Foundation of Chinese Art, 1982).

TEXTILES

Ayer, Jacqueline, *Oriental Costume* (London: Studio Vista, 1974).

Baker, Muriel and Lunt, Margaret, *Blue and White: the Cotton Embroideries of Rural China* (London: Sidgwick and Jackson, 1978).

Burnham, H. B., *Chinese Velvets. A Technical Study* (Toronto: University of Toronto Press, 1959).

Camman, Schuyler, *China's Dragon Robes* (New York: Ronald Press, 1952).

Capon, Edmund, *Chinese Court Robes in the Victoria and Albert Museum* (London: H.M.S.O./Victoria and Albert Museum, 1970, reprint).

Chung, Young yang, *The Art of Oriental Embroidery* (New York: Charles Scribner's Sons, 1979).

Ecke, Tseng Yu-Ho, *Chinese Folk Art in American Collections. Early 15th–early 20th Centuries* (New York: China Institute in America, 1976).

Frozen Tombs. The Culture and Art of the Ancient Tribes of Siberia (exbn cat.) (London: British Museum Publications, 1978).

Hommel, Rudolf, *China at Work* (Cambridge, Mass.: M.I.T. Press, 1969, reprint).

Lattimore, Owen and Eleanor (eds) *Silks, Spices and Empire* (New York: Dell Publishing, 1968).

Mailey, Jean, *Chinese Silk Tapestry: K'o-ssu* (exbn cat.) (New York: China Institute in America, 1971).

Vollmer, John E., *In the Presence of the Dragon Throne. Ch'ing Dynasty Costume (1644–1911)* (Toronto: Royal Ontario Museum, 1977).

Wilson, Verity, *Chinese Dress in the Victoria and Albert Museum* (London: Victoria and Albert Museum, 1985, forthcoming).

PERIODICALS

Many periodicals devoted to Far Eastern art and archaeology cover the categories included in the present volume. The following is a short list of the major titles.

Artibus Asiae, Ascona, Switzerland 1929–
Arts of Asia, Hongkong 1971–
Bulletin of the Museum of Far Eastern Antiquities, Stockholm 1929–
Early China, Berkeley, California 1975–
Gu gong bo wu yuan yuan kan, (Palace Museum Journal, in Chinese), Beijing, 1958–60, 1979–
Oriental Art, Hongkong 1948–
Transactions of the Oriental Ceramic Society, London, 1921–
Zi jin cheng (Forbidden City, in Chinese with English captions), Hongkong, 1980–

INDEX